# Warthog

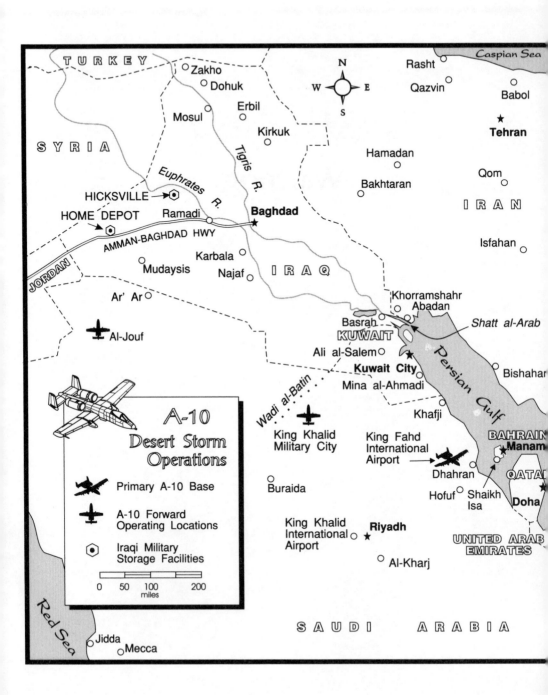

A-10
Desert Storm
Operations

Primary A-10 Base

A-10 Forward
Operating Locations

Iraqi Military
Storage Facilities

0   50  100        200
        miles

TURKEY
Zakho
Dohuk
Erbil
Mosul
Kirkuk

SYRIA

Euphrates R.
Tigris R.

HICKSVILLE
HOME DEPOT
Ramadi
AMMAN-BAGHDAD HWY
JORDAN

Baghdad

IRAQ

Karbala
Mudaysis
Najaf
Ar' Ar

Al-Jouf

N
W        E
S

Rasht
Qazvin

Caspian Sea

Babol

Tehran

Hamadan
Bakhtaran

Qom

IRAN

Isfahan

Khorramshahr
Abadan
Basrah
KUWAIT
Ali al-Salem
Kuwait City
Mina al-Ahmadi

Shatt al-Arab

Persian Gulf

Bishahar

Wadi al-Batin

King Khalid
Military City

Khafji

King Fahd
International
Airport

Dhahran

BAHRAIN
Manam

Buraida

Hofuf    Shaikh
         Isa

QATAR
Doha

King Khalid
International
Airport

Riyadh

Al-Kharj

UNITED ARAB
EMIRATES

SAUDI        ARABIA

Red Sea

Jidda
Mecca

# Warthog

## Flying the A-10 in the Gulf War

William L. Smallwood

BRASSEY'S
Washington • London

Library of Congress Cataloging-in-Publication Data
Smallwood, William L.
  Warthog: flying the A-10 in the Gulf War / William L. Smallwood
    p.  cm.
  Includes index.
  ISBN 0-02-881021-X  Paperback ISBN 0-02-881123-2
  1. A-10 (Jet attack plane) 2. Persian Gulf War, 1991. I. Title.
UG1242.A28S53  1993
358.4'383—dc20                                                    92-23201
                                                                      CIP

10  9  8  7  6  5  4  3  2  1

Printed in the United States of America

TO FOUR HOG DRIVERS WHO GAVE IT ALL:

MAJ. JEFF WATTERBERG

CAPT. STEVE PHILLIS

1st LT. PATRICK OLSON

1st LT. ERIC MILLER

# Contents

# Preface

This book was researched during the summer of 1991, just after all the A-10 pilots who flew in the Persian Gulf War returned to their home bases: RAF Alconbury in East Anglia, Great Britain; Myrtle Beach Air Force Base in South Carolina; England Air Force Base in Alexandria, Louisiana; New Orleans Naval Air Station (home of a reserve squadron); and Davis-Monthan Air Force Base in Tucson, Arizona. Despite the black clouds hanging over them—three of the bases were being closed, five of the seven squadrons were being deactivated, and about 40 percent of the A-10 inventory was heading to the bone yard—the pilots remained full of enthusiasm for the airplane and its capabilities. More importantly from the standpoint of the researcher, they still had vivid memories of their Gulf War experiences and the squadrons were still largely intact. During a roughly three-month series of visitations to those bases, I managed to interview 143 of the pilots who flew the A-10 in the Gulf War. This book tells their story and, to the extent possible in such a narrative, in their own words.

The names and deeds of all those who helped me are recorded in the acknowledgments. I hope the reader will peruse this list to appreciate those who made this book possible. However, before the story begins, I want to relate here a deeply moving experience I had with two of the pilots who are on that list.

It was a Monday morning in mid-September and I was making my third visit to England Air Force Base. A month earlier I had confirmed with Col. Dave Sawyer, the wing commander, that I would be returning on that Monday. Because of his hectic schedule, however, which, besides running the wing, included all of the dismal PR chores associated with closing the base, he had forgotten that I was coming. He had declared this particular Monday a "stand-down" day, a military euphemism for a holiday given at the commander's descretion when performance goals are exceeded.

However, he was in his office that morning, and when I came in was apologetic, and he immediately went to his deputy for operations, Col. Dick Lemon (who was also on the job), and asked whom they might call to help me—someone who would not mind sacrificing the holiday.

I objected when I heard what they were planning. "It's not that big a deal," I said. "I can go to my room and review notes, then take a run and relax for the day—maybe even take in a movie."

The Colonels persisted. Said Sawyer, after another conversation with Lemon, "No way. You've come all the way down here and we're going to help you. And we know just the guy who will be happy to do it."

Lemon made the call and I felt relieved after hearing his side of the conversation. Whoever was coming seemed to be enthusiastic about the idea.

I went to the 76th Tactical Fighter Squadron and waited until a small man in casual clothes drove up and unlocked the door. Sawyer and Lemon had given me the name: Maj. Jeff Watterberg, and I walked up and introduced myself as he opened the door. We chatted for a moment and then went to his little office, which was decorated with plaques and mementos from his career. Among the awards, I noted that he was the distinguished graduate of both his ROTC class and his undergraduate flying training class. A large picture of his wife was prominently displayed on his desk, and on the wall behind his chair was an enlargement of a photo taken as he stepped from the ladder of his airplane after returning home from the Gulf War. All during the interview, which lasted almost three hours, my eyes kept wandering back to that photo on the wall. I was captivated by the poignancy of the image, which recorded just one microsecond of the man's life—he with his arms spread to receive the embrace of his wife and children whom the photographer had captured in various stages of sprinting to reach him—the teenage daughter leading the race. Later, when he left to take a break, I walked behind his desk to look more closely at that photograph, marveling at how lucky he was to have had someone capture what must have been one of the happiest moments of his life.

On and on he talked, not so much of the war and his role in it, but about the A-10 itself and how proud he was to have been in the first small group out of pilot training to fly it. I was fascinated as he related how he had learned to fly at 100 feet, navigating with a map in his lap while following streams and power lines, using windmills and barns as checkpoints. When the topic turned to the future role of the A-10 in national defense, his fiery dark eyes took on a new intensity as he gave a discourse on flexibility as the key to air power, and how the A-10 and its pilots were, in his opinion, the most flexible of them all.

I am sure I was frowning when he moved on to the controversial topic of which airplanes should be kept in the inventory and which ones sent to the boneyard. I did not (and do not) consider myself qualified to evaluate such an argument. And at that stage of my inquiry I was almost certain that I did not want to get into that controversy in the book I planned to write. But just in case, I said, "Jeff, you're getting into some heavy duty criticism here, and I would like to interject a 'no attribution' statement into my notes at this point just to protect you should I . . ."

That was as far as I got. Unlike most of the other pilots who occasionally strayed to the same controversy in their interviews, but who did so cautiously and fearfully lest I should write something that might endanger their careers, Jeff Watterberg cut me off. Politely, but curtly, he said, "All that no attribution stuff may be okay for some, but not me. I am saying all this to you and I would say the same to a congressman, a staffer, or your publisher. I believe in the A-10, not because I fly it, but because I love my country and I want what is best for it. . . ."

I generated twelve pages of single-spaced, typewritten notes from the tapes of that interview, and when it was over, without bothering for lunch, Jeff started calling some of his squadron mates and arm twisting them to come in for interviews. One of them, a pilot who had been shot down and held as a prisoner of war (POW) in Iraq, had been pestered by the media for months, and when Jeff mentioned that he was going to call him next, I objected. "That guy has had enough pressure; don't call him on his day off," I insisted. Jeff agreed reluctantly, but, speaking with his authority as the squadron's assistant operations officer, he vowed that I would not leave the base without talking with the ex–POW.

Several pilots volunteered to come in that afternoon, making the day as productive as I had planned. The next morning I drove to Shreveport for an interview, then went back to Alexandria to find that Jeff and the leadership of the 74th Tactical Fighter Squadron, the other squadron that had fought in the war, had booked me solidly for the next two-and-a-half days.

I was scheduled to interview the ex–POW on Thursday at four o'clock and at five o'clock, his wingman, 1st Lt. Eric Miller. After that, I had to drive to New Orleans to prepare for interviews scheduled there the next morning with the "Cajuns," the only reserve A-10 squadron that flew in the war.

At the appointed time the ex–POW, whose name and experiences the reader will encounter in the narrative, joined me in one of the squadron's small briefing rooms. There, while three hours passed without either of us realizing it, I listened and tried to comprehend the criminal and depraved treatment this young man had experienced. Beaten mercilessly, his shoulder had been repeatedly pulled out of joint, and, in agony, with his shoulder finally broken, he had been forced to live and sleep in the the wastes from his kidneys and infected bowels.

It was almost seven o'clock when I looked at my watch. "It's late—way past the time I was to interview Eric Miller," I exclaimed, as we walked back to the Ops (operations) counter through the dim and deserted squadron building.

"Don't worry about Eric," said the ex–POW, and as we rounded the corner, there was Eric Miller, darkly handsome like a 1940s movie star, standing at the Ops counter, waiting patiently.

"I'm really sorry, Eric," I said. "We just got carried away and, quite frankly, I forgot about you."

"That's no problem, sir," he said politely. "I understand."

I looked at my watch again. I wanted to interview Eric Miller but I also had to get to New Orleans, which was five hours away. "If you have to go, sir, I understand. I'll make myself available at another time," Eric said.

The problem was that I was leaving England Air Force Base for good. There was no way I was coming back again; I had a contract and a book to write with a deadline ominously close. I had already talked to Eric briefly during an earlier visit when he was getting ready to fly. But he had been part of an important event in the war and I definitely needed more details. Finally, I made the decision. "Eric, would you mind hanging a phone receiver on your ear for an hour or so? I have to go and I can't come back, and the only option I can see is to do the interview by telephone. Can you live with that?"

Eric smiled modestly. "Absolutely, sir. We'll do it by telephone any time you say."

With that as a parting comment, I left Eric and the ex–POW standing in the parking lot and was off to New Orleans where I interviewed twenty-two of the Cajuns during their long weekend of active duty.

The next day, as I was driving to San Antonio to catch my plane, I heard a newscaster on the radio reporting that two A-10s from England Air Force Base had collided in midair and that both pilots were reported killed. A sick feeling went through me. I had met so many fine young men at that base. Who could it have been? I stopped at the first available telephone and called Sgt. Bob Pease in the Public Affairs Office. "Bill, they were from the 76th squadron," he said, knowing that I had just spent most of the past week there. I swallowed hard and listened as he continued, "It was Maj. Jeff Watterberg and Lt. Eric Miller. All we know at this time is that they collided, the planes exploded, and they probably died instantly."

I did a lot of remorseful thinking about those two young men on the way back to my home in Idaho. Jeff Watterberg—so intense and so dedicated, and that picture on the wall—the children and wife so thrilled by his safe return from the war, and now. . . . Eric Miller, the brilliant astrophysics major at the air academy, the perfectionist, the modest, dedicated, conscientious wingman whom everybody admired. . . .

But I had a book to write, and for professional reasons, I wanted it to be a good one. So when I returned home I threw myself into what seemed like a gigantic task of organizing a story out of more than 1,000 pages of notes, and of experiences related by 143 pilots, most of whom were young men, just as enthusiastic and just as dedicated as Jeff Watterberg and Eric Miller. As I was contemplating the enormity of the task, with piles of three-ring notebooks stacked on my desk, I realized that my motivation for doing a good book was now more than just professional. I became aware that I was emotionally involved with the story, and that I wanted to write a book that would do lasting justice to the Jeff Watterbergs and the Eric Millers who fought in that war.

That I was emotionally involved was a frightening discovery. It has been said numerous times that writers must be cold and objective and avoid emotional involvement with their stories. Well, perhaps that is true. But reader, please be aware that the motivation for telling the story that you are about to read has an emotional component. And I make no apologies for that.

# Acknowledgments

It was 1980 and I was north of Las Vegas, Nevada, in a Mooney 201NS at 800 feet, bucking a strong southwest headwind on my way to Phoenix, when two strange-looking aircraft passed me on the right. I imagined that both pilots waved, although they weren't close enough that I could be certain. As they disappeared in the distance, I was puzzled. What the hell kind of ugly planes were those? This was at a time in my life when I was reading scientific journals on such topics as the bioenergetics of mitochondrial cristae rather than *Aviation Week*, but my curiosity was aroused. Soon I was reading and asking questions, and for some perverse reason—maybe because the rugged and ugly, barrel-shaped P-47 "Jug" was my favorite plane during World War II, and I had to defend it to my boyhood friends who admired the svelte, pointy-nosed P-38s, P-51s, and Spitfires—I became an admirer of the A-10 Warthog. So, to the two pilots who flew past me that day, whoever and wherever you are, thank you for the introduction.

During the air campaign in the Persian Gulf War I knew the A-10s were in the thick of the battle and when the war was over, I contacted a friend who was the F-111 wing commander at Mountain Home Air Force Base, Idaho. To Col. Vic Andrews I said, "Vic, you were in the A-10 community for quite a while; how do you think they would react if I got a contract to do a book on what they did during the war?" His reply got me going: "Bill, I think that's a great idea. I know both wing commanders, Sandy Sharpe and Dave Sawyer. When you get ready to do it, I'll contact them both and do what I can to support you."

That was the start and it snowballed after that. Lieutenant Colonel Mike Gannon at Air Force Public Affairs endorsed the project and arranged official support. Next, I obtained a contract with Brassey's, and while still in Washington D.C., a friend who was attending the War College at Fort McNair, Lt. Col. (now Col.) Skip Bennett invited me for lunch and said that he would arrange for two of his classmates, both Hog drivers, to join us. There I met Lt. Col. Darrel Whitcomb and Col. Charlie Thrash, oldtimers in the A-10 community, who for well over an hour, gave me background, names, and much good advice. (While I was at the Pentagon, another friend, Col. Dick Hellier, also gave me very helpful advice.)

I started visiting the two main air bases, at Myrtle Beach, South

Carolina, and Alexandria, Louisiana. I was greeted warmly by both wing commanders and from the beginning to the end, they did everything they could to help me. They made sure I had the complete freedom to interview all their pilots, they gave me long interviews themselves, accepted dozens of phone calls after the visits, and both men read and commented critically on nearly all of the manuscript. To Colonels, and soon-to-be Brigadier Generals, Sandy Sharpe and Dave Sawyer, thanks for everything.

Now for the pilots who gave interviews, reviewed chapters (and in three cases the whole book!), took and furnished photos, good-naturedly answered my calls on evenings and weekends, and, in general, did anything I asked to help make this an accurate account of their war. To the following who were in or attached to the squadrons below, *milla esker*—a thousand thanks.

• *the 74th Tactical Fighter Squadron, the Flying Tigers:* Col. Tom Lyon, Lt. Col. Jim Green, Lt. Col. Mike Wilken, Maj. Jeff Watterberg, Capt. Steve Barbour, Capt. Matt Cavanaugh, Capt. Arden Dahl, Capt. Ralph Hansen, Capt. Eric Paul, Capt. Mike Isherwood, Capt. Mark Koechle, Capt. Dave Feehs, Capt. Eric Stoll, Capt. Kent Yohe, Capt. Lee Wyatt, Capt. Mike Mangus, Capt. Kevin Jens, Capt. John Russell, Capt. Scott Kelly, Lt. Dave Lucke, Lt. Bryan Currier, Lt. J. J. Krimmell, Lt. Pat McAlister, Lt. Don Henry, Lt. Cliff Grafton, Lt. Tom Norris, and Lt. Dave Ure.

• *the 76th Tactical Fighter Squadron, the Vanguards:* Lt. Col. Gene Renuart, Capt. Rich Biley, Capt. Karl Buchberger, Capt. Rick Griffin, Capt. Al Hicks, Capt. Blas Miyares, Capt. Tim Saffold, Capt. Eric Salomonson, Capt. John Scott, Capt. Dale Storr, Capt. Bob Sullivan, Capt. Ernie Brown, Capt. Ward Larson, Lt. Darren Hansen, Lt. John Marks, Lt. Eric Miller, Lt. Matt Murray, Lt. Jim Schmick, and Lt. Dan Dennis.

• *the 355th Tactical Fighter Squadron, the Falcons:* Col. Hank Haden, Lt. Col. Rick McDow, Lt. Col. Joe Barton, Lt. Col. Danny Clifton, Lt. Col. Chuck Fox, Lt. Col Con Rodi, Maj. John Bingaman, Maj. A. J. Jackson, Capt. Bob Buchanan, Capt. Jim Cobb, Capt. John Dobbins, Capt. Leon Elsarelli, Capt. Jeff Gingras, Capt. Rob Givens, Capt. Carlos Honesty, Capt. John Marselus, Capt. Mike McGee, Capt. Leslie Rohlf, Capt. Mark Roling, and Capt. Jeff Wesley.

• *the 353d Fighter Squadron, the Panthers:* Lt. Col. Rick Shatzel, Lt. Col. Ron Kurtz, Lt. Col. Mike Parsons, Lt. Col. Tom Essig, Maj. Dan Swift, Maj. Scott Hill, Capt. Tom Dean, Capt. Don Fann, Capt. Tom Wilson, Capt. John Whitney, Capt. Dan Mulherin, Capt. Randy Goff, Capt. Dave Hanaway, Capt. Eric Sobol, Capt. Larry Butler, Capt. Greg Henderson, Capt. John Nachtman, Capt. Paul Johnson, Lt. Stephan Otto, Lt. Jeff Scott, and Lt. Rob Sweet.

• *the 511th Tactical Fighter Squadron, the Vultures:* Lt. Col. Mike O'Connor, Lt. Col. Keith Bennett, Maj. Wayne Pepin, Capt. Rick Turner, Capt. J. C. Carter, Capt. Kevin Kriner, Capt. Gregory Benjamin, Capt. Joe Nuti, Capt. Dave Tan, Capt. Tommy Atkins, Capt. Paul Rastas, Capt. Eric Offill, Capt. Todd Sheehy, Lt. Todd Decker, Lt. Jeff Clifton, Lt. Brad Whitmire, Lt. Dan Greenwood, Lt. Richard McKinley, and Lt. Greg Engle.

• *the 23d Tactical Air Support Squadron, the Nail FACs:* Lt. Col. Bob George, Lt. Col. Jeff Fox, Capt. Jerry Stophel, Capt. Greg Wilhite, Capt. Ted Bale, Capt. Mike Bartley, Capt. Jerry Deemer, Capt. Bob Ginnetti, Lt. Scott Stark, Lt. Quentin Rideout, Lt. Ed Norwesh, Lt. Sean Kavanaugh, Lt. Scott Fitzsimmons, Lt. Bob Morse, Lt. Jeff Cowan, Lt. John Fitzgerrell, Lt. Dean Lee, and Lt. Mark Register.

• *the **706th** Tactical Fighter Squadron, the Cajuns:* Col. Bob Efferson, Lt. Col. Greg Wilson, Lt. Col. Tom Coleman, Lt. Col. Craig Mays, Lt. Col. Jack Ihle, Lt. Col. Doug Findley, Lt. Col Johnny Alexander, Lt. Col. Lee Brundage, Maj. Sonny Rasar, Maj. Jim Rose, Maj. Jim Venturella, Maj. Larry McCaskill, Maj. Greg Durio, Capt. Todd Nilsen, Capt. Bob Swain, Capt. Phil Farrell, Capt. Mark Habetz, Capt. Larry Merington, Capt. Jim Callaway, Capt. Dave Duncan, Lt. Will Shepard, and Lt. Mark White.

Numerous others generously gave interviews or helped me in other ways during the research and I would like to thank the following: Col. Buck Rogers, Mr. Tim Walker, Capt. Tom Trask, Lt. Col. Fred Offutt, Capt. Frank Hinson, Capt. Tony Huelin, Sgt. Jim Protzmann, Lt. Joel Hylen, Navy Lt. Devon Jones, Capt. Don McGough, Maj. Frank Green, Maj. Keith Michael, Dr. Robert Sanitor, Mr. Joel Thorvaldson, Army Capt. Mike Winstead, Army Capt. Joe Gerard, Mr. Vincent Tizio, Capt. Jeff Eggers, Capt. Lary Korn, Lt. Lisa Rappa, Jim and Dale Kiser, and Sgt. Glenn DeTour.

Special thanks are due the maintenance and armament personnel at England Air Force Base who, for three hot summer days and with great patience, tried to educate me regarding all aspects of their support role during Desert Shield and Desert Storm. They knew that the pilots were going to get all the glory, but they didn't care because they were satisfied in their own minds that they had performed well above and beyond their duty. Here are the names recorded in my notes and my thanks to others I cannot name: C.M. Sgt. Wilson R. Ewing, Jr., Sr.M. Sgt. Luis Salinas, M. Sgt. Dave Craby, Sgt. James Hargrove, Sgt. James Wolf, Sgt. Ron Wright, Sr.M. Sgt. Ernie Bellerd, Capt. Dan Regan, Lt. Dan O'Hair, Sgt. Ricky Galloway, Sgt. Bryan Vincent, Sgt. Lanny Orr, Sgt. Keith Durgan, Sgt. Chuck Spurlin, Sgt. Mark Holaway, and Sgt. Victor Smallin.

At each base I was assisted by the Public Affairs Office and I would like to acknowledge the specific help of Capt. Becky Colaw, Capt. Anna Palutti, Capt. Keith Tackett, Sgt. Bob Pease, and especially T/Sgt. Linda Mitchell, who went to a lot of trouble helping me locate quarters and an automobile while at RAF Alconbury.

I am very fortunate to have a knowledgeable, enthusiastic editor on this project and I want to thank Don McKeon for the helpful guidance he has given me.

I also want to thank the field guys at Silver and McGraw for making it possible for me to do all of my research—they know who and why.

On the home front, special thanks are due Doris Bills, who did an outstanding job transcribing my tapes, Mike McLean, who read with a critical, discerning eye, William M. Smallwood, who consulted with me on all phases of manuscript production, and Patricia Smallwood who, as always, copyedits the manuscript and sustains me in every way.

# Warthog

# 1

# Terror in the Night

*"After flying through those thunderstorms for an hour, three feet off Rutkowski's wing, I had to pry my fingers off the stick, then fly with my left hand for a while."*
— Capt. Tim Saffold

It was almost midnight when Capt. Matt Cavanaugh saw the lightning flashes. He was flying on the left wing of a KC-135 tanker over the Atlantic Ocean, about 1,200 miles east of the Virginia coastline. He was in the second of four cells of A-10s, each cell of six aircraft flying in formation off the wings of a tanker, headed for Saudi Arabia.

Iraq, with the world's fourth largest army, had just overrun the small, oil-rich kingdom of Kuwait. Now its massive armored forces were poised near the Saudi border, ready, it appeared to President George Bush and his military advisers, to strike southward. Without the intervention of the United States and other Saudi friends, such a move was certain to be successful because of the Saudis' limited defensive capability. In addition, a strike southward, where the world's largest oil reserves were but a day's march away, was a move that now seemed irresistible to the cash-starved Iraqis, burdened with massive debts incurred during their eight-year war with Iran.

In recognition of this grave threat to Saudi Arabia, President Bush and the leaders of a hastily assembled coalition of allies were rushing forces to the region to deter such an invasion. The A-10s were among those forces. Their specialty was tank killing, but with the awesome ground attack weapons they carried, they could be a deadly force against any threat to friendly ground troops. They were on the way to Saudi Arabia to become part of an aerial line of defense. Should Saddam Hussein, the outlaw military dictator of Iraq, decide to strike southward, they would be there, along with other assault aircraft, to attack the Iraqi armor and provide close air support for the embryonic assembly of Coalition ground forces now rallying in defense of the region.

Off in the distance the lightning discharges were getting brighter and more frequent. On his Victor (VHF) radio Matt Cavanaugh could hear his friends in the cell ahead chattering excitedly about the line of thunderstorms they were penetrating. They had already moved into a close V-formation with their tanker, flying 3 feet from their tanker's wings and from each other. Like ducklings behind their mother, they were weaving blindly through the thick, turbulent clouds, relying on their tanker's radar to lead them through the least violent parts of the storms. In Cavanaugh's cell they were talking with each other over their short-range Fox Mike (FM) radios. For awhile they chatted about last night's party in Myrtle Beach, South Carolina, where they had rested after their flight from home, which was England Air Force Base in Alexandria, Louisiana. It had been a good party, although as Cavanaugh later said, "Nobody really got smoked or lit their hair on fire even though we knew this was probably the last booze we would see for awhile. There was a definite feeling of tension among the guys. I myself figured, knowing the number and kinds of SAMs [surface-to-air missiles] the Iraqis had, that if we went to war, 20 to 25 percent of us were not coming back. The other guys had those kinds of numbers in mind, too—we had talked about it—so there was a definite cloud hanging over the celebration. Besides that, we knew we had a twelve- to thirteen-hour flight ahead of us and we were not about to go out and paint the town the way fighter pilots would if they were on a regular TDY [temporary duty]."

They knew that it would be a long, tiring flight. The A-10 is a slow, stick-and-rudder, no-computer airplane. It is primitive and ugly in comparison to other Air Force fighters and, unlike other fighters produced since the fifties, it had no autopilot. Also, the trim mechanism—the devices that allow the pilot to get the plane into a stable position where it can be controlled with the least amount of effort on the stick and rudder—is the subject of one of the standing jokes about the A-10. The trim mechanism is said to be so bad that when the aircraft is being fired at by AAA (ground-to-air-antiaircraft fire), there is no need to perform violent evasive maneuvers, or "jink." Instead, all the A-10 pilot has to do is turn loose of the controls and let the plane fly "hands off."

In addition, they expected the flight to be boring, so they brought along Trivial Pursuit cards and the Battleship game, and some had wired their Walkmans into the Fox Mike radios so all the pilots in the six-ship cell could share musical entertainment.

But this night there had been no opportunity to play their games. Flying over the black Atlantic, where there were no lights for horizon clues, was a demanding task that few of them had ever experienced before. And no complaints were heard about the lack of musical entertainment. Just the routine aviator's task of keeping wings level and the plane in its proper place in the formation was demanding enough to require near-total concentration.

Then there had been the night air-to-air refuelings. In Matt Cavanaugh's cell they had already done three of them, which was more than any of the pilots had done in the previous two years. No pilot likes the night refueling experience. But when spatial disorientation, or vertigo, hits—when the pilot's brain sensors say the plane is in a position that differs from reality—then the night refueling process becomes a nightmare. Several of the pilots in the cells that night had experienced mild vertigo, which they call "the leans," and they had serious trouble moving up closely behind their tanker and engaging the tanker boom in the receptacle above the nose of their plane.

A pilot in one cell narrowly averted disaster because of severe vertigo. During the night his brain sensors had convinced him that his plane was in 130 degrees of bank, which meant that he felt like he was flying almost completely upside down. (With 90 degrees of bank the wings are perpendicular to the earth.) It was only after numerous failures and the patient coaching of his cell leader—who also happened to be his wing commander—that he got on the tanker and possibly avoided a fuel-starvation flameout of his engines and a long, lonely glide into the desolate waters of the Atlantic.

"Gold 73, Bemo 21. It looks a little bad up ahead. What are you painting?" It was Capt. Mark Koechle, the cell leader on Uniform (UHF) radio talking to the tanker crew, asking what they were seeing on their radar.

"Bemo 21, Gold 73. We're painting lots of stuff at our ten and two but nothing much straight ahead."

Matt Cavanaugh, who was Bemo 23 and on the opposite tanker wing from Koechle, scanned from ten to two o'clock and saw repeated flashes of lightning. There appeared to be no difference between the two positions; the whole frontal area looked sinister and dangerous.

"Bemo flight, Bemo 21. Hey guys, let's move it up into close on the tanker." Mark Koechle didn't like what he was seeing ahead of them and the tanker's position lights were starting to grow fuzzy. This meant that the tanker was moving into clouds. He ordered his flight of six to move into close formation—to change from a separation of about 250 feet to within 3 feet of each other.

Matt Cavanaugh moved up on the left wing of the tanker and established its red position light just in front of his right wingtip. He had to concentrate intensely to hold that position and he tried to shut out all other thoughts.

But they flooded in despite his efforts. He couldn't help worrying about the two lieutenants who should be off his left wing—they had announced their presence but he didn't dare swing his head around to confirm that they were there. They were the only two lieutenants in the squadron who had been allowed to fly on this mission. At the party the night before and again during the earlier part of the flight he had teased them unmercifully about who in the squadron or wing he had angered enough to have gotten stuck with both of them on his wing. Now their lack of experience was no joking matter. If either of them suffered just a two-second lapse in his concentration or made a quick, jerky move on the control stick, any or all of them could end up as a fireball heading into the Atlantic.

He also had personal problems crowding his thoughts. He was from an old Nebraska family that still owned the land that had been homesteaded by his great-grandfather. But his father, who had been a fighter pilot in the Korean War, elected to be a crop duster rather than a farmer and ended up getting killed when Matt was only nine years old. That left Matt's mother with four boys and a girl to raise by herself, and like many families who suffer such a loss, they all became very, very close through the years. Thus it was a severe blow when Matt learned just before his deployment that his oldest brother—also a crop duster—had crashed and suffered second- and third-degree burns. Matt's last report was that his brother was in no danger but he would lose one of his fingers and would have to endure numerous skin grafting operations.

And his thoughts were heavy with matters of the heart. He had finally met the girl "I wanted to start my own family with." Her name was Melanie, and when he kissed her good-bye at the plane, she said that she would be there when he returned. Those happy words were echoing in his mind and had buoyed him throughout the flight. But even though he had the classic fighter pilot's attitude about flying in combat—that it won't happen to me—the ominous survival statistics, which he believed, weighed heavily on his mind. Like many of the young men and women heading to the Persian Gulf, he wondered why, when his future was suddenly looking so bright, he had to be heading to a potential war that could end it all.

The lightning was becoming more intense, and at first the flashes of light reflecting off the clouds allowed him to momentarily see the entire tanker and the three A-10s tucked up in tight formation on the tanker's right wing. But a few minutes later, as the tanker moved into the roiling, churning air in the core of the thunderhead, the brilliant flashes of lightning blinded him, and after each one, it was like going from bright sunlight into a dark theater. Squinting anxiously, he had to struggle to relocate the faint and, because of the dense clouds, nearly obscure red position light on the tanker's wing.

The up- and downdrafts grew more violent and as he fought the turbulence with his rudders and stick, he grew angry at the tanker crew for taking them into such a storm. *There is no peacetime mission which allows intentional flying into thunderstorms: Chapter Eight, Air Force Regulation 60-16.* That was what he was thinking; thunderstorms are off limits, period, unless you are in a war. *Is going to a war an excuse for flying through one?* He fought the control stick and silently cursed. *What are those assholes sitting up there fat, dumb, and happy in that tanker trying to do to us?*

He had been watching the buildup of ice on the leading edge of his right wing and had added power to compensate for the drag it was causing. Now he was startled by new elements of the storm. Large pellets of hail began cracking against his windscreen and although he could not see the impacts, the hailstones were denting the leading edges of his wings, even through the thick ice accretions.

Suddenly he felt the tingling of an electric shock in his right hand and a brilliant flash of lightning appeared to have struck the tanker and sheared off its left wing. Within seconds, while he was trying to sort out the bizarre black and white images dancing on his retinas, a violent gust tossed his plane upward with such force that his plane might as well have been a balsa wood and tissue-paper model of itself.

When his vision returned, Matt realized that he had completely lost sight of the tanker and he responded to the emergency reflexively with a lost wingman call to his flight. The lost wingman call is a well-drilled emergency procedure whereby the pilots—in this case, Cavanaugh and the two lieutenants flying off his wing—are to maneuver their planes in a prescribed way so that a collision is avoided.

But Cavanaugh had no chance to even think of flying a new heading and altitude. (For that matter, neither did the two lieutenants on his wing; at the same instant he went lost wingman because of a severe updraft, they were on the other side of a wind shear and were slammed in the opposite direction by a violent downdraft.) As his vision recovered enough to scan his instruments he saw that his 23-ton airplane (including 8,000 pounds of fuel in external auxiliary tanks) was climbing at 5,000 feet per minute—an incredible rate for a heavily loaded plane that will barely stay airborne when it is over 20,000 feet.

The vertical velocity was all he managed to see. This time a lightning bolt struck the nose of his plane and the dissipating electric energy shot through the stick and throttle into both of his hands. It was only a tingling sensation; that was the good news. The bad news was that the lightning had blown out all of his interior lights. Now he was in a violent updraft, out of control, hammered by hail, and he had no instrument references to know whether he was right side up or upside down. Nor did he have any clue as to the position of the other aircraft. He could have been on a collision course with any of them.

Cavanaugh was the squadron's functional test pilot, a job that required him to test fly all the aircraft after they went through a major maintenance program. This was a standard two-hour test regime that included high-G aerobatic maneuvers and, as a finale, a screaming 90-degree dive straight down from 35,000 feet. (He was able to struggle up that high with a minimum load.) Now, he used every millisecond of experience that he had gained during those stressful flights. He fought his brain, which seemed to be congealing like cold syrup. He forced himself to recite and execute the procedures for such a situation. He took his feet off the rudder pedals and planted them flat on the floor. He neutralized the stick and held it in the center position. Then, while he felt the plane hurtling through the sky and the harness digging into his shoulders, he summoned raw will power and forced himself to bend over and grope for the flashlight that he carried in the right lower leg pocket of his G-suit.

When he reached it, he knew that there was no use shining it on the horizontal situation indicator (HSI), which depicted a small airplane and its relation to the ground, horizon and sky. He knew that this instrument, along with the other primary attitude instruments would be inoperable because of the electrical failure. Instead, he shined the light on the tiny standby attitude indicator in the upper-left quadrant of the panel, which was powered by a gyro that would keep it operational for another nine minutes. That is when he discovered that the plane was right side up.

With the flashlight, Matt checked the altimeter and saw that he was climbing through 23,000 feet, which was 5,000 feet higher than he had been on the tanker. Then his scan took him to the backup "whiskey compass," a notoriously erratic instrument almost impossible to read accurately during violent maneuvers. He studied the wide oscillations of the compass and when he averaged them, he decided that he was still heading roughly 090, which was the original eastward route of the tanker.

Then the monster spit him out. He looked up and saw an array of stars and realized that he had been ejected from the back of the thunderhead. Flying with the flashlight between his knees, he turned off his radio, light switches, and all the other devices in the cockpit that used electrical energy. With that accomplished, he did another scan with the flashlight, made the necessary stick and rudder adjustments, then put the flashlight back between his knees and began punching in all of the circuit breakers that had popped when the massive electrical discharge surged through the plane.

Then the test, and it was a scary one, because if the radios and navigation instruments had been fried by the lightning, and if he could not somehow find the flashing lights of one of his fellow airmen—at the time he believed the tanker might have lost its wing and gone down—he would be hopelessly lost in the middle of the Atlantic, unable to call for help, and . . .

He constrained himself from thinking of the alternatives and set about doing what he had to do, which was to turn on the electrical instruments and radios one by one to see if they would come on line. He did that and started breathing again. The lights came on, the gyro instruments spooled up and functioned properly and, most satisfying of all, his radios came on and he heard his wingmen talking to the tanker. The tanker had survived. His wingmen had survived. He had survived. Clear skies were ahead and all he had left to do was get on the radio and talk his way back into the formation.

Then, because they were fighter pilots to the core of their souls, they laughed and joked about the "sporty" moments in the storm. And, in loose formation again, they relaxed and began teasing the tanker pilots for not knowing that their radar was malfunctioning between the headings of ten and two o'clock. And they flew on through the night, listening to the music that they had wired into their Fox Mike radios. And hours later, as dim light appeared on the eastern horizon, they watched in awe as the purplish green fingers of electricity danced up their windscreen like a laser show—St. Elmo's fire, one of the more spectacular of nature's wonders to be experienced by the aviator.

Then there was the sunrise over the water, awesomely beautiful and serene after a night of terror. And there was yawning and stretching and vain efforts at twisting in their seats to find more comfort in the cramped space they had occupied for ten hours.

As the August sun rose and the light slowly grew to a blazing intensity, their thoughts turned to their ultimate destination and the fate that awaited them. A poet among them could have imagined they were in a David Lean script, modern day Lawrences charging forward to save a righteous Arab kingdom from another tribe of black-hearted, ruthless, Arab warriors.

But at this time in their young lives they were not much inclined to poetry and make-believe visions of grandeur and righteousness.

They were fighter pilots, trained to Olympian standards in the art and science of killing and keeping from being killed. The blazing sunlight and their television-enhanced images of a shimmering desert triggered thoughts of how they would dive on tanks and kill them while shoulder-fired SA-16 missiles were boring through the sky toward them, and while radar-guided streams of fire from Russian- and Chinese-made ZSU 23-4s were reaching for them like fingers of death.

And if there was room for any romance to be crowded into all their grim thoughts, they would be thinking of the beloved plane they were flying.

Beloved? An airplane? A piece of machinery?

Absolutely.

# 2

# The Airplane

WARTHOG: "A rather hideous animal . . . "
—*Encyclopedia Britannica*

The CBS program "Sixty Minutes" did a segment on the A-10, essentially saying that it was a near-useless airplane, unwanted by the Air Force and the pork-barrel project of self-serving politicians protecting lucrative defense contracts in their districts.

Who knows what the Air Force itself has said about the airplane? The pilots who fly it—an obviously biased crowd—say that their plane has been maligned for years because (their words) it doesn't have a pointy nose, go Mach snot, or fit the gleaming, high-tech image the service would like to portray. And, they say, their plane is always the butt of jokes from the pointy-nosed fraternity within the fighter community. Hey, do you know what the airspeed indicator in the A-10 is? It's a calendar. And, did you hear that an A-10 had a bird strike? It finally caught one from behind.

Then why did the Air Force acquire the airplane in the first place?

The answer to that question depends on whom one asks. Those who are not fans of the plane say that it was forced upon the Air Force by the Army. After the A-1 Skyraider—the propeller-driven Vietnam workhorse that gave the Army the kind of close air support (CAS) they desired—was given to the Vietnamese and taken from the Air Force inventory, there was nothing available to do the job—at least, the way the Army wanted it done. Of course, so the story goes, they—the Army—would be happy to design and build a special fixed-wing airplane that would have all the desirable features for CAS. *And, of course, they would be happy to fly it and maintain it themselves.*

Horror of horrors: the Army in the fixed-wing aviation business! Never, unless it was over the dead bodies of Frank Andrews, Hap Arnold, Tooey Spaatz, Ira Eaker, and all the others who fought for years to extricate themselves from the tentacles of Army control and gain Air Force independence.

Hell no! [Air Force generals pounding on the table—so the story goes.] We'll draw up specifications. We'll call for a design and proto- types. Then *we'll* buy and fly and maintain those suckers. Yes sir! We'll do just exactly what you guys in the Army want . . . [in a low voice] if we have to.

Is there any truth to that story? The author heard similar versions numerous times but no one with authority wanted his name associ- ated with it.

And who really cares at this point if the child was wanted or not? Despite the fact that she was born ugly (blame the pilots for the gen- der!) and did not get any prettier when she matured as the Air Force's dedicated CAS airplane, she did get invited to the big dance. And those who scoffed may not be praising, but even her worst critics will admit that the ugly girl gave a good performance in the Gulf War.

So when was the ugly child conceived?

In the late 1960s Air Force planners drew up preliminary specifi- cations for the ideal CAS airplane and they asked the aircraft indus- try to come up with proposals. In those specifications the planners incorporated all the lessons that had been learned about flying air- to-ground combat, especially in Vietnam. In essence, they advised the industry to throw away their preconceived notions about an attack aircraft and start from scratch with seven main consider- ations.

1. The plane has to be able to operate out of short, primitive air- fields.

2. It should be reliable and easy to maintain in the field under wartime conditions.

3. It must be able to carry a large amount of ordnance and specifi- cally must be able to kill tanks and other armor.

4. It must have sufficient range to loiter "on call" near the battle- field, and when needed for CAS it should have enough remaining endurance to find the target, identify and confirm that it is, indeed, enemy rather than friendly, and then destroy it.

5. It must fly at least 350 knots, but be maneuverable enough to turn tightly over the battlefield so that the pilot will not lose sight of the target when visibility is low.

6. It must be survivable; it should be able to take damage from ground fire and still return to base with a healthy pilot.

7. It should be a low-cost airplane in comparison to prices being quoted for supersonic jet fighters, and cost overruns, such as had occurred with the F-111 and C-5 programs, were not to be allowed.

By the deadline in August 1970, six companies had submitted proposals for what the Air Force called the A-X (attack, experimental) program. Within a short time, the list had been narrowed down to two finalists: Fairchild and Northrop. The Fairchild proposal was put together by the Republic Division of Fairchild Industries—Republic being the company that manufactured the P-47 Thunderbolt, the F-84 Thunderjet, and the F-105 Thunderchief. These planes had major air-to-ground roles in World War II, the Korean War, and the Vietnam War, respectively.

A key factor that influenced the original design of the A-X was related to geopolitics. Vietnam was making the headlines, but as U.S. policy shifted from nuclear deterrence as the sole means of stopping a Warsaw Pact invasion of Central Europe, the military scrambled to develop conventional weapons that could do the job. Thus, thoughts about the role of a future CAS airplane moved from the jungles of Vietnam to the Fulda Gap of Germany. Instead of fighting off a battalion of North Vietnamese overrunning a mountain outpost, planners saw the need for a plane that could help destroy the hordes of Soviet tanks that were in massed positions in Eastern Europe. (The Apache helicopter gunship was under concurrent development. It would move with the army and attack on frontal assaults but would be vulnerable behind the lines where the A-X could continue to attack.)

A major question for the A-X planners was what weapon could the A-X use to kill those tanks? Could bombs do it?

No way. It is too difficult to hit tanks with iron bombs, especially if the tanks are moving. Smart bombs—bombs guided by laser targeting beams—were just then being developed, as were Maverick "fire-and-forget" missiles. Neither of them could be considered as a viable weapon system for the A-X.

That left one option: some kind of cannon. Cannons were used very effectively in World War II, and anybody interested in the history is urged to read *Stuka Pilot* by Hans Rudel. This intrepid warrior killed hundreds of tanks on the Eastern Front with two 37mm cannons mounted under the wings of his Stuka.

A comparatively recent event was also on the minds of the planners. During the 1967 Arab-Israeli War, the Israelis mounted 30mm cannons on some of their fighters, and this weapon was highly effective against the Soviet-made tanks, which their enemies were using.

The reason it was effective is because the Israeli aircraft were able to attack the tanks from the sides, rear, and top where they were lightly armored.

So the A-X had to have a cannon, and to be effective it had to have a very high rate of fire. This precluded recoil-operated guns and left the Gatling-type gun as the only alternative.

When designers began looking at the specific power and velocity needed to effectively kill tanks at anything but point blank range, however, another problem arose. To make a Gatling gun with sufficient muzzle velocity, and to have accessory space to carry enough ammunition to be effective, the gun system would be as long and heavy as a full-sized Cadillac automobile—and this was in the early seventies when Cadillacs were *big and heavy!* This monster gun, bigger than anything ever before considered, somehow had to be stuffed inside an airplane.*

So, in Dr. Robert Sanitor's words—he was head of the aircraft design team—"We literally sat down and designed a plane around the gun that we had to have."

The gun that was ultimately designed and incorporated into the A-10 is a seven-barrel Gatling, manufactured by General Electric, and capable of firing 3,000 to 4,000 rounds per minute. The reason for the variance is that the gun fires fifty rounds the first second and, after the inertia is overcome and the barrels are rotating, it fires seventy rounds per second. Do not let these numbers sail by without thinking about their significance. Imagine the shell that is used in such a gun. It is about 1 foot long and weighs up to 2 pounds. Now try to imagine a gun mechanism that can load, fire and unload fifty or seventy of these in one second! Is it any wonder that engineers stand in awe of the genius of Richard Gatling whose design for such a gun was patented over 150 years ago?

Another major problem for the designers was how to power the aircraft. The conventional jet engines available at the time were fuel hogs. The danger of the CAS mission dictated that the A-X had to have two engines for survivability. But with two jet engines gulping fuel, especially at the low altitudes the A-X would be flying, there was no way the plane could carry enough fuel and ordnance to meet Air Force specifications.

Turboprops, where jet engines are mated to propellers, were more efficient but had disadvantages that ruled them out. Propellers are

---

* The Gatling gun eventually developed, the GAU-8/A, loaded, weighs 4,029 pounds and is 19 feet, 10 inches long.

sensitive to battle damage. In addition, with the large engines and propellers necessary for design performance, the distance they would have to be mounted out on the wing would create problems should an inflight engine failure occur. The pull of the good engine would create adverse yaw, making it difficult for the pilot to maintain directional control.

Fortunately, the designers had another option. A new jet engine called the turbofan was just coming into general use. Airliners were using it and General Electric was developing a smaller version for the Navy's new S-3A antisubmarine warfare plane. The turbofan has several characteristics that made it attractive to A-X designers.

It is very fuel efficient—much more so than the traditional turbojets being used by military aircraft. The smaller engines that GE was developing for the Navy promised to be efficient enough for the fuel economy A-X planners needed.

The turbofan has a big blade in front of a much smaller-diameter jet turbine. The turbine burns fuel and provides the power to turn the big blade. However, the volume of air that is shoved backwards, and that provides propulsion, is much greater than what comes out the back of the turbine itself. Engineers call the turbofan a high-bypass engine because most of the air going through the engine goes around the turbine instead of through it.

The turbofan engines also made the A-X more survivable. For example, bird strikes, which are common at CAS altitudes, usually do relatively little damage to turbofan engines. The strong titanium blades of the fan chew up the bird and the pieces usually flow past the turbine in the bypass air. Turbojets, on the other hand, are easily damaged by bird strikes because the bird is always sucked through the turbine.

In addition, fan jet engines are much quieter than turbojets. That turned out to be a tremendous advantage in the Gulf War because the night fighters could operate as low as 5,000 feet and not be heard by the enemy. "We were flying a stealth fighter, too," joked one of the night fighters.

Another safety feature of the turbofan is its low heat signature—a military term meaning that the engine exhaust heat is much lower than from ram-jet engines. (Most of the exhaust is cold air that has bypassed the turbine.) This means that infrared tracking missiles, such as those fired from handheld SAMs, have a much more difficult time locking on to the turbofan exhausts. In fact, one of the tactics pilots use to defeat such missiles is to turn their tails away from the missile so that the heat signature is much reduced or nonexistent.

The bad news about the GE fan jet engine that was eventually selected for the A-X was its lack of power. When the engine became operational, it never quite produced as much power as its engineers predicted. And, according to Vincent Tizio, who was responsible for much of the overall A-10 design, the Air Force could never afford the more than $100 million GE wanted for boosting the power 10 to 15 percent. The net result was an A-X and, later, the A-10, that is considered by most of its pilots to be underpowered. According to Tizio, it has enough thrust for takeoff but the fan blade is just too big for the turbine and too much air goes through the bypass. This causes it to perform like a propeller plane, which loses thrust with both speed and altitude.

Once the designers decided on the engines, their next step was to decide where to place them. Under-the-wing placement, like on the Boeing 737, was not a good option. The under-wing area was needed for ordnance. Their ultimate placement, canted upward from near the back of the fuselage, had several advantages. The potential yaw problem after an engine failure was negligible because the engines were mounted close to the centerline. Also, the high position of the engines, which Tizio calls "real suckers," decreased the probability that foreign objects thrown up from rough-field operations would get sucked through the turbine. Another advantage relates to the large volume of gases that are expelled from the gun when it fires. Placing the engines above the fuselage takes them out of the major gun-gas flow. (According to the mechanics some of the gun-gases still get into the engines and the residue sticks and creates a crud problem. But during service in the Saudi desert, when everybody was worrying about abrasive damage from sand, the mechanics were ecstatic. The ingested sand cleaned out the gun-gas residue "slick as a whistle," and one of the headaches they were dreading from so much combat firing of the gun turned out to be a non-problem.)

So the practical problem of engine placement was solved. But at what expense aesthetically! From the front view some say the big round engines look like the bug-eyes of a dragonfly. Others moan that no self-respecting jet airplane should look *that* unstreamlined.

But Joel Thorvaldson, a retired Air Force fighter pilot who worked on the design, just laughs when the plane's double-ugly reputation is brought up. "You don't hear the pilots running it down because it's ugly," he said. "They love it. It's beautiful to them."

He is right, of course, and one of the reasons they love it is because of the survivability that was designed into the plane. In fact, when one looks at an A-10 and disregards the engines and the placement of the gun, almost everything else one observes is there because it contributes to survivability.

Take the double-tail configuration, for example. If one of the vertical fins or rudders gets blown away, the plane can fly almost as well with the one that remains. The same goes for the horizontal stabilizer and elevator. Also, when the plane comes back with one or more of the tail components missing, the parts can be cannibalized from any other A-10 and used on *either* side—the tail components are symmetrical. (Actually all parts of an A-10 except the canopy are interchangeable and cannibalization—the taking of parts from one aircraft to use on another—is a routine maintenance procedure.)

An additional advantage of the double tail is that the vertical fins and rudder shield the engines' heat signature from the side, thus making the plane less vulnerable to heatseeking missiles.

The landing gear is another example of built-in survivability. All three of the wheels retract forward against the force of the slipstream—the air streaming over the plane. That's no problem at the low speed of takeoff, and it is a real advantage if the motors that operate the gear are shot out. All the pilot has to do in an emergency is to release the gear locks manually and the wheels fall down. They are then forced backwards and locked in place by the power of the slipstream.

The fuel tanks are another example. There are none in the outer wing where the large surface area invites AAA damage. Most of the fuel is in a large fuselage tank, and because of the slab sides and narrow width of the fuselage, the area of exposure to ground fire is minimized. However, some fuel is in tanks in the inboard section of the wings but they, like the fuselage tank, have dual protection. They are lined with a self-sealant, which is a safety throwback to the way rugged World War II gas tanks were constructed. Also, they have a foam-type material inside that prevents the formation of a gas-air mixture that an incendiary bullet might ignite. In addition, the fuselage tank is circular, and for reasons even engineers have trouble explaining, this shape tends to negate the possibility that a high-explosive shell would rupture the tank.

In tests before the A-X was finally accepted, mockups of the plane filled with fuel were fired at with incendiary and high-explosive bullets and not once did the fuel ignite. The same kinds of tests were done with the A-7—an existing air-to-ground attack plane that Congress thought might do just as good a job as the A-X. The A-7 tanks ignited and burned every time they were struck.

There are many other survivability features that are not visible. The control system is an example. There are dual hydraulic systems that operate the controls. But unlike other combat aircraft of the era, where the dual hydraulic lines ran side-by-side and were highly vulnerable to a single strike, the hydraulic lines in the A-X were placed in widely separate positions. In addition, a manual cable system was also designed into the plane. With both hydraulic systems shot out, the pilot can switch over to the manual flight control system called manual reversion. This cable and pulley system activates the trim tabs on the controls, which, in turn, cause the controls to move the way the pilot wants them to go. When flying the plane in manual reversion the pilot is not going to win any dogfights. But there are two A-10 pilots who survived heavy battle damage in the Gulf War and were able to fly home and land because of that system.

The pilots don't like to admit it, but the survivability feature they probably love the most is the huge chunk of armor that surrounds them, which they call the "titanium bathtub." The pilot literally sits inside thick slabs of titanium bolted into a bathtub-shaped container. During interviews, when many of the pilots told of combat missions during which they experienced heavy AAA fire, they often unconsciously slumped a little lower in their chairs. "And so you hunkered down a little lower in the titanium bathtub, right?" said the author after he began to notice the reaction. "Right," most of the pilots said, grinning. One pilot went on to say, "That was the warm-fuzzy we always carried with us."

The first Fairchild A-X flew in 1972, and in the fly-off competition with the Northrop plane, which was built more like a conventional fighter, the Fairchild A-X won, but not by much. The Northrop plane was cleaner, handled better, and was more stable. However, the survivability that was designed into the Fairchild plane was superior to its competitor, and its external engines, as ugly as they were, promised to be easier to maintain than the competitor's engines, which were buried in the wing roots. An additional factor in favor of Fairchild was that its plane was less expensive and much closer to being what would come off the assembly line than Northrop's prototype. The latter factor was good leverage on Fairchild's part because the Air Force leaders didn't want any more trips before Congress with cost-overrun tabs.

About six months after the Air Force made its decision to go with the ugly child, an officer writing about it in a professional journal wondered what it might be named. He then recalled that Republic's F-84, which on hot days sometimes could not get airborne, was called the Groundhog, or just "Hog." When the swept-wing model of the F-84 appeared, also with ground-loving characteristics, pilots called it the "Super Hog." Since the Republic F-105 was also a ground lover and called the "Ultra Hog" by pilots (later the F-105 became much better known as "The Thud") the writer wondered if the A-10, which promised to be the meanest and ugliest plane ever to join the Air Force, should perhaps be called the "Warthog."

The Air Force leadership choked on that name and Fairchild dutifully came up with something much more distinguished. Wanting to capitalize on the immortal reputation of the rugged P-47 Thunderbolt that was so effective as an air-to-ground warrior in World War II, they decided to invite two WW II Thunderbolt pilots, both highscoring aces, to a ceremony and christen the plane the "Thunderbolt II."

So the Air Force leadership was happy and Fairchild was happy.

Then the planes started coming off the production line and at Davis-Monthan Air Force Base in Tucson, Arizona, pilots began to show up at the new A-10 training squadron. Most were pilots who had just stepped out of speed-of-heat, supersonic hot rods and they looked in awe at the ugly machine the Air Force said they were going to fly.

"Don't worry, we'll let you put a sack over that mother before you get in and fly it," said the instructor pilots (IPs) to assuage the egos of their tormented students.

After that, the IPs had no worries. In fact they smiled to themselves as the new pilots taxied away for their first flight. In the plane alone—there were no two-seaters used to train pilots—they soon graduated from straight and level flight and were rolling and diving and, in general, responding with amazement at the nimble way the big plane was able to maneuver. On their 360 overhead approaches—the fighter pilots approach to landing where they roll 60 to 90 degrees sharply, almost violently, over the center of the runway—they learned to throw out 40 degrees of dive brakes and snap the plane into an approach that looked almost as pretty as the overheads they had flown in their fast movers.

Hmmm. Not too shabby, they thought. It's gawdawful ugly, but . . .

Lieutenant Colonel Jim Green, commander of the Flying Tigers—one of the night fighter squadrons that fought in the Gulf War—can continue the story. He flew F-4s for three years, then spent six years as an aggressor pilot in the Air Force Fighter Weapons Wing—the Air Force's equivalent to the much more publicized Navy Top Gun School. After a staff job, "I put down on my request sheet F-15, F-15, and F-15 because I thought I was an air-to-air god—that's all I knew and all I cared about.

"Then my assignment came down and it was to an A-10. I couldn't believe it. In my staff job in personnel I wondered who I had ticked off. I decided to fight it. I called my former boss and said, basically, 'Please help me; I'm doomed.'

"Well, it so happened that my former boss was an A-10 wing commander—in fact, when we worked together he would rib me about my air-to-air hot rods and I would kid him about flying such a slow, ugly bird. And now he got back at me. 'Jim,' he said, 'I think you got the perfect assignment.'

"That settled it; I was doomed for sure. However, I had been out of the cockpit for four years and the more I thought about it, the more anxious I became. It *was* a fighter, after all.

"Then I started flying the plane and that was the start of a love affair. Right off, I was surprised at how the thing could turn. As an air-to-air guy that was my trade; that is how you kill people and win. I found that I could pull as good as anyone. That really surprised me.

"Also, I remember my first ride. Right away I told the IP flying with me, 'Hey, I can land this thing.' And it was a piece of cake. I had the stick and the rudders and the throttles and that's all. And all of a sudden I found that flying was not work; it was just fun.

"Another thing that helped the love affair was the way the plane employs its weapons. In the air-to-air world you get a film-kill, watch the guy you killed do an aileron roll acknowledging he's dead, and that's it, except for watching your film and that's not all that exciting. During a career in that business you might fire a missile once.

"In this plane I went out to the range and shot the gun and dropped bombs and I got immediate feedback. I either hit the target or I didn't, and when I got back and debriefed, I was immediately being judged in comparison to my fellow pilots. In the air-to-air world I had all kinds of systems helping me do the job. In this plane it was just me; I either did the job or I didn't do it. I had to work. I *really* had to work. I liked that. I liked the challenge, and I liked the excitement of seeing smoke from the bombs and sparkles when the gun is on target. And in six months on the range, I employed more ordnance than I did flying as an aggressor for six years.

"My romance with the A-10 intensified during the Gulf War. That's when I truly began to appreciate its survivability and dependability. In the war some of the planes took incredible damage, yet they flew home. I went out on thirty-eight missions. I shot forty Mavericks without a bad one, didn't have one gun jam, and every time I hit the pickle button my ordnance left the plane. And when a plane was scheduled to fly five straight days, it flew five straight days. Had I scheduled an F-4 for five days, it might have taken off three times; it would have had a maintenance problem that might or might not have gotten fixed, and it would have had a ground abort for some reason. In the Gulf our planes just didn't break very often, and if they did, the maintenance guys fixed them immediately.

"And now? I absolutely love the plane. I look forward to my practice missions, and I always check the schedule to see if I'm going to the range. Out there I'm challenging myself against all the other pilots who are trying to score, and they are guys who are just as competitive as I am. I like that."

Versions of the preceding story were related by several pilots who left the "fast-movers." Basically, they all liked the simplicity of the airplane. It was a pure, World War II-type, stick-and-rudder airplane, with no computers, and a mission that relied totally on the pilot's skill when delivering ordnance.

And the nickname the pilots finally decided to use for the airplane? It certainly isn't "Thunderbolt II," the nickname Fairchild convinced the Air Force to accept. The pilots almost gag when they hear someone use that name.

In principle they liked the nickname "Warthog" and they have semi-officially adopted it because it symbolizes what they perceive to be the airplane's two key characteristics; like the real warthog, it is both mean and ugly.

However, one never hears the pilots themselves using that nickname. "Warthog" is strictly for polite company (and for book titles). Within the community of pilots they shorten the name, perhaps because they *want* a chip on their shoulders because of its ugliness. The pilots call their airplane the "Hog," and, proudly, they call themselves, "Hog drivers."

In August 1990, the Hog drivers got their first opportunity to take their Hogs to war and show what they could do.

# 3

# The Initial Deployment

*"I felt this blast of heat when I got off the plane and I thought I was standing in the exhaust of the engines because they were still running. I was wrong; it was just Saudi Arabia in August."*

—*1st Lt. Bryan Currier*

At the bases in Korea, Great Britain, and the United States, the training schedule was frenetic. The pilots flew all the time, practicing the dreaded worst-case scenarios over and over. The North Koreans were coming. Or the Russians were coming. Throw your plane and your body into the breach. Get down there and help those poor guys on the ground who are getting the snot beat out of them. Shack that command post with your bombs. Nail those tanks with your gun. And it didn't matter that the bombs had tiny charges and the command post was a mark on the ground, or that the tanks were rag targets. Scores were kept, an accounting was made, and the competition increased in intensity as it moved up from squadron to wing and, yearly, to the all-Air Force "Gunsmoke" competition where the best-of-the-best of all fighter planes and pilots is determined.

The training exercises take many forms, even today as the threats around the world seem diminished. Sometimes a squadron will fly off to a remote location and operate around-the-clock under simulated combat conditions. Also, about every third month, a squadron will go through an exercise called a sortie surge. This is an intense training exercise designed to pressurize the operation—in which planes fly four or five sorties a day and ground crews hot pit the planes—they load bombs, gun, and fuel while the plane's engines are running and an observer's stopwatch is ticking. By putting the squadron operation under pressure during a surge, the weaknesses show up and commanders can make the fixes.

*The more you sweat in peacetime, the less you bleed in war.*

That Chinese motto (which is actually on the shoulder patch of one Warthog squadron) is the basic rationale for all this training. Every operational fighter squadron in the Air Force has a "checkered flag," which is its own unique battle order. Their checkered flags require them to deploy to some trouble spot in the world, ready for combat, often within twenty-four to forty-eight hours after being alerted, and usually with all necessary support people and every bolt, nut, bullet, and light bulb needed to sustain the combat effectiveness of the squadron for thirty days. In other words, they sweat during peacetime so they can get to a combat theater, then fight and *win*.

And doing just that, as a peacetime exercise, was what was on the mind of Col. Ervin ("Sandy") Sharpe, the commander of the 354th Tactical Fighter Wing at Myrtle Beach Air Force Base, South Carolina, when Saddam Hussein rolled into Kuwait on August 2, 1990.

Said Colonel Sharpe, "I was gearing up for a training deployment of one of my squadrons and, even though our checkered flag was in that region, I had not even thought that we might have to fight Iraq some day. Our scenario that we trained for always involved a conflict instigated and backed by the Soviets. So it was a real surprise to me when Saddam moved into Kuwait, and even then it didn't hit me that we might end up fighting him.

"Then I heard rumblings that we were going to send forces over there to try and prevent him from invading Saudi Arabia. However, I only began to take this seriously after I heard that the First Wing at Langley [Air Force Base, Virginia], an F-15 wing, was put on alert. Then, about the seventh of August I picked up the secure telephone and heard from a colonel on the newly formed battle staff at TAC [Tactical Air Command] Headquarters that, Yeah, it looks like you guys are going, too.

"I immediately got my deputies together and we started looking at our readiness. We were in pretty good shape. We were expecting an ORI [Operational Readiness Inspection—the ultimate higher headquarters inspection that commanders dread the most] at any time so my guys were as close to being ready as any unit could be in peacetime.

"Starting about the eighth, we stopped all flying and went on a twenty-four-hour schedule, getting the planes ready for deployment, and taking care of all the other support and logistics problems. I was on the phone a lot during this time and learned that TAC only wanted two of my three squadrons. I protested—the guys in the third squadron had trained just as hard for this and wanted to go—but TAC had already decided to take two squadrons from another base. Those ended up being two squadrons from England Air Force Base in Louisiana."

The days crept by and the pilots waited with mixed emotions. They hated the idea of leaving their families and going into a war from which they stood a good chance of not returning. But the idea of flying against a real enemy had been such a major part of their lives for so long that they were eager for the challenge. They wanted to know if they, personally, had the right stuff. They wanted to know if they could hold up under the pressure of combat and fight effectively with their airplane.

And definitely they were affected by the "Warthog factor." They had been the ugly ones in the fighter community for years. They knew that the pointy-nose fighters were going—the F-15s, F-16s, F-111s, and F-117s; now, it seemed like they, too, were going to be invited to the party. They had misgivings and fears—they all admit that—but when it came down to personal feelings about the matter, they would have been terribly disappointed if TAC had canceled their deployment.

Finally, on August 14 the pilots in the Panther Squadron were called to a meeting by Lt. Col. Rick Shatzel, their commander. It was eight o'clock in the evening and the hammer had fallen. "We're going for sure," he said. "We're leaving at 1600 tomorrow and we're going to Saudi Arabia for an indefinite period. And that's all we can tell you."

Unlike the Army, where the senior officers stay behind the lines in command posts, the Air Force has a tradition where the senior officers get out in front in their planes and lead. Thus, in the first six-ship cell that departed, the wing commander, Col. Sandy Sharpe, was flying lead, with squadron commander Rick Shatzel on his wing. In addition, two spares were to follow until the first refueling in case one or more in the six-ship cell had to drop out.

The second of the two spares never made it. Capt. John Whitney was just breaking ground and putting the wheels in the well when he noticed the plane yawing to the left. "I was at 48,000 pounds," said Whitney. "I had the works on it, and being the heavyweight that it is, I just assumed that the yaw was the result of the heavy load. It was quiet up there and I didn't realize what had happened until the big clue bird, the master caution light, flashed on. Then I saw the left engine instruments winding down. The aircraft and I were only a couple of hundred feet above the ground, losing airspeed, losing altitude, and to make it even worse, I was over the crowd of onlookers that had gathered at the departure end of the runway to see us off. With all that weight I knew I was going down unless I could jettison stores, but I couldn't do it over those people. Somehow I kept it airborne and, in the last seconds before I would have gone in or ejected, I went feet wet [got over the ocean] and pickled the fuel pods and travel pod. That got rid of almost 9,000 pounds and I managed to stagger along above the water on one engine. After that, I was able to climb a little and eventually got back over the field. After I got rid of that weight, the plane handled as advertised and the single-engine landing was strictly Dash-1 [as described in the aircraft operating manual]."

The other seven planes went up the coast to the Norfolk, Virginia, area, tankered, then turned east and headed out over the Atlantic. Their immediate destination, Moron, Spain, was still more than thirteen hours away.

After the first refueling and all six planes ran satisfactory fuel checks, the spare, Capt. Gus Kohntopp, turned back and began a lonely flight home. The others droned on into the night behind their KC-135 tanker, which, at the blistering speed of 250 knots (or less), had to use partial flaps just to stay airborne.

Then the gremlins went to work and the misery of the night commenced.

In Colonel Sharpe's cell, Capt. Tom Wilson was flying in the number five position (second off the left wing of the tanker). Said Captain Wilson, "Our weather briefing said that we were going to have clear sailing but when we got out over the Atlantic, there were buildups all over the place and we had to tuck into close formation on the tanker and on each other.

"Then, as we were going in and out of clouds and I was struggling to stay on Hendo's [Capt. Greg Henderson] wing, he suddenly goes into a 60-degree bank to the left. I didn't know what was going on; I wanted to stay on his wing but I didn't want to lose sight of the tanker. I yelled, 'Hendo, turn right, level your wings.'

"He came back and said, 'Thank you,' and leveled his wings. It was weird; he was one of our most experienced pilots. Then, after a few minutes he did it again. I followed him, talking to him all this time, and we actually lost sight of the tanker for a few minutes."

Captain Henderson picks up the story: "Right after the first refueling I noticed a fuel odor but I put it out of my mind. I didn't realize it then but the receptacle seal was bad and fuel was leaking into the cockpit area whenever I took on fuel. I was breathing those fumes and, after three more refuelings, my blood was loaded with that stuff. My first symptom was a severe headache. What was insidious was that my brain was not functioning well. I thought I was dehydrated so I drank water. Then I started feeling really tired and I was having a hard time flying a heading. The three things—severe headache, nausea, and extreme fatigue—were a triple-whammy and by the time I was trying to get on the boom [of the tanker] the fourth time, I was seeing two or three of them—now, I don't even know how I did it. That time, after I came off, I announced that I was having a little problem and that I didn't need anybody on my wing. That's when Tom [Wilson] started watching me and when he saw me go into the 60-degree left bank. By then I was totally out of it. I couldn't reason, could barely fly, and I thought for sure that I was going to pass out. We were in and out of clouds and I remember looking down through a hole and seeing a brightly lit ship on the water. I was ready to punch out and let them pick me up. Then I started weaving around again and Tom talked me back. Finally, I got violently ill and threw up all over the cockpit."

Captain Wilson continues, "We talked to Hendo and among ourselves and decided that he was completely hypoxic [suffering from the lack of oxygen] because he had been breathing fuel vapor. After he got sick, seemed to be able to communicate a little better. We got him on one hundred percent oxygen and that helped . . . "

"I was in a bad way," said Henderson. "We were in and out of the weather and right out in the middle of the ocean—maybe three-and-a-half hours from the Azores. But the vomiting had helped and my flying improved. Then, during the next refueling, I went on one hundred percent oxygen, depressurized the cockpit, and used ram air [outside air] to purge the cockpit for a few minutes—then repressurized and was able to cut back on the oxygen. [He didn't have enough oxygen to stay on 100 percent for the remainder of the trip.] Later, as we got closer to the Azores, Colonel Sharpe wanted me to take someone and divert to the Azores. But by then the headache and nausea were not as bad and I figured I could live with the tiredness and still fly. I said that I wanted to continue, mainly because I was afraid I might miss a war."*

In the third cell back the gremlins had attacked all six planes. (The cells had departed at thirty-minute intervals.) Captain Eric Sobol, flying in the number five position, was straining to see his wingman's red position light when " . . . the absolutely beautiful

---

* In a later crossing Capt. David Feehs of the Flying Tiger Squadron suffered and endured a similar problem]

weather that had been forecast suddenly went bad. We hit the clouds without warning and lead called for us to tighten up. Fanspeed [Capt. Don Fann] was six and on my wing. He had me in sight but I could not find Gils [Capt. Kim Gilbert] who was in number four position, just off the left wing of the tanker. So Fanspeed and I go lost wingman and Gils is calling for us and trying to get us back on the tanker. Unconsciously, while he was looking back over his left shoulder, Gils had gotten into a 30-degree left bank so when he looked right toward the tanker, he was looking up and he lost it. Then he calls lost wingman, but without realizing it, he had rolled on over and was flying inverted.

"Fanspeed is still tucked in on me and I'm alternating between the gauges and looking out for Gils when suddenly I see a whole canopy full of A-10, inverted, out in front of me. So now I'm thinking, is he inverted or am I? I quickly checked the gauges, saw that I was straight and level, then yelled to Gils to get on his gauges. I repeated it a couple of times, then he does this barrel roll up and around us and ends up in trail. Then, as Fanspeed and I are trying to find the tanker, three goes lost wingman, then two and then one. So, it's pitch black, we're in heavy clouds and turbulence, and the sky is full of planes that can't see each other. And I'm thinking, hey, it's Wednesday; we found out we were leaving Sunday so that night and Monday and Tuesday nights I got very little sleep. Now I'm exhausted, in heavy weather, with no radar or autopilot, and everybody is lost wingman. I'm wondering how it could get any worse.

"But it did. First, I started seeing flickering in my peripheral vision, like it might be the strobe lights of one of the planes. But when I would look, I couldn't see anything. Then somebody called out St. Elmo's fire and I realized, when it started coming up the nose and over the canopy, that that was the flickering I had seen. This was distracting and having never experienced it before I wondered if it might short out my electronics. While I was thinking about that and trying to get back on the tanker, my airspeed indicator started winding down. It went from 210 indicated down to 30. My first reaction was to think I'm in an insidious climb so I pushed the nose over. My VVI [vertical velocity indicator] did a full-scale deflection and the big hand on my altimeter was spinning, telling me that I was descending wildly, out of control, and that is when my own gyros tumbled [when he experienced severe vertigo]. For about ten seconds I was ready to pull the handles [eject] and sit out in the Atlantic in a one-man life raft. But Fanspeed stayed with me and talked me though it, and I righted the plane and fought the vertigo. Then, feeling around the cockpit, I found that my lunchbox had knocked off my pitot heat switch and also that a circuit breaker had popped. I realized then my pitot tube [tube on wing through which ram air drives the airspeed indicator] had frozen over. When I put them back on line, I got my airspeed indicator again and ten minutes later we were out of the weather and looking for the tanker and our wingmen. When we landed at Moron, after thirteen hours and fifty minutes in the air, I was so exhausted they almost had to lift me out of the cockpit."

The first cell landed in Moron at around two in the afternoon and the other three cells arrived at thirty-minute intervals thereafter. Maintenance crews had been flown in, and in 100-degree heat on the ramp they began inspecting and repairing squawks on the planes. (Some pilots landed with low oil pressure lights flashing because of the oil consumption on the long flight.) The weary pilots were taken to a hotel where, despite air conditioner problems, most fell asleep.

Back in Myrtle Beach the Deputy Wing Commander for Operations (DO), Col. Hank Haden, was organizing the departure of the remaining pilots, along with all the support personnel and equipment. He was to depart the morning of August 17 on a C-5 transport from the Military Airlift Command (MAC). On board with him were about thirty key support personnel. They flew in the top deck in relative comfort, above tons of equipment in the main cargo area. The plan was for Colonel Haden and the other key people to be in Saudi Arabia several hours before the first Warthogs arrived so they could make some of the necessary preparations.

The C-5 was to be followed later in the day by two C-141s, which would be loaded with personnel and equipment. Captain Tom Dean, who had contracted conjunctivitis from one of his children two weeks prior and was scratched from the list of pilots who would fly over, tells about the experience.

"First they loaded all this equipment—stuff like the dragon, which loads bullets into our gun. The whole middle part of the plane was packed with equipment and stuff on pallets. Then thy herded about a hundred of us into folding web-mesh seats along the sides of the fuselage. There was no way one could get comfortable in those seats, so when we got airborne, most of the people unbuckled and laid on or under the equipment. The temperature dropped from one hundred degrees to about forty and everybody was scrambling through their bags looking for a jacket. It was so noisy, especially in the back where I was, that we had to use EARS [a brand of foam ear plugs] to protect our hearing. And to go to the bathroom—what a mess. First, it was almost impossible to walk fore or aft because of all the bodies. They had one enclosed toilet on a pallet in the front—one with a seat. The women used that until it clogged up. The other was an open half-toilet on a pallet in the back that the guys had to use right in front of everybody. That thing had a leak that we didn't know about and one of our pilot's personal bags, with all his flight gear and helmet, was stashed by it and got soaked. It was not a pleasant trip.

"We landed at Torrejon Air Force Base outside Madrid, Spain. It was after dark and we were scheduled to be on the ground for about four hours. When I crawled off the plane, I was amazed as I looked down the flightline. It looked like every C-141 and C-5 in the world was sitting on that ramp. It really made us realize that a massive buildup was under way.

"They herded us into a big hangar and we got a nice surprise. Inside there were base personnel—wives and dependents mostly— serving cookies, cakes, drinks, and every kind of homemade food you could imagine. And even though it was in the middle of the night, they were bouncing around, friendly and cheerful, trying to do everything they could to make our layover more pleasant. It made us all feel good to see this kind of support and enthusiasm for what we were doing.

"Most of us tried to nap on the cots that were scattered around the hangar. But a lot of the Army guys who had come in on other planes sat on the cots and cleaned their weapons before they laid down. This impressed me, and it made me realize how serious this deployment really was."

Meanwhile the four cells of Warthogs had departed Moron, led by the squadron commander, and were over the Mediterranean flying eastbound. Their route on the twelve-hour flight would take them north of Libya, south along the Nile Valley of Egypt, then, without a tanker to lead them, eastbound over the Red Sea and into Saudi Arabia. They had latitude and longitude coordinates for their destination, which was the unfinished King Fahd Royal Airport 20 miles from Dhahran. But the inertial navigation system (INS) they use for guidance is not reliable after several hours of flight. So they went back to fundamentals and used the same techniques that Lindbergh had used in 1927 to cross the Atlantic. Said Capt. Don Fann, who was in the third cell, "We used heading, time, distance, and a black line on the map. We also tried to use eyeballs, which is a part of the technique, but in that barren desert it was useless effort."

The C-5 arrived at King Fahd at about 7:30 in the morning on Sunday, August 18. Colonel Hank Haden describes what he found: "When I first heard where we were deploying, I thought we would be near some kind of civilized area. But I was wrong. There were two 13,000-foot runways, some ramps and taxiways, and the King's unfinished private terminal. And this was all sitting right out in the middle of the most barren desert area you can imagine. There was nothing in the way of civilization for miles around."

Colonel Haden borrowed some vehicles from a special operations force that was already on the base. Then, with a logistics specialist who came up from Riyadh, he began to prepare for the arrival of his two squadrons.

Meanwhile, in the air over Saudi Arabia, the pilots were talking among themselves about the scare they had experienced. "We were just leaving Egypt and crossing the Red Sea," said Capt. Tom Wilson, "when we saw these fighters coming at the speed of heat toward our six-ship, and if you don't think I had butterflies in my stomach sitting there saying, what are those, what are those. It turned out that they were Navy F-18s. They just wanted to pull up and give a friendly wave and that was it—but it sure got our attention.

"From then on," said Wilson, "we just motored along over some of the most awesomely desolate country in the world. We were checking our INSs [Inertial Navigation Systems], but after twelve hours they weren't accurate. We just kept trucking until Colonel Shatzel calls out that two long parallel runways are at our twelve [o'clock position—straight ahead]. 'That's got to be it, boys,' he said, and it was. We landed and pulled off the runway to a taxiway, but we didn't know where to go. Finally we taxied up to this unfinished terminal where a bunch of guys with turbans were looking hard at us. I'm looking at them like, are you good or bad? I didn't know. There was absolutely nobody else in sight—no friendlies, I mean. Then this bus pulls up and it was our guys there to greet us with water, which is all we wanted at the moment."

Colonel Sharpe climbed down the ladder to meet his DO, Col. Hank Haden. Said Sharpe, "I'll never forget that look on Hank's face nor what he said. He looked at me with a kind of overwhelmed look and said, 'Boss, you ain't gonna believe this . . .' Then he went on to tell me that there was nothing there but a few metal trailers for housing. There were no support services, no fuel, no bombs, no Maverick missiles, and no gun ammo except what we had carried with us—we came over with fully loaded guns.

"But we hit the ground running and picked up where Hank had left off, doing the kinds of things that would get us operational as soon as possible. We made arrangements with the civilian contractor to get one meal a day in his chow hall—we could get by with MREs [Meals Ready to Eat—military combat rations] for the other two meals. Also, after all four cells were on the ground, we called General Horner [the theater air commander] to let him know that we had arrived.

"About eight that evening General Horner called us back and said, 'Sharpe, a U.S. Navy ship just shot across the bow of an Iraqi ship trying to run the blockade. There is absolutely nothing between you and 4,000 tanks massed on the Kuwait border and they may be coming south tonight or in the morning. If they do, you're going to have to attack them with what you've got and try to delay them. I can't tell you where to go or how to get away after that. You'll have to figure that out. Also, get your people on the ground ready to evacuate if they keep coming south.'

"I was beat physically—in the past I had crossed the Pacific twice and the Atlantic eight times, but I'd never flown a fourteen-hour sortie and I'd never experienced anything so physically tiring as this trip, flying without an autopilot and in conditions, for much of the way, that demanded every ounce of concentration just controlling the airplane.

"Then came this message from Horner. I immediately called the pilots together and told them exactly what Horner had told me. Then we talked over the situation, which was not good. When we landed, our planes had about 6,000 pounds of fuel, which is enough for two hours of cruise or an hour and a half on a cruise/combat mission. In addition, we had a full drum of ammunition for the gun—1,150 rounds of combat mix, which is five armor-piercing rounds to one high-explosive round—an ECM pod [Electronic Counter Measures—for jamming and fooling enemy radars], a pave penny [for receiving laser target information from troops on the ground] and two AIM-9s [heatseeking air-to-air defense missiles]. That was it. Against tanks we only had the gun; once we shot the gun out, we were through until we could get more fuel and ordnance—and at that time I had no idea where we could do that.

"Sometime before I laid down to catch a quick nap, I managed to get [Col.] John McBroom on the phone—he was commander of the First TAC Wing at Dhahran—and he said he would send some fuel tankers over at dawn—it was about an hour's drive for them—and I felt a little relieved. If he [Saddam Hussein] didn't attack until morning, we could go fight and at least get back home.

"Finally, I went to my room, got out my chem [antichemical warfare] gear and laid down. But the situation looked grim . . ."

# 4

## New Tactics

*"There was absolutely no doubt in my mind that we were going to war the next morning."*

—*Capt. Dan Mulherin*

As tired as they were, not many of the pilots went right to bed. Said Capt. Greg Henderson, "We had this pilot in the squadron who was also a flight surgeon—one of three in the Air Force—and he briefed us on the chem gear that we were issued. We had had these chem warfare briefings at home, but it seemed like they were always on a Friday afternoon when we were more concerned with getting the squadron bar open—so we hadn't paid a helluva lot of attention to any of them.

"It was different that first night at Fahd. [Major] Pete Demitry was briefing us on how to use that stuff and it was like a religious meeting—I mean, the guys were asking, 'Now is this the way it goes?' referring to the gas mask or chem suit and 'You take this pill when?' We knew he [Saddam Hussein] had Scud missiles and about 500 fighters that could deliver gas weapons. So we were dead serious. Some of the guys actually went to bed that first night in the chem coveralls that were issued."

Most went to bed but few slept. With four of them jammed in a 10-foot by 10-foot room, and as keyed up as they were about the mission they might fly in the morning, they spent most of the night just talking.

Then there were the F-15s. They were taking off from Dhahran throughout the night and they were coming over King Fahd in full afterburner. Aside from the noise, which the pilots eventually got

31

used to, there was the worry that the roar might be from Iraqi jets attacking the field. There was no warning device in operation and, according to Capt. Tom Dean, "About half the guys would rush out when they heard the roar of jets and start scanning the sky. Mostly it was just curiosity, but some were concerned that Iraqi jets might get past the CAP [combat air patrol flown by the F-15s]."

The pilots who were not on alert that night nor scheduled to go on alert at five o'clock the next morning, went to work in the command center. Their main task was to prepare maps—a ritual for Warthog pilots because they are so dependent on the folded map in their lap as they fly at 100 to 500 feet above the ground, navigating by roads, streams and terrain contours.

The squadron had been given one area map that had contact points, which pilots program into their INS and use for navigating to and from targets. During the night the mapmaking crew broke out the contact paper, which is used to line the maps so that information can be written and erased and so they will not wear out. They proceeded to mark the contact points on the maps so all the alert pilots would, in the words of one mapmaker, "be playing off the same sheet of music."

At about four in the morning, just as the eastern horizon was beginning to lighten, twelve new alert pilots went out to the ramp and "cocked" their planes. They started the built-in auxiliary power unit (APU), then, with that power, fired up the two engines. Then instruments were checked, radios were checked, and the contact points near the area where they were going to fly and attempt to intercept the Iraqi armor were programmed into the INS. Finally, they shut everything down and lowered the canopy, which was a sign to ground crewmen that the plane was ready to roll.

Then they went to the command area, settled down next to the telephone, and began debating whether or not it was really going to happen.

Some were negative. "Naw, that guy is a plodder. He doesn't do anything dramatic. I read what he did in the Iran war. He'd attack, go a little ways, then stop and consolidate for a week or two. He's not a Patton; he's a McClellan."

Most—including many who had been skeptical before—were convinced that they were on the brink of war. "Yeah, you say he's a plodder, but look what happened in Kuwait. Bam! He's in there. No screwing around. He had the whole country before the Kuwaitis knew what happened. Now he's got all that armor on the border ready to move south. This is desert, man; he can cut those tanks loose and he's past here in a heartbeat. And he's filthy rich again with Saudi oil. I say he's coming. He'd be nuts not to." That was the majority opinion.

As the debates continued, the sun rose, blistering hot in a sky that would not see a cloud for almost two more months. And it was ominously quiet. Outside, the silence was only occasionally broken by the roar of one of the tanker trucks from Dhahran, or the yell of a ground crewman alerting everyone within earshot to look off in the distance at the camels meandering around in the desert.

The phone seldom rang in the command center and when it did, all eyes were on Colonel Sharpe or Colonel Haden, who took the calls. Most of the time the calls were unimportant. "Just somebody in Riyadh needing some information. And, no, there's no sign that he's moving south yet. They say not to worry, we'll hear it from them first."

The sun beat down relentlessly, and the heat became intense. And as the morning crept slowly by, the anxious pilots on alert were like Gary Cooper in *High Noon*. They were waiting for a gang of outlaws to come rolling into their territory, and although they were far outnumbered and outgunned and had no desire to become dead heroes, their fate was already decided. They were going to fight despite the odds because that is what they had hired out to do.

Some say he blinked, that he realized that he was going to have to kill Americans if he moved south and that would start a war he did not want.

Others say he was just biding his time, waiting for the Americans to get called back home—that on CNN he was seeing American protesters with "No Blood for Oil" posters. Iraq had the poor Arab nations such as Jordan on its side because they were jealous of the rich Kuwaitis and Saudis. So why take a chance fighting the Americans in August? Why not wait till America tears itself up in controversy, then turns tail as it did in Vietnam? Then he could move into Saudi Arabia on his own timetable, without fighting the Americans.

Whatever the rationale, the Iraqi tanks and planes stayed in Kuwait, and the Warthog pilots sat night and day on alert, waiting for an attack that did not come.

Nobody knew that that would happen, of course, and General Horner did what any responsible commander must do: he strengthened his forces; he requested that two more squadrons of A-10s be sent to the Gulf. The Falcons from Myrtle Beach were already on the way. They would be on the ground in Saudi Arabia the next day, giving him forty-eight A-10s to throw against an armored invasion. With the two squadrons from England Air Force Base, which had been on alert for a week, this would double his assets, giving him ninety-six A-10s ready for battle.

The problem was how to get the two squadrons from Louisiana over there. The cargo and troop carriers of MAC already had tasking beyond their capacity because of the massive buildup of Army forces that was underway. And Strategic Air Command (SAC), which controls the tankers, had a problem because of all the other fighter aircraft that were being called into action. Also, providing tanker support for the A-10s was an additional problem because they were much slower than the other fighters and needed three times as many tankers to get them across the Atlantic and the Mediterranean.

Colonel Dave Sawyer, the energetic and voluble commander of the 23d Tactical Fighter Wing at England Air Force Base, was working a hectic schedule trying to get his two squadrons under way. Said Sawyer, "MAC was just overwhelmed, then I got this call on the twenty-first saying there's going to be tankers for us and that we would be leaving the next day. We immediately went into action. We configured the 76th [76th Tactical Fighter Squadron—the Vanguards] with tanks, flew the planes and tank-checked them. Then they called it off; they had a higher priority; the tankers had to take some Navy planes across.

"In the meantime I had called [Col.] Sandy [Sharpe] several times. I asked him what he needed us to bring and he said that he didn't need any more maintenance guys—our first plane was supposed to be full of them—but he did need contracting and pay people and he badly needed civil engineers who could get building and paving done. I said, fine, we'll do it. Then I got on the phone to tell headquarters what I was taking and they said I couldn't do that. I said, 'Watch me.' I knew that reasonable people would prevail.

"I also had a personal problem. Since two-thirds of my wing was going over, I felt I should go with them. But Sandy was already over there and what would my presence do to the command structure? I called several people at Ninth Air Force and at TAC and told them I planned to go with my guys—that this is what I had been training for during my whole career. They said, 'Hell yes, that's where you should be.' They were all fighter pilots. They knew how I felt.

"Then I called Sandy and told him I was coming and that I hoped it wouldn't be a problem for him—I outranked him by about two years, but he was the host wing commander. He said, 'Come on over; it's not a problem.' He was very gracious and said we could work it out.

"I had worked with Sandy when he was vice commander. When I was commander of the 602d Tactical Air Control Wing at Davis-Monthan in Tucson, I had taken a squadron of OA-10s [A-10s used for forward air control] to Myrtle Beach for an ORI. We worked closely together on that exercise and got an "outstanding" rating, which is rare. Also, the past spring during a wing commanders' conference, Sandy and I were in the same foursome that won the golf tournament, so we knew each other socially as well. I liked Sandy personally and I felt confident that with his attitude, we could work it out.

"Finally, on Friday the twenty-fourth they called and said they had tankers for us and that the 76th [Vanguards] would depart on Monday the twenty-seventh and the 74th [Flying Tigers] two days later on the twenty-ninth. I hung up the phone and quickly ordered the tanks put back on—we had taken them off so we could practice our tactics while we were waiting—and tank checks to be flown. Then I told the squadron commanders that the guys could tell their wives when they were leaving so they could make the most of their last weekend home.

"I went on Monday with the 76th and flew to Myrtle Beach. Then the next night we crossed the Atlantic and it was probably the hardest flight I ever made. We flew through thunderstorms and one of the guys in my cell had vertigo so bad I didn't think we were going to get him on the tanker boom.

"We arrived at King Fahd on the thirty-first and the very next day General Horner came up to inspect the field. Sandy and I got in the car with him and he brought up the subject of command—already some of the folks there had me pegged as the new vice commander. Horner, whom I had worked for before and who knew me well, didn't make a fuss over the matter. He just said, 'You guys work out whatever command structure you want—you guys figure it out.'

"After he left, Sandy and I both felt good that he trusted us enough to leave us alone, knowing that we would work out a command structure that would get the job done. So he and I sat down together and quickly decided that there should be one commander who just happens to be two persons. In other words, we decided upon something that I believe is unique in the history of warfare; we decided that two people would share command but that they would speak with one voice.

"That bothered our people somewhat because, after all, there is fierce competition between wings and it is always 'they' and 'us,' whenever there is commingling of the troops. But we were absolutely adamant that there was not going to be any of that while we were commanding. We divided up the command responsibilities under us between the two wings—his DO would take one shift, night or day, and my DO would take the other—that kind of thing.

"Between us we also worked out some areas of responsibility. Because he was the host wing commander, he was clearly responsible for base support functions, although, as a courtesy, he never did anything important without consulting me. Later, when the Cajuns [a reserve squadron from New Orleans] and the OA-10s came in, Horner gave me specific responsibility for them because I had worked with reserve units in the past and I had been the first commander of the OA-10s. However, when the Vultures from RAF Alconbury [a squadron of A-10s from England] came in about that same time, Sandy took direct responsibility for them.

"And sure, there were some initial problems. Our planes had teeth [those of the 23d Wing were in the direct lineage of the original Flying Tigers] and theirs didn't. We thought we were better than them and they thought they were better than us. But all that is normal—Sandy and I knew that—and we were determined that we were not going to let this kind of petty rivalry get in the way of the job we had to do. We divided up our people as fairly as we could, balancing authority between the wings, and we integrated personnel from both wings into the support groups. We felt that if we showed a strong united front at the top, that we could pull it together down at all the lower levels. And, from that day on, that is how it was. When problems were bucked up to the top, Sandy and I would close the door, work things out between us, then come out together and announce a decision. If there were orders and directives to be signed, both of our signatures went on them. Sandy put it well when he described us as one commander who just happened to be two persons."

The A-10s from Myrtle Beach had been on alert for twelve days when Colonel Sawyer's first squadron arrived. During the first few days of that alert period, the tension was high and the pilots expected to go into action on a moment's notice. But when the invasion didn't come, and intelligence reported no further pre-invasion activity along the Saudi border, the suspense level dropped. And, as the long, brutally hot days started to creep by more slowly, the pilots began thinking about home and families and another scenario, less foreboding, but more depressing. What if Saddam decides just to sit on the border for several months or even a year, waiting for the American people to tire of the situation? What happens to us if he does that?

Colonel Hank Haden, the officer in charge of wing operations at that time, knew that the pilots were soon going to get bored and restless. So, around the twenty-third he started them flying on a limited basis and, at the same time, he put the pilots who weren't flying to work with ground crews that were improving the facilities.

The flights were two-turn-twos, where two ships would go out in the morning, fly for about an hour, then return, and another two-ship flight would depart. In Haden's words, "The flights were plain vanilla; just routine local orientation flights to give the pilots some flying time and to allow them to familiarize themselves with the local area. We were careful to fly every plane during those days because we wanted to make sure they were all Code-One [in perfect condition]."

The work he set them to was not nearly as enjoyable as the flying. They filled sandbags and built revetments around equipment and around huge fuel bladders that had been airlifted to the field and filled by tankers from Dhahran. And, in an operation that went on twenty-four hours a day, the pilots pitched in and helped the enlisted folks build "tent city," which became the housing area for all enlisted personnel and, eventually, for the pilots who came later in the year.

When Colonel Sawyer's two squadrons arrived on August 31 and September 2, they were the new kids on the block compared to the "veterans" who had been sitting on the precipice of war for twelve days. Immediately, they became the "Alex guys," because their home base was in Alexandria, Louisiana. To counter that, the "veterans" were called the "Beach guys," because of their home in Myrtle Beach, South Carolina. And even though the Beach guys had really had it "hanging out" for a few days and were justified in talking up the potential danger they had faced, the Alex guys had their own stories. Most of them had flown through vicious thunderstorms in their trek across the Atlantic and they, too, had earned respect for what they had survived.

Of course, the enemy that they were brought over to fight did not go away. He was still there, looting, killing and committing general mayhem in Kuwait City while thousands of tanks were still poised and ready for an invasion of Saudi Arabia. And daily, as alert crews were briefed on potential threats should they be launched into combat, the danger of the enemy grew more ominous.

Iraq, according to the intelligence briefings, had purchased thousands of SAMs from the Soviet Union. Some were the old SA-2s, the radar-guided, "telephone-pole" missiles that pilots who flew into North Vietnam had to evade. But they also had the much more sophisticated radar-controlled SA-3s, SA-6s, and SA-8s—the latter two being extremely dangerous, according to Israeli pilots who had flown against them in previous conflicts.

The Iraqis also had SA-7s, SA-9s, SA-13s, SA-14s and SA-16s, all infrared (IR), heatseeking missiles. Of this group, it was a toss-up for many pilots between the SA-13 and the SA-16 as to which one was more dangerous. The SA-13 was vehicle-launched, dangerously fast, and ubiquitous in Kuwait, while the SA-16 was shoulder-fired, did not leave a smoke trail to be spotted as it streaked toward its target, and it was reported that it would not always "bite off" on the flares that the A-10s released as a defensive measure to fool IR missiles.

So, on paper at least, the Iraqis appeared to have as great an air defense threat as the Soviet-equipped, Warsaw Pact forces would have had if the dreaded Central European scenario had unfolded. In reaction to that danger the A-10 pilots and their leaders treated any potential battleground involving the Iraqis as a "high-threat" environment.

The term "high threat" has a very special meaning to pilots in the A-10 community. It means that when they fly in that environment they must do so with very specific, well-rehearsed tactics—tactics that, years earlier, had been refined and formalized into tactical doctrine.

The high-threat tactics can be summarized in two words: stay low. The idea behind the tactics is to fly low, from 500 to as low as 100 feet, to avoid being seen by enemy radar. By escaping radar detection the enemy does not know you are there, and radar-guided SAMs and AAA cannot be used to target you. Then, when close to the enemy, the A-10 "pops up" just long enough to identify the target and shoot the gun, fire a Maverick missile, or drop bombs. Then it dives back down and egresses the target area at low altitude.

While practicing high-threat tactics, A-10 pilots learn to use "terrain masking" as they fly to and from their targets. They study their maps before a mission and plan their routes so they can fly low and use valleys, hills, and even clearings in forested areas as places to hide from the enemy.

In the worst-case scenario, as when Warsaw Pact forces would have come rolling into Germany, all of these terrain features were in abundance. And, while practicing, especially in wooded, stream-cut regions of South Carolina and Louisiana, the pilots, day in and day out, were able to train realistically for the "big one."

However, during September and October, as the number of training sorties were increased and as pilots became more familiar with the desert environment, it soon became apparent that they were going to have to throw away the tactics book and look for something new.

All of the pilots, at one time or another, had trained in the desert around Tucson, Arizona—that is where pilots transition from whatever else they have been flying. But that desert, they discovered, was totally different from the desert in the Middle East. In the Sonoran Desert of Arizona there were mountains everywhere that could be used as navigation checkpoints. Also, the terrain features were irregular so there was almost always a place to hide as you approached a theoretical enemy position. Most important of all, the air in Arizona was like glass; on most days they could see for a hundred miles or more.

None of this applied to the deserts of Saudi Arabia or in the potential combat theater of Iraq. The land was flat and, with the exception of the "wadis," or dry streambeds, and the occasional oasis inhabited by a family or two of Bedouins, there was almost nothing the pilots could use for low-altitude navigation or for terrain masking. "Where do we hide?" became a recurrent question as pilots reported to commanders and commanders began discussing tactics with their leaders.

Then there was another problem. The sand in Saudi Arabia is not like sand on the beach, which is made up of coarse grains. The sand in the Saudi desert is extremely fine, almost powdery, and, as a consequence, is often in motion when the wind is blowing—which is most of the time—and, because of its fine structure, it tends to remain suspended in the air, even during periods when the air is relatively calm. So, besides the lack of terrain features, the pilots found a second problem. Visibility was nothing like it was in Arizona, often dropping below three miles when gusty winds were blowing. Also, there was often no visible horizon that the pilots could use as a guide for keeping their wings level. In many cases during bright, sunlit days, they had to fly on instruments the same way they would if they were in clouds.

The commanders worried about the latter problem, especially with pilots out in the desert trying to fly low. They were concerned that a pilot would bank and turn while flying visually and fail to realize that he was near the ground. The fear was that a pilot could misjudge the location of the ground and  catch one of his wings. So they upped the minimum altitude to 500 feet, and the question, Where do we hide? became even more vexing for those who were responsible for specifying tactics in a desert war.

Slowly it began to dawn on the commanders that a desert war had to be fought with different tactics. Several factors influenced this awareness.

Kuwaiti pilots came down to Fahd to visit and brief the pilots on their experiences fighting the Iraqis. They emphasized that the Iraqis weren't 10 feet tall—that, yes, they did have all of those dreaded weapons, but they were very poorly trained for the most part and didn't always know how to use them.

Then there were the Sparkvarks, EC-130s, Prowlers, and Weasels that were on our side.

Sparkvark is an EF-111 (the nickname for the regular F-111 is "Aardvark") packed full of ECM gear—the EC-130s (a varient of the

C-130) and the Prowler (a Navy four-place A-6) are equipped similarly. When they fly in the vicinity of a battlefield, they can jam
enemy radars and radio communications between AAA sites.

The Weasels are mostly F-4Gs equipped with sophisticated radar-
detection gear and HARM missiles. Whenever a radar site becomes
active, the Weasel locks it on and fires a HARM missile that guides
in on the radar signal. In other words, should an Iraqi radar SAM
start tracking one of the A-10s when an F-4G is nearby, it is, in pilot
lingo, "good-bye Akhbar."

So why fly low? The pilots and the commanders began to wrestle
with that question. None of them were so rigid in their thinking that
they would stay low because that is what they had always done.
Aside from the cover and visibility problems, flying low was dangerous because it put planes down where small arms fire and some of
the deadliest AAA would be effective.

Gradually, as pilots and commanders questioned the need to
fly low, tactics began to evolve toward high-level flying. But then
the question became: How high? The answer they worked out was
pragmatic. They wanted to fly high enough to stay out of most of the
AAA fire.

The deadliest of the AAA weapons they had to face was the ZSU-
23-4. This is a Soviet-designed, four-barrel, radar or optically guided
23mm machine gun that literally sends out a hose-stream of bullets.
In Vietnam its predecessor (a two-barrel version) was used against
our fighters with devastating effectiveness, and at that time the
weapons were only guided optically—by eyeballs and the skill of the
gunner. The radar-guided version, which the Iraqis were known to
have in abundance, was much more frightening because even ill-
trained gunners could shoot down planes when the computerized
sighting mechanism is fed with radar information.

The other major AAA threats were the 37mm and 57mm guns,
which were optically guided but fired shells that detonated in the air
and sent out metal fragments, or "flak."

As all these threats were evaluated, the problem was to arrive at a
compromise altitude where they could fly high enough to avoid the
worst of the AAA, but low enough to employ weapons effectively
against their targets.

The problem in making that decision was that they did not have
enough knowledge about high-altitude employment of their weapons.
In other words, from how high can one kill a tank with the gun or a
Maverick missile? Of course, they had some statistics in their tactics
manual, but their validity was suspect because they were not based
on battle experience. Also, several variables could influence the
effective distance. Shooting the gun from a steep dive of 60 to 70
degrees almost straight down on the target was one tactic. That one

might be effective when triggering the gun at an altitude of 12,000 feet. But when shooting the gun from 12,000 feet at a 30-degree dive angle, the actual distance or "slant range" to the target is much greater and the bullet trajectory has a higher gravity component. Then there is the wind, which was a major factor in the desert. Above 10,000 feet the winds were often over fifty knots, which made shooting and bombing from those high altitudes a much more difficult problem, especially for pilots with little high-altitude experience.

So, again the question: how high? During the autumn months, as they flew and experimented and discussed the problem, an answer finally evolved. They could maneuver over enemy territory at 15,000 and avoid all AAA except the 57mm guns (85mm and 100mm would also be effective, but they expected little of that). Also, at 15,000 they were almost out of the threat envelope for the shoulder-fired SAMs. About the only way the deadliest of them, the SA-16, could reach them at that altitude was when it was fired from directly below, a negligible probability.

Thus 15,000 feet was a reasonably safe maneuvering altitude. But what about employment of their weapons? What dive angles would they use and at what altitude would they shoot, fire Mavericks, or drop bombs? In their terms, what was the "pickle" altitude?

They decided they would start their dive at 15,000 and use a steep dive angle—45 to 60 degrees, depending on the preference of the pilot. And they decided that 10,000 feet was low enough as a pickle altitude to be effective with their weapons. That way, if they pickled at 10,000 and pulled out at 8,000 they could stay above the effective range of small arms fire and the streams of bullets from the deadly ZSU-23-4.

Such was the reasoning and those were the "ceiling" and "floor" altitudes that the commanders had in mind should war break out. However, there was one important caveat. It was understood by all the pilots that if friendly ground forces were in contact with the enemy and in danger, all ceiling and floor altitudes were to be forgotten. Under those circumstances the pilots were to use whatever tactics they thought necessary to save the soldiers on the ground.

So the low flyers of South Carolina and Louisiana, who joked about feeling like they needed oxygen whenever they flew above 500 feet, now began feeling like they were flying in the ionosphere. It was a surprise to all of them that they would be doing this, and none of them liked it. But they also knew it was safer, and doing it meant they were more likely to return home alive after the combat. And home was very much on their minds, especially after they had been in the desert for several weeks with no action.

# 5

# The Night Hogs are Born

*"When he [Lt. Col. Rick McDow] asked, 'What do you think about us being the night guys?' I looked at him and wondered what he had been smoking or drinking . . ."*
—Lt. Col. Joe Barton

Right after Col. Sandy Sharpe arrived in Saudi Arabia, he called his headquarters at home and told them to get him everything that had been written on Iraq as a military power, especially anything that told how the Iraqis had fought in their war with Iran. Soon he was deep into several books and, "I got a feel right there for what this enemy was going to be like. I was pretty much convinced he wasn't 10 feet tall. He wasn't even 5 feet tall. He was probably more like 3 feet tall and I felt we could get away with a lot more than most people were thinking at the time. He didn't have the leadership out there because they were so tightly controlled by him [Saddam Hussein], personally—and he wasn't a soldier—Schwarzkopf said that from the beginning. I also had the feeling that the will to fight wasn't there [among his troops], particularly when he said he was putting old guys and young kids on the front lines.

"Then I got to thinking how we could fight him and it was pretty apparent that the Army, when it cut loose, would be fighting a mobile, twenty-four-hour-a-day kind of operation. The Army has been evolving toward night operations for several years. They're equipped to do that. They want to take the night sanctuary away from the enemy.

43

"And where would we be in that kind of fight? We were strictly day-VFR [visual flight rules] guys and I was concerned that the Army would move out at night and say, 'Where were you guys? We've been planning on doing this for years. Why haven't you kept pace to provide the air cover we need?'

"I felt very uncomfortable about that and wanted to cut that question off before it was asked. Also, you have to realize that I've been a night guy for my whole career. I flew two tours in Southeast Asia, both at night, then I was with the Stealth program from day one and spent five years in the desert flying the A-7 and 117 at night. I knew what it takes to fly night combat. It takes a dedicated night pilot and he must live nights.

"So, with that concern about doing our job for the Army, and with my background, knowing the advantages of night fighting, I brought up the subject to General Horner on his next visit. I said, 'General Horner, intuitively I feel that General Schwarzkopf is going to want night cover—night close-air support. If that is the case, I want, right now, to put a squadron on nights and get it prepared to fly the night mission.

"He didn't hesitate, he said, 'Okay, do it.' And that's what I did."

"Dave [Sawyer] was with me when I discussed that with Horner and later we talked about it. He wasn't very enthusiastic and didn't particularly want either one of his squadrons involved. Then we talked it over with our DOs, [Colonels] Hank Haden and Tom Lyon, and we all were pretty much in agreement that one of my squadrons, the Falcons, would be the best one because they had a lot of mature, experienced guys, and their commander, [Lt. Col.] Rick McDow, had night combat experience in Southeast Asia—he was actually shot down over there and was a POW in Hanoi—so he was a very mature leader."

Lieutenant Colonel Rick McDow continues the story. "Colonel Haden called me in one day and told me that General Horner was going to need some night CAS if our Army got engaged up there. He said, 'What do you think?' The idea was totally foreign to me at the time; I had never thought along the lines of fighting full-time at night. I told him that I wanted to think it over for awhile and we left it at that.

"It didn't take me long to make a decision. I remember going back to the squadron and looking at the intel map and seeing all the Iraqi defenses and fortifications and what I saw was not too distinctly different from what I saw in Vietnam. When you start counting everybody who can shoot at you in the daytime, you can easily get up into the tens of thousands of weapon systems that can engage you every time an eyeball can see you. If you look at what they had to engage us at night, you get down to significantly less than one hundred."

So, Rick McDow said, "yes," to Colonel Haden, then called his squadron together in one of the big "temper tents"—aluminized canvas tent designed to shed heat—and broke the news. There are various descriptions of what happened next. The flight commanders and pilots were essentially in shock. Their reaction was, "This is stupid! You've got to be crazy, out of your mind. . . . sir."

There was emphasis on the "sir." For "Falcon One" was a highly respected commander—his assistant Ops officer, Maj. A. J. Jackson calls him, ". . . without a doubt the finest warrior I have ever seen."

In the squadron meeting, after the rumbling died down, McDow patiently explained to his pilots why he had volunteered them for such a mission. He said, as he had several times before, that his goal was to lead them into combat and then lead them *all* home.

The pilots listened respectfully. The message: "If you can't be seen, you can't be shot at," seemed abstract to them because their minds were on the more basic problems. Said one, "The Hog was a bitch to fly at night—we learned that coming over that black hole in the Atlantic. And then we were going to fly the thing in combat, diving at 60 degrees, with four-G pullouts. No way. We thought it was stupid."

Captain Mark Roling, the squadron weapons officer, had talked to McDow briefly before the meeting so he was able to coolly survey the reactions of his fellow pilots. According to him, "Out of the thirty-six pilots, I'd say he might have convinced five of them that flying nights was what we should do. I'd say that eighteen or so—the biggest portion—were just in awe of the whole idea, too shocked to respond. However, a big minority, say thirteen, were saying outright that this was stupid, this was dumb."

So for the next several weeks, the pilots of that squadron had something else to think of besides the question, "Honey, when are you coming home?" They had something new to occupy their minds, which, expressed in their terms, went something like, "How the hell do I stay alive doing this crap?"

The first night out, one of them came close to not staying alive. Said Rick McDow, "We were flying a wedge formation and the guy on my wing was keeping my lights in sight through his quarter-panel. He got into a left bank without realizing it—he was flying off me instead of his instruments—and he started descending. He didn't know it because he was still keeping me in the same place in his view. But he thought I was in a left bank, descending. So he called, 'Lead, check your altitude; you are descending.'

"I called back and said, 'No, I am straight and level at 8,000, check your altitude. What is it?'

"He checked his instruments and said, '3,000 feet.' He suddenly realized what he had done, so he leveled his wings and pulled up, but before he did, he saw 2,000 on his altimeter. The terrain we were over went up to sixteen-hundred. In another second or two he could have been dead."

McDow called his pilots together for a meeting after that first flight and, according to one of his pilots, did some "hard debriefing." He stressed the importance of keeping the instrument scan going, and, to eliminate the problem his wingman had had, mandated that there would be no more wedge formation flying at night. From that time on they were to fly only in trail, where one follows the other.

That irritated the pilots. If there is anything sacred in the fighter pilot credo, it is for flight lead and wingman to keep each other in sight. That is impossible for the flight lead when the wingman is in trail. However, as McDow pointed out to his disgruntled pilots, in a combat situation there would be no lights on, so the wedge formation was not an issue—they wouldn't be able to fly it in combat anyway, so they might as well get used to flying in trail. Later, after some of the pilots continued to object, "He did the 'read my lips' number and that finally ended the argument," said one of the pilots.

So the Falcons went out at night in trail and they began to practice tactics in the strange new environment. At first they dropped practice bombs after a gentle, 30-degree dive, pulled straight up, and tried to resist turning their heads quickly over their shoulder to see their results—it was quick movements of the head that brought on vertigo.

But how did they see their targets at night? At first, they used methods pioneered in World War II. They had a flare, the LUU-2 (called a Lou-two), with a parachute that opened automatically at a preset altitude. The heat of the flare warmed the air under the chute, creating a lift effect like a hot-air balloon, so that the flare dropped very slowly. Under the flare, the target was illuminated as in daylight, and they bombed and strafed as they would during the day.

At about this time the pilots made a discovery that eventually had a great impact on the war they eventually fought. They found out that the IR Maverick could be used as a FLIR (forward-looking, infrared night vision device).

The Maverick missile has a television camera in its head. The image the camera sees is projected on a green, four-inch-square TV monitor on the right side of the pilot's instrument panel. The angle that the camera looks down from the plane can be controlled to a limited degree with a "slew button" on the right throttle handle. The pilots knew all this, of course. They had used practice Mavericks on their ranges at home, and they had acquired targets on their screen, locked them on, and dummy-fired the missiles.

A few of them had also shot a live Maverick or two, especially those who had gone to Weapons School recently. But, said Capt. Mark Roling, who had recently graduated from that school, "It was stressed in Weapons School and it was stressed in all the IR texts that the missile is *not* to be used as a FLIR. And I stressed that myself when I got back to the squadron. Guys, you keep your head up, you acquire the target visually through your windscreen, then—and only then—put your head down, watch the TVM [television monitor], lock on the target, and fire. I stressed to the guys, you do not fly around with your head down, trying to find targets with your TVM. That's a good way to hit something or somebody and get killed."

Added Capt. Mike Isherwood, another Weapons School graduate, "In the daytime that's a good way to get shot to pieces because you're motoring along, head down, flying in a straight line, and that makes you predictable to the gunners."

So that was the general attitude, until they started flying nights out over friendly Army troops who were now deployed north of them. Typically, they would be flying along, playing with their slew buttons, occasionally searching the area in front of them through the camera in their IR Maverick, and then, "Hotel Sierra [Hotel stands for "holy"]! Look at that tank!"

And the wingman, also looking through his Maverick, would reply, "Wow, I see it! And look at those tracks; you can see 'em for a mile!"

Then they came back and debriefed and the chatter was exciting because the other pilots had made the same discoveries. They would talk it over and go back out the next night with their video cameras running—every plane had one—and they would search for some of the friendly armored targets (the Mavericks were not wired and it was impossible to fire them), lock them on and simulate firing the missile. Then, when they returned to the squadron, they pulled the video tape and, together, reviewed and critiqued their work.

They learned a lot during the first weeks they did this. At first some of them locked on to sand dunes, vegetation, and especially camels, which showed up hot and bright white on their screens. But they improved quickly, and after a few weeks of night training, they had thrown away the textbook and were using their Maverick missiles as FLIRs. However, there were some inherent problems with this method of searching.

One has to do with the viewing angles of the TV camera in the Maverick. It can only look forward at a 3-degree or a 6-degree viewing angle (the angle selectable by the pilot). That is an extremely narrow view and to appreciate just how narrow it is, compare that view with what we can see normally with our own eye scan. Without moving our heads, we can scan about 100 degrees in front of us. So the problem, when searching with a Maverick, is that the pilot is flying along with his head down, and his field of view is about the same as if he were looking through a soda straw. It was very difficult to find widely spaced targets because they couldn't be seen unless they were almost directly off the nose of the plane.

The other problem with using the Maverick as a search device was that it is a weapon meant to be used against the enemy. When it is fired, the pilot is left sightless in the dark.

Besides learning of the value of the Maverick as a FLIR, the Falcons made another discovery while out flying at night. They were constantly working with Army ground controllers while they practiced and they decided to do a test to see how low they had to be before their engines could be heard on the ground. They thought they would have to be fairly low because they knew their engines were relatively quiet. But they were surprised to learn that the magic number turned out to be 5,000 feet. Above that altitude, the ground controllers said they could not be heard.*

As the weeks went by, positive things began to happen to the Falcons—things that made them feel that maybe their commanders weren't so stupid after all.

At the beginning some of the pilots deeply feared flying combat-type maneuvers on instruments. But they all learned rapidly and soon they were comfortable on "combat gauges."

Learning that they could use the IR Maverick as a search instrument helped remove doubts about their potential effectiveness at night. After a few missions using the Maverick, they became confident that they could search, find, lock-on, and kill any Iraqi target.

Perhaps the most encouraging was the realization that they were flying a semi-stealth fighter. Their planes were dark green, which at night might as well be black. And they were quiet. They could loiter over ground troops indefinitely, and as long as they stayed above 5,000 feet, no one on the ground would know they were up there. They weren't true stealth fighters, of course; they joked that their

---

* Other A-10 pilots, especially those flying night missions in Korea, had occasionally used the Maverick for searching. Also, others had observed that the A-10 was inaudible above 5,000 feet. These facts were unknown to the Falcon pilots, and in the strictest sense they should only be credited with rediscovering them.

radar signature was like Mount Rushmore. But, if the war kicked off and the Sparkvarks did their job, and the Weasels did their job, and the effectiveness of the enemy radar was diminished—well, maybe those worrisome casualty statistics that flitted across their minds while they were alone with their thoughts in bed—just maybe they wouldn't come to pass after all. Maybe old man McDow did us a favor after all. Maybe.

# 6

# Boredom and its Antidotes

*"Psychologically, Desert Shield was a lot more difficult than Desert Storm."*

—Capt. Rich Biley

They were young, they were aggressive, and they were trained to knife-edge sharpness. They had come to fight and they were ready to fight. They were some of America's finest, ready to defend a nation threatened by a brutal dictator. They were well-educated and they knew their history. They knew that their fathers and grandfathers had journeyed to far-off nations and had fought and died to help peoples victimized by such a tyrant. Defending or liberating an underdog from oppression was a part of their American heritage in which they took pride.

Now, they, too, were in a far-off land, poised to defend an underdog nation and fight a dictator spawned in their generation. They were proud of themselves for being selected for such a worthy endeavor. They were eager to strike another blow for American ideals, and they didn't care what the war protesters at home were saying. They believed in what they were doing and they were ready to add another proud chapter to their country's history.

But by October and November they were getting damned tired of the underdog's attitude. The commanders were keeping a brave face, of course, because they knew the extreme fragility of the coalition that their leaders were building. They had studied Middle Eastern history and culture at their war colleges and other leadership schools. They knew that the American presence in the Gulf was, as one salty old pilot said, "Like a painted whore in an old-fashioned country church."

The pilots knew that, or at least they should have known, because they had been hammered on the subject of cultural awareness and sensitivity since they arrived. And, for the most part, they believed in what they heard; they believed that they should make as small a footprint on the Saudi landscape as possible.

They believed all that in the abstract, but damnit, when they came back from a rugged training mission, tired and sweaty, they believed even more strongly that they should be able to relax with an ice-cold beer. They knew Saudi tradition was dead set against alcohol, but they were American fighter pilots with their own tradition that went back to World War I. And, with all due respects to Charles Schulz, they were not into the Snoopy scene—mademoiselles for company, yes, but no root beer, thank you.

What made their forced abstinence harder to bear was their belief that the Saudis really did not expect them to make such a sacrifice. They believed this because some of them had been invited to American homes in the region and had seen that all of the houses built for foreigners, set exclusively in walled-off compounds, included a small room for an alcohol still. The room was plumbed with hot and cold running water but it was not large enough for a washer or dryer, so they claimed it could not have been designed for any other purpose. Of course, the visiting pilots sampled the product, which was a choice between "brown" and "white," the former a whiskey-like potion and the latter a homemade version of gin. It was well known that the Saudis tolerated this bibulous activity. The counterpoint was that tippling outside the compound invited harsh retribution.

The pilots were also irritated because their brethren flying out of Bahrain just a few miles away were not burdened with such penance, nor were the pilots flying out of Qatar. These were Muslim cultures, too, and the pilots wondered why, if those Muslims weren't afraid of revenge from Allah, the Saudis should be so uptight about it all.

The egregious dictum that aroused their anger was General Order Number One, which prohibited, among other things, possession of alcoholic beverages and any form of pornography. The leaders who authored this missive were no doubt aware of how Americans in the past had ignored a much more noble doctrine—one that was ultimately enshrined in the American Constitution as a result of action by the Temperance Union—but they had their job to do. They wanted to cement the coalition of Christian–Muslim nations, and they didn't want any damned Coors or Jack Daniels around to dissolve away bonds. So, that's it guys; forget that stuff and play our game or we're going to send you home.

Now, the thought of going home might have been attractive to some pilots, but to the Hog drivers that would have been a terrible fate, and just the thought of being sent home sent shivers through their bodies. They had been invited to the party; they had flown through hell to get there; and by damn they were going to stay and take their ugly girls out on the dance floor and show all their friends with their pointy-nosed dollies what their ugly girls could do.

They did not want to be sent home, but they were fighter pilots, and guys in that fraternity were not used to letting threats intimidate them. After all, they were looking at *real* threats on their intel maps every day. They were looking at SAMs and AAA poised and ready to kill them in a thousand different ways. They walked with Frankenstein and Dracula and Jack the Ripper through dark corridors every night in their thoughts. Were guys like these going to be intimidated by a temperance order that (1) they didn't believe in, and (2) they didn't think was necessary? The answer for many of them was: hell no.

But what they would do is try to protect their commanders—guys, for the most part, they genuinely liked and respected, but who were caught in the middle. The pilots did not want those guys, or their commanders, to incur Schwarzkopf's temper, which, it was rumored, was world class. So they didn't create any scenes. They didn't file any protests. They didn't complain to their chaplains or congressmen. They just set about using their abundant resourcefulness to circumvent the order in their quiet ways.

It probably started out in tent city with the enlisted folks—that according to a seasoned, old, senior master sergeant who wishes to remain nameless. Of course, those folks didn't need handbooks of organic chemistry to know what to do; this was a generation nourished on years of "M*A*S*H*" and its reruns. One simply finds some kind of fruit, adds sugar, yeast, and water, and waits. The little microscopic squiglies, the yeast cells, will go right to work on the sugar. They'll attack it, molecule by molecule, and break it down into alcohol. And they'll keep doing that until they commit suicide— until the concentration of alcohol reaches a toxic level that kills them. Then, the patient brewmaster will wait till their dead little bodies settle and entomb themselves on the bottom of their workplace. The impatient brewmaster will send someone to Dhahran to an aquarium store to buy a filter and use the tubes and charcoal for filtering the corpses from the brew. Either way, give or take a technique or two, the result is an alcoholic potion with a drinkable quotient proportional to the needs of the tippler.

The only problem was that nobody told them that the little yeast beasties create a lot of waste as they do their noble work. When that sugar molecule is broken, a carbon atom falls in love with two oxygen atoms, unites in a scandalous marriage, and drifts off into the delicious freedom of space. A problem arises, however, when too many of these hybrids are produced. The space gets more and more crowded, and as that happens they begin hammering each other. And as the crowd continues to grow, the violence increases as does their frenzy, and if they are in a container where they cannot escape, that container had better be strong; otherwise they are going to keep battering it until it erupts and sets them free.

And if that happens in the middle of the night, when rumors of terrorist attacks are rampant, and folks are sleeping with guns and helmets within reach, well. . . .

It did happen. It happened in tent city when the guys first started their illicit enterprise. One nameless sergeant collected fruit from his MREs, had his friends bring sugar packets from the mess hall (the mess folks were soon wondering why the troops had suddenly developed such an appetite for sugar), had some driver bring him yeast from Dhahran, put his mixture in a plastic water bottle and capped it. Then the little beasties did their job just like they were programmed to do, and the little carbon dioxide molecules did their thing, and . . . a whole bunch of sleepy troops dove under their beds, or grabbed helmets and guns, and an embarrassed sergeant had a royal mess to clean up. Fortunately, tent city was far enough away from the commanders. . . .

He tried it again. Only this time he would give the carbon dioxide molecules more room to roam. He loaded in the fruit saved from more MRE's, along with water, sugar, and yeast, then attached a condom to the neck of a water bottle with rubber bands. Again the beasties worked for him, and the condom expanded, shockingly and obscenely, until the pressure outgrew the strength of the rubber bands. The good news was that there was no explosion; the bad news was that the brew cascaded over the sides of the bottle and the sergeant had another mess with nothing to drink to salve his disappointment.

He did it a third time, with a tight-fitting balloon acquired somehow from Dhahran, and, for his pioneering, product-manufacturing research, it is reported that his grateful colleagues, when they partook of his elixir, voted to beam him up to the NCO's Nirvana.

It didn't turn out as well for the officers—at least not for one of their major efforts.

Two enterprising Hog drivers heard that the local Americans, Brits, and French had all the beer they wanted. All they did was buy a certain brand of non-alcoholic beer—one with screw caps on the bottles—add yeast and sugar, recap the bottles, wait two weeks, and *voila!* It wouldn't be what they enjoyed at home in their squadron recreation room, but with their palates' memory deteriorating in log-phase downward, they were assured they would smile all the way to the urinals.

"Great idea," said one of them when he heard how it was done.

"Sierra Hotel!" [Hotel stands for "hot"] exclaimed the other. "Let's do it!"

"Should we buy a six-pack and experiment?"

"And waste two weeks?"

"You're right. We might be dead by then."

"Let's get a whole bunch."

"Yeah, like three or four cases."

"How about five or six?"

"Hell, if we're doing that, let's get enough to last."

"Ten cases?"

"Sounds good to me."

So on their first trip into town, while their friends were shopping for gold and trinkets to take home to wives and girlfriends, our two would-be brewmasters were purchasing the seven-foot stack of beer cases that would end up towering above them in their room.

Then they went to work. At first they opened one of the bottles and leisurely dumped in the yeast-sugar mixture they had been advised to use. Instantly, like a volcano, the liquid erupted and doused them. Well, okay, if that's the way you're going to behave. . . .

Soon they were sitting in the middle of the floor, one with his flight gloves on—because unscrewing the caps was tearing up his hands—and the other poised above the bottle, ready to drop in the virile ingredients, while milliseconds later the other would ram the cap down and frantically screw it tight to stop the eruption. With proper timing and their fighter-pilot reflexes working for them, most of the time they were successful. However, there were drippings, and both pilots swear on their Hog driver's honor that some of the spillage remained on the floor and refused to evaporate during the whole time they were stationed in the Gulf.

They were supposed to wait two weeks but their needs were acute and they tried a bottle after eight days. The story was told with screwed-up faces, and their phrases like Delta Sierra and Hotel Papa really don't need to be translated. It was bad, bad.

So they waited another week and cautiously, hopefully, sniffed, then took a small taste. The lines weren't as deep in their facial expressions, and they bravely sampled another swallow or two. But it was still bad.

They let another three weeks go by, thinking now that they had not put in enough yeast or sugar, and tried it again. This time they each managed to get down a full bottle. But *real* beer it was not. In fact, it was so detestable that they tried to forget their folly, for which they were being needled regularly, and returned to Pepsi, which at least had an enjoyable taste.

Then their memories were jogged in the middle of the night when one bottle exploded, causing a chain reaction that blew up one whole case. There were eight rooms in the trailer and unofficial reports say most were vacated in ten seconds. (By their tenth-year reunion the time will probably be an Olympic-class record.)

That did it for number two pilot—he was the wingman—his cohort was Lead. They were jammed in a ten-by-ten room and their other accumulations (which will be described in the next part of this story) were about to crowd out their roommates. So Two takes it upon himself to go on a cleaning spree and get rid of the brew. But where? He couldn't put it outside and take a chance that it would explode. Finally, he decided that the toilet was the only place, so he lugged the cases to the middle of the trailer where the bathrooms were located and began the dismal work of opening and emptying the spoiled fruit of their labor into a toilet. Like it or not, the Saudis were going to have their underground terrain blessed with devil water.

But before Two completed his labor, Lead arrived, questioned his action, then succumbed glumly to his friend's decision. He was even helping him when another pilot came to use the facilities. He, too, questioned them, then decided to salvage two six-packs "just in case." Somehow, he knew there were hard times ahead. That gave Lead an idea, so he, too, decided that some should be saved and he kept back a six-pack.

Almost two months later, just before the real war started, the friend who had rat-holed the two six-packs was suffering severe withdrawal after a particularly hard training mission. Having exhausted all other options (and there were several) he thought of the brew he had saved. He wasn't anxious to try it; he remembered the descriptions of how bad it was. But when you're desperate . . .

Five minutes later, while Lead and Two were lying on their bunks reading some of the smut that had been smuggled into the country, the friend sauntered into the room. Then comedy became tragedy. The friend, who was holding one of the bottles, announced rather quietly that the brew he had in his hand was one of the finest and most potent beers he had ever had the pleasure of drinking.

Tragedy, yes. But shed no tears for Lead and Two. Their brew-making was just Act One of the drama for they were about to discover "Crystal Light."

Lead had this friend he called "Timmy," who had been a fraternity brother in college, and who was now "TJ" in an ultraconservative Eastern Establishment company. One day Timmy received this letter from his old friend, Lead, telling him what hell was like in the desert. "Well, that struck a chord with me," said Timmy, "because he told about the things he couldn't get over there. He was amazed, he said that there wasn't a corner drugstore where he could get Skoal—he chewed the stuff—and he lamented that they couldn't have any form of alcohol or pornography. The more he rattled off, the more my interest peaked in doing what I could do on the home front to help my warrior friend.

"The first thing I did was to go out and buy a *Penthouse* and a *Newsweek*. I switched covers, and not to brag, but I did a professional job because I'd heard that people were hung by their thumbs if they were caught with contraband and I didn't want that to happen to my buddy.

"Then I got on the phone. I found out Skoal was manufactured by the U.S. Tobacco Company in North Carolina. I called them and they directed me to the marketing department in Connecticut. There I got a product manager who agreed to donate ten cases of Skoal—1600 cans, I believe—if I could figure out a way to get it over there. At that time there was a twelve-and-a-half pound limit on packages, so that option was out. Then I really went to work, and after lots of sleuthing around the air bases, I found this sergeant who was sympathetic and just happened to know of a pallet of supplies that was going over there—a pallet with a little extra space. I immediately called the marketing guy and he had the cases on a truck that same day. Three days later the sergeant called quite distraught. 'I thought you said you wanted to send some tobacco,' he said. 'Hell, man, I can't even move in my office for all this stuff.' We chatted and I assured him that it was a terribly important cause and, seeing the light, he agreed and in a day or two my friend, and all the other Skoal-users in the Persian Gulf had one of their needs satisfied. I also sent the sergeant a nice bottle of scotch for his above-and-beyond effort for the cause.

"By then I was becoming very paternalistic about those guys over there, so everywhere I went I began thinking of how I could get things to them. I knew that the alcohol prohibition was their most acute problem and I got on that right away. At first, I took 11 x 14, padded mailing envelopes, slit the sides and removed the stuffing. Then I filled a Ziploc bag with scotch, taped the edges with clear, polypropylene tape, tested it by pounding it, and inserted it in the space where the stuffing had been. Finally, I put a computer company's sales pamphlet inside, addressed it to my friend, put 'J. Daniels' on the return address, and mailed it. A week or so later I got a call from my friend. He was ecstatic but he had had a close call. After cutting open the envelope and finding just a computer pamphlet, he stabbed the envelope in frustration. He reported that the next words in the bunkroom were, 'Hold it; don't anybody move a muscle.'

"I did several of those but I knew my friend was dying for a cold beer and I was frustrated; I couldn't think of a way to get beer over to him. They took the weight limit off the packages and that really got me thinking. One day, while in the market with my wife, I happened to notice the Crystal Light (a soft drink powder) cans and suddenly a light bulb went on. I lifted one—it's like a small tennis-ball can—and my wife thought I was crazy when I speculated that a beer can would fit inside. Well, I tried it as soon as I got home. I got a Budweiser can about two-thirds of the way in, but that was it. It wouldn't go any farther. And I was defeated, crushed. Then, sometime during the middle of the night, I was lying awake, trying to think of what I could do, and it hit me: Coors cans have a different shape—they're slimmer! I charged out of bed, got under the counter where I had a six-pack of Coors, and I almost cried when that puppy slipped right in that can. It was a perfect fit.

"But then, how was I to replace the plastic, tamper-proof seal that I had removed? That's when my wife came to my aid. One of her companies made the stuff—it's a plastic that shrinks when heat is applied. With my prodding she quickly requisitioned an emergency supply, we got out the trusty hair dryer, and it worked! When we finished, the can looked like it had just come from the store. So we got the Coors lifeline in operation.

"About this time I began worrying about the food they were eating over there. I knew it had to be camel meat and figs, right? Well, one day I was leafing through one of those little catalogs with executive gifts and I see this ad for Phalzer Brothers where you can buy gourmet steaks and have them shipped to a client. I jumped right on the phone and called them in Burr Ridge, Illinois. I got past the order clerks and got a guy who said there was no way they could ship steaks to Saudi. Well, I finally worked my way up to the president, Bill Cronin, and asked him point-blank: If I can arrange the shipping, would you donate some steaks for those guys?

"He didn't even hesitate. He said, 'Absolutely.' Then I went to work in the military channels. I didn't go back to my sergeant friend who did the Skoal—he had risked enough already. But let's just say that I lived on the phone for awhile. And in the process, I got hold of a Navy commander that ripped me a new one. How dare I try to do something special like that for one squadron when there were thousands over there needing food! Oh, he was a mean one.

"Finally, I made a connection. Yes, there is a plane going to that region and, yes, if you will furnish the dry ice and get them here, we'll see that they get on. I called Bill Cronin immediately and he was happy. He suggested the 10-ounce steak, which was their finest, then said he would pass me over to his secretary and that I was to tell her how many I wanted. But, before he did that he came up with another thought. He said that his inventory was overloaded with Macadamia Nut Crunch and did I think the guys would like some of that. I didn't know what it was but I wasn't about to turn it down. I said, 'Sure,' and then the secretary came on. She asked how many steaks I wanted. I gulped a couple of times and asked, hesitantly, '150?' There was no quibbling. 'That's fine,' she said, 'and the Macadamia Crunch?' I said, 'Oh, I don't know,' and she said, 'Well, why don't I send a case today, and a case every week afterward until you tell me to stop. All right?' That was all right with me—but then I forgot I'd said that until I got a report after the War that they had cans and cans and cans of Macadamia Crunch and more overweight fighter pilots than in the whole Air Force.

"But the steaks were the thing—I couldn't believe the generosity of that company. They Fed-Ex'd the steaks to me immediately. I then bought dry ice, put on my cloak and dagger, and headed for the secret rendezvous 290 miles away. Then, after exchanging passwords and countersigns . . ."

They got the steaks from Timmy—with a plastic bag of Pinch scotch taped inside the carton. And they got cases of Macadamia Nut Crunch (there were fifty cans per case). And they got 400 pounds of domestic items donated by the employees of Caesar's Palace in Atlantic City, courtesy of Timmy's arm-twisting. And they got a 1,000-gallon plastic swimming pool that Timmy thought they needed. And the list goes on . . .

But Timmy wasn't the only benefactor. Packages began flowing into the base after the weight limit was lifted. And they were loaded with mysterious things.

One pilot, for example, received a package from his wife and it was labeled "Sanitary Items." He opened it to find a toothbrush, toothpaste and a bottle of Listerine. Puzzled, he showed it to his roommates. He couldn't figure out why she had sent the Listerine. "Maybe you better smell that," the most astute of his roommates suggested. He did, and smiled. It was fine scotch.

Then the AT&T long-distance lines grew heated. There was suddenly an epidemic of bad breath breaking out everywhere in the pilot community. And the manufacturers of Listerine, Plax, and Scope would have been blessed if they could have used the pilots' pleas for their commercials. The pilots told their wives that they were desperate—that their friends had quit speaking to them because of their breath problem.

Some wives were reluctant. They, too, had heard stories of how the Saudis hung people by their thumbs and chopped off important appendages. They were not going to jeopardize their loved ones just so they could make their breath sweeter.

But there were many wives who were as gutsy as the pilots, and soon, after Myrtle Beach, South Carolina, and Alexandria, Louisiana, stores got in more green food coloring—there was an instant run on it—there were bottles of mouthwash proudly displayed everywhere, and the pilots were once again speaking to each other in close quarters with confidence.

Oh, there were a few problems. Over in tent city an enlisted guy or two over-imbibed and created a scene that the security police could not ignore. They were sent home, and after that, there was some resentment whenever they [the enlisted men] heard party-noise coming from one of the pilots' rooms. The pilot who reported this said, "A little of the resentment might have been justified because we did have an occasional get-together. But alcohol had nothing to do with what they heard most of the time. Lots of times we'd just get together and laugh and whoop and yell because that's the way we were. We tried to have fun whether we had booze or not—and most of the times it was not."

The autumn days were creeping by and nothing warlike was happening. The pilots didn't have television yet, but they kept their ears glued to the radio, alert for anything that might have a bearing on how long they were going to stay over there. But they heard nothing significant, and their commanders convinced them that they were as much in the dark as the pilots.

So as the days crept by, seemingly at a pace that was getting slower, the pilots became more aggressive in taking advantage of other outlets for their pent-up energies. Some built furniture in a wood shop that had been created and stocked for their use. This enterprise resulted in ingenious creations, including a bunkroom storage cabinet with a two-chute soft drink dispenser.

Many played on the volleyball, basketball, and softball teams and ". . . there was lots of running. For some guys it was just a way to stay in shape and pass the time, but for several of us there was a more serious motive. We knew that if we got shot down in the desert, survival was going to be tough, and just the little edge the physical conditioning would give us might make the difference."

So, even though they were talking incessantly about home and when they might get there, they were also aware that a heavy black cloud was still hanging over Kuwait.

Before, it had been Saudi Arabia that was in danger of invasion. Now, with ground troops deployed along the border and with the buildup increasing dramatically day by day—buildup they could see because of their training missions—they could feel the subtle change of emphasis as they listened on their radios to the pronouncements from Washington. The talk of the Saudis being in danger was diminishing and the protesters slogan, "No Blood for Oil," didn't seem pertinent any more. What they were hearing now were atrocity stories out of Kuwait and the banner topic had shifted. The goal now seemed to be the liberation of Kuwait, which, if they became involved, would be an act of goodness and of mercy, and have nothing to do, at least directly, with the Saudis or their oil.

Meanwhile, some golf clubs had arrived and one of the contractors had created a small, makeshift golf course out in the desert—with sand greens, naturally. So, for the really superior athletes among the pilots, the queen of all the sports became available. There was only the minor nuisance of dealing with 30-knot winds, sandstorms, and the hassle of carrying their little piece of Astroturf around with them. . . .

# 7

# From Defense to Offense

*"Gentlemen, you are going to make history. . . ."*
—*Brig. Gen. Buster Glosson*

"When are they going to let you come home, honey?"

She just kept asking that question. And no one could blame her. She was working at a full-time job, yet trying to raise little Suzie, who has had chicken pox and pinkeye in the last two months, and little Matthew, who had just broken the neighbor's window and has already lost two pairs of glasses since school started. And besides all that, she's tired of being alone. She's tired of female company. She wants a man around the house, even if he does come home on Friday evenings a little glassy eyed.

And besides that, just what are you doing over there? Do they• really need you?

Fortunately, for most of the pilots, the wives didn't get past the basic question. For they knew why their men were there, and they knew that they wanted to come home just as much as they wanted them home. They said that in their letters, and they said it in the marathon, budget-busting phone calls that were, for most families—and for the first time in any of America's wars—the communications link that bound them together.

The "when are you coming home" problem got a little more touchy in November. Administratively, the pilots were on temporary duty (TDY) for a ninety-day period. That was the standard way the

Air Force handled all short-term deployments. Ninety days was going to be up soon, however, and for some of them it would be right at a crucial time, for a family at least: Thanksgiving. So, despite what the United Nations was or was not resolving, and despite whether sanctions were going to drive Saddam Hussein out of Kuwait or not, the question for many of the pilots was more fundamental: Are they or are they not going to rotate us in time to get home for the Thanksgiving holiday?

Rotate? That meant bring A-10 pilots from other bases to take their place. They could have done that easily. There were plenty of A-10 pilots who were dying to get over there—the Warthog Factor was a universal affliction.

Also, rumors and questions were rampant. "I hear the F-16 squadron at X is going to rotate and we were here before them. How come?" That kind of thing.

Then Secretary of Defense Dick Cheney announced, as a result of numerous inquiries, that the question of TDY and rotation was up in the air and being evaluated. As soon as the pilots heard that on their little radios, the anxiety quotient went up a notch.

What they did not know was that Gen. "Stormin'" Norman Schwarzkopf was doing some of his stormin'. He was adamantly opposed to any rotation and he was letting everybody know it.

He had a good reason to be against it. He, like the other senior commanders, had lived with the Southeast Asia experience. And while there were many counterproductive policies in that war, one of the worst, for commanders at least, was the rotation policy. Said Col. Sandy Sharpe, "That policy guaranteed that we were always fighting with inexperienced people. In war you need experience and, sure, you can take a few new guys and upgrade them, acclimatize them, teach them the unique targets, threats, and routes. But the turnover factor can overwhelm a unit and divert your attention from the mission. In a long war, that has to happen to some degree. But we weren't planning on a long war. So Schwarzkopf was adamant. He wanted all the experience he could get, and when he went to war, he wanted 100 percent of his people fully ready. Of course, he wouldn't have experience in the theater if he started rotating people."

Schwarzkopf got his way. Cheney passed down the word that there would be no rotation and, as Lt. Col. Gene Renuart, the Vanguards squadron commander, put it, "The word came down to us that, 'Boys you can forget all about rotation for now. Nobody is going home. You're here for the duration. Enjoy your turkey dinner.'"

"That was healthy," said Renuart, "because guys then knew they weren't going home until the job was over. Also, that helped at home because they had something definite now to tell their wives. They would come home when the job was done and not before. That was hard news for the wives, but it also took away a lot of the uncertainty. They could then focus ahead just like the pilots were doing. Life would be difficult, but they knew where they stood."

From the day that policy was announced, every man and woman over there shifted into a lower gear, the gear of determination, the gear that would grind them over peaks and valleys, through sand and fire.

And they focused. It was no longer a broad image that was in their mind. The no-rotation policy was a powerful magnifying glass that focused all their pent-up anger and frustration on one single person: a man with a bushy moustache, lots of teeth, and shifty eyes. Saddam Hussein. Not since the days of Adolf Hitler had one man so single-handedly aroused the passions of American fighting men and women. Saddam Hussein was the man who invaded Kuwait and encouraged his troops to pillage and rape. Saddam Hussein was the man who willed 400,000 men to stand and be ready to fight a holy war against the infidels. And, now this, the ultimate transgression of them all: He had stepped directly between all these Americans and their homes.

Buddy, when you do something like that, you're begging for trouble.

That's what any American could have told him, had he had sense enough to ask. But he apparently glided through the weeks of November and December sublimely ignorant of the power and resolve of the forces massing against him, more fascinated, perhaps, by CNN images of shouting, screaming, wild-eyed protesters being dragged from the White House lawn than he was by intelligence reports from his generals.

The Warthog community wasn't doing any gliding. They were in full military power and wishing for afterburners.

They were flying day and night, practicing, modifying, refining tactics that would allow them to attack Saddam's armor but evade his myriad threats so that they could come back and do it another day, and another day, and another, until his forces were beat to a pulp—obliterated—totally destroyed, so that he could never do it again—providing his arms merchants were similarly dispatched, or otherwise rendered inoperative.

Nobody with any authority was saying all of that in polite company. The sanitized language was that all we wanted was Saddam out of Kuwait. But that was not what was in the hearts and guts of the Hog drivers. And that probably could be said for the thousands of grunts up near the Kuwaiti border who were living in the sand and the wind and who hadn't had a shower for a month or more. Saddam was standing in the way of their homes, too, and it is probably safe to say that violent mayhem and total destruction of his war machine were more important to them than just running him out of Kuwait. They had already had more than enough of desert living. They had no desire to come back. Ever.

At the start of all of our wars, whenever aircraft were used as weapons, battle planners, usually under hectic pressure, were always responding to aggression that had been initiated against the United States. The air offensives in other wars were always counterblows thrown at an enemy that had bloodied us, and when we lashed back, we were seldom afforded the luxury of fighting on our terms. That would also have been the case had the Central European scenario unfolded, or if Saddam had moved south after taking Kuwait. We weren't without battle plans, of course, but the attacker is the one who dictates the time over target (TOT) and the scene of the battle. There is no way a defensive battle plan can be a precise document.

In Riyadh, down in the "black hole" where war planners were working, Gen. Chuck Horner's air staff was making history. For the first time ever, the United States, with coalition forces, was preparing a precise, preemptive air campaign that would be launched against another nation. Instead of being victims of a surprise, brutal attack, as most of the coalition nations had been to the likes of Goering and Yamamoto's air-battle planners, the United States was deciding the TOTs and the battle scenes. Horner's planners were told to strike first, strike fast, strike hard, and use all available assets as effectively as possible.

Representatives from all of the different aircraft communities were involved in the planning process. The Eagles and Strike Eagles, the Aardvarks and the Sparkvarks, the Harriers and the Intruders, the Buffs and the Spectors—their pilots, and pilots of all the other aircraft in the theater, were all down in the black hole, joint architects of the most massive air campaign ever created.

And where did the Warthogs fit into the big show?

They didn't. The planners wanted the Warthogs sitting on the ground for the opening night and the matinee and for all the other initial performances. That was just what one would expect if one could believe all the bad things that had supposedly been said about the Hogs, right?

Well, according to Capt. Mike Isherwood, who was one of the Hog drivers involved in the planning, the ugly-girl affliction wasn't really the problem. "The planners simply felt that the A-10s should be held back and saved till the Army kicked off. The doctrine was that the Hog stayed within 20 miles or so of the ground forces and did CAS, period. It was not a deep interdiction plane. It wasn't envisioned for that and the planners felt that, with all the threats the Iraqis had, the Hogs would get creamed if they were sent on strike missions very far behind the lines. They were too slow for that mission, and it was estimated that four or five of them would be lost every day. The Army would not like that because when they got ready to move, the planes they were relying on for CAS would be attrited."

Colonel Dave Sawyer picks up the story from there. "In my opinion it was Gen. Horner who turned the thing around for us. I think when he saw that the Army wanted us to stand down during that initial phase of the air war, he said, 'Baloney, those guys can carry six Mark 82s [500-pound bombs], four Mavericks, 1,150 rounds of 30mm. They can beat the crap out of that artillery and that armor that you are so damned worried about. Let's let them in; we'll work them at the borders and increasingly deeper.'"

Continues Sawyer, "Gen. Buster Glosson came through on October 24, and Sandy and I had lunch with him at the hospital. He was talking about the day-one frag [Air Tasking Order, or ATO—the overall plan] and he asked us if we thought we could take out radar sites on the Iraqi border. He said there were so many of them he didn't have enough assets to take them all out. He said there wouldn't be any radar SAMs—those things would eat our lunch—and that the threat would be mostly 23mm and 57mm triple-A. We said, 'Hell yes, we can do that; throw us in that briar patch.'

"Later, Sandy and I went down to Riyadh for a tactics meeting. All the interdiction guys had this big, top-secret package, the day-one frag that Glosson and the black hole had been working on. We didn't get one and we asked, how come? They said we're going to stand down for the first three days. We said, 'Bullshit, we could be creaming them along the border. There are no radar SAMs down there. You guys are supposed to take them out, anyhow—the Weasels are supposed to take them out early on.'

"I'm confident we put that idea in their minds because, later, Glosson came back to us and asked us point blank. He said, 'I'm thinking about putting you out on those radar sites.' We said, 'God, put us in the frag. You are going to have a bunch of pissed-off fighter pilots if you don't put us in, especially if we sit on the ground for three days and then, after all hell breaks loose, we have to go offensive.'

"That must have helped because, in early January, we went down for a final tactics conference and talked about the day-one frag, and guess what? Sandy and I got a package. We are alive, and we are a part of the big boys now. At least we thought so until the ATO came in. We opened it up—it was top secret—and there it was, the whole plan laid out, where every plane was going and what it was going to do. But there was nothing for the A-10s and we couldn't understand it. Then [Col. Hank] Haden or [Col. Tom] Lyon—one of the DOs called our guy in the black hole down there, Lt. Col. Bob Lane, and he said it was just an oversight—that our ATO was on the way."*

In the meantime, General Horner was hedging his bet. If he was wrong and the A-10s took some big hits during those first days and there weren't enough of them left to help the Army when it kicked off . . .

Orders went out for two more squadrons of A-10s and six more OA-10s (six had come over in October) to deploy, which would increase the total from 102 to 144.

The Vultures, based at RAF Alconbury, in Great Britain, was one of them. This squadron had been poised on the north flank, ready to leap into a Central European battle, but since the Warsaw Pact was in the process of self-destructing, it seemed safe to uncover a little of that flank.

The second squadron, the Cajuns, was an Air Force Reserve squadron. These pilots were much older. Many had combat records in Southeast Asia and were now flying for companies like American, Delta, United, and Federal Express—and getting their kicks by flying the Hog in their free time and during extended-period summer tours. (The group also included pilots from diverse backgrounds and locations, including a business executive from Atlanta—the squadron commander—a veterinarian with two practices in rural Louisiana who also flies for United, and a television reporter from Cleveland.)

The OA-10s were from the squadron of Nail-FACs, based at Davis-Monthan. Their name, Nail-FACs, dated back to Vietnam when a gutsy group of guys using the call sign "Nail" began flying as FACs [Forward Air Controllers] in the little single-engine Cessna O-1, marking targets with Willie Pete [white phosphorous rockets], and calling in air strikes on the enemy. Coincidentally, the Cajuns were well versed on that heritage; six of them had been FACs in Southeast Asia, and two of them had been Nail-FACs in the same squadron.

---

* Major General Buster Glosson reviewed this chapter and said, "I understand Sharpe and Sawyer's perception but they were wrong. We wanted the A-10s in from the very beginning but CENTCOM [Central Command] fought us because they were worried about an Iraqi attack when the air campaign started. They wanted the A-10s held for defense against Iraqi armor if they attacked. But we argued and won.

But were they actually going to war? Or were they chips being shoved into the pot of a high stakes poker game? That depended upon whether the fellow who was holding the poker hand and shoving in the chips was serious or was bluffing.

As it turned out, he was dead serious. When President Bush issued his now-famous ultimatum—"Get out of Kuwait by January 15, 1991, or we're going to come in and kick you out"—he had drawn a line in the sand. Although the pilots had listened anxiously to the congressional debate over the matter, and had argued among themselves over whether the country would have the resolve to do what they, themselves, believed was right—which was to destroy Saddam's ability to make war—they were not surprised at Bush's firm stance. Bush was a former military pilot. He belonged to the fraternity. Perhaps that helped them believe in him. But something else was happening that had an even greater impact.

They were being buried in letters of support. Tons of letters, most of them addressed "To any Serviceman in the Gulf," had been arriving for weeks. They were from old folks, business executives, secretaries, farmers, factory workers, teenagers and third-graders. And they were 99.99 percent supportive. "Go get 'em guys; we're sayin' a prayer for you. And God bless America."

First Lieutenant Lisa Rappa, adjutant of the Panthers, said that her squadron alone received over 1,400 letters, ". . . all of which we answered, not only as a matter of principle, but because we appreciated the support. I still correspond with about forty of those folks [one year later]."

Then, just before Christmas, another squadron of pilots received an unpleasant surprise. It all started after Colonels Sharpe and Sawyer had been talking to their DOs, Colonels Haden and Lyon. What is the best way for us to use these 144 planes we're going to have?

The air campaign, as they knew it then, was a twenty-four-hour-a-day campaign. The Iraqis were not going to get any respite. The pressure would be on them day and night, the latter especially because it would shut down their logistics. Night truck convoys would be knocked out when they tried to move south from Baghdad and resupply troops in Kuwait, for example.

Realizing this, the colonels looked at the number of planes again. They had twenty-four tasked for night operations—the Falcons, which were Beach guys. That left 120 planes for day tasking, yet, by next month when they expected to go to war, the nights were longer than the days. They saw that the numbers didn't jibe with the job they anticipated. If they were going to carry their weight in the impending air war, they needed another squadron ready for night operations.*

Sawyer volunteered. "Not because I was wild about it; I wasn't," said Sawyer. But the Beach guys already had one ready for night operations and I felt that we should share the load."

Sawyer talked it over with Tom Lyon, his DO, and they agreed that the Flying Tigers would be their first choice. They had a new commander, Lt. Col. Jim Green, but he was capable and seemed to have the squadron running well. But mainly it was the experience level in the squadron that swayed them; they had more overall experience than the Vanguards, the other Alex squadron. Lyon agreed that he would call Jim Green in and see if he wished to volunteer.

Jim Green readily admits that he was not enthusiastic about the idea. He had come from the air superiority world, flying aggressors for six years in the air-to-air combat regime where it was eyeballs against eyeballs. At night he felt semi-blind, like he needed a white cane.

But he was a good soldier and, after talking it over with his Ops officer, Lt. Col. Mike Wilken, he called a squadron meeting. According to the guys who sat through the meeting (the author interviewed twenty-six of them), he performed a masterful feat of consensus leadership.

"Guys, I've just been told that we need another night squadron. I've been given the chance to volunteer us. Frankly, I'm not wild about the idea. Why don't you tell me why we should do this." That was the lead-in. From then on he listened.

And he heard a lot. First, the flight commanders—A, B, C, and D, spoke. Negative. Negative. Negative. Negative. The whole damned idea is stupid. The Hog was designed as a day-fighter. We'll blunder around at night and kill ourselves. And we won't be effective. We know how to do CAS in the day. Let us fight in the day and we'll kick ass. We'll do it big time.

The Warthog Factor was also at work. Two of the captains, Kent Yohe and Dave Feehs, voiced strong objections. "Hell, the war'll kick off, the day guys will go out and beat the snot out of them and we'll sit on the ground. The war will be over in two or three days and we'll be nothing but a bridesmaid. We've sat around for months waiting on this and we'll never get to fly the Hog in combat. The whole idea sucks."

---

* General Glosson says that he encouraged Colonels Sharpe and Sawyer to bring up another night squadron.

There were three Weapons School graduates who would be flying with the squadron and they spoke next. Two of them opposed. Then Capt. Mike Isherwood, who Jim Green says is a general running around with captain's bars on his shoulders, spoke his piece.

Says Isherwood, "I was strongly in favor of the idea and I told them I thought they were all wrong. I told them that we should definitely do it. Then I went into some of the rationale. The reduced threats, the fact that they couldn't see or hear us. . . . things like that. So there was the safety factor. They wanted to fly combat in the Hog but they also wanted to get back to their families. I stressed that by flying at night we stood the best chance of getting everybody home.

"I also stressed the needs of the Army. I said that the Army was going to fight at night, that they were going to need good pilots to support them, and that the Tigers were, in my opinion, the best qualified to accept that role.

"Also, there was the effectiveness factor. They wanted to be effective and they were afraid they couldn't do much at night. From my Weapons School background I knew about the IR Maverick, and although we were hammered to never use it as a search device, I knew what the Falcons had learned. I believed that at night, if we flew around with our head down in the cockpit looking at the TVM, we would be relatively safe from the gunners. With the radar threats taken out—which they were supposed to be—the only way they could get us is with barrage fire [unaimed AAA fire, shot straight up, the gunners hoping a plane will fly through it], or by IR SAMs, but they would have to know we were up there.

"I had a more difficult problem countering what Yohe and Feehs had said about not getting into the war. I had been working with planners in the black hole down in Riyadh and I knew the complete battle plan. I felt certain that Iraq was not going to cave in after a couple of days, and I knew that there was lots of tasking for all the Hogs. But that was top-secret stuff and I had to hedge around what I knew, yet try to convince those guys that they were wrong—that they were not going to sit on the ground—that they were going to get plenty of action."

Then Green took over and basically turned the squadron around. "If we do end up doing this, how do you think we should go about it?" The suggestions flowed. Ideas were seconded and reinforced. Everybody contributed, adding bits and pieces. "Well, if we are going to do it, I think we should . . ." Eventually, Tiger pride showed itself. "Well, if they want the Flying Tigers to do it . . ." The meeting ended. Green reported to Lyon. "Affirmative, sir."

On December 24, Christmas Eve, the first Tigers climbed the ladders and flew off into the black night. But they were not invading a new realm; they did not need white canes. They had huddled with the Falcons, who had been flying around in the dark since October. "Here, this is the way you mask that TVM to keep the green light from blinding you. . . ." "Here is how you use the air-to-air TACAN to keep track of each other. . . ." "Here is how you calibrate the Maverick to get your best lookdown, shoot-down angles for target acquisition and lock-on. . . ." "Here, right on page so and so in this Sporty's Catalog [an American mail-order general aviation supplier] is this lighted kneeboard and this little red, gooseneck lamp. We found they work great. Call 'em and they'll Fed-Ex 'em right out . . . ." It was a cram-course called Night Lessons Learned 101, and twenty nights later, on January 12, Jim Green reported to Tom Lyon that the Tigers were MR—mission ready.

On Christmas Day Bob Hope came through and put on a show for them—which they appreciated. "But after that," said Col. Sandy Sharpe, "the visitors stopped coming. That is when I fully realized that, yeah, we're going to war."

The Vultures from RAF Alconbury were supposed to leave on Christmas Day. But the fog was so thick they couldn't get out. They wanted to go the next day, but that was Boxing Day, a British holiday, and the air controllers didn't think much of that idea. Then, on the morning of the twenty-seventh they got airborne. They flew to Sigonella in Sicily, laid over and rested, then flew directly to Fahd.

Captain Eric Offill, famous for his Hog cartoons and as one of the Lost Wingmen, a group of rock-and-roll musicians in the squadron, decided that he should make a tape recording as he flew down. He thought his wife and, someday, his kids, would appreciate hearing what he observed. "But when I came back," said Offill, "I listened to about fifteen minutes of that tape and I had to turn it off. It was too depressing. My voice was depressing—I hadn't realized how down I was. But not only that, I relived in my mind seeing the guys in formation with me, and I remembered thinking that the formation wouldn't look the same coming home. I couldn't help wondering how many of us would make it back. As Hog drivers trained to fight in Europe we lived with the probabilities. We expected to take some big hits."

The Cajuns took off from NAS New Orleans in the afternoon of New Year's Day, and on their pass over the city they flew over the Sugar Bowl where thousands of football fans looked up and gave them a cheer. They were followed by a cell of six Nail-FACs flying OA-10s out of Tucson.

For most of the Cajuns, flying "across the pond" was old stuff. Most had done it eight or nine times, deploying to their Central European Scenario forward operating location (FOL) in Denmark.

Said Lt. Col. Craig Mays, Federal Express captain and the squadron operations officer, "We train for this all the time. We do mobility exercises where we do all the packing and that stuff. So when they said, 'Okay, you guys are going to Saudi Arabia,' I just said to [Capt.] Jim [Callaway—the mobility officer], 'We're going,' and it was out of my mind; I didn't have to worry about it.

"We flew over in a nice, gentlemanly way," said Mays. "We motored over to the Azores, relaxed, then flew to the Med and on to Fahd. It was my eleventh crossing; the weather was good, so it was no sweat. We got to Fahd on the sixth of January and when we hit the ground we were one-hundred percent ready, with chem gear and everything. Colonel Sharpe met us and called some of us to the side. He said for us to get our shit together in a hurry—they had IPs ready to give us local checkouts and to bring us up to speed on command and control and how everything was going to be run during the war.

"For me, personally, what I experienced was a great relief. I had been concerned, that because we were a reserve squadron, they might treat us like we were some raggedy-ass militia moving in on them. But they treated us like big kids. They were very happy to have our experience. With our guys who had fought in Southeast Asia we more than doubled the number that they had with combat experience. One of the first things they asked is whether some of our veterans would mind talking to their young guys, telling them what it would be like to get shot at. We were happy to do that. We were pleased to be a working part of the operation."

It was a countdown now—the days remaining until the President's deadline. Ten . . . nine . . . eight . . . seven . . . six . . . five . . . four . . . three . . . then a meeting was called by Sharpe and Sawyer. It was for pilots only, in one of the small hangars.

It was 1500 hours on Sunday afternoon, January 13, 1991, Saudi Arabian time when Brig. Gen. Buster Glosson advanced to the front and looked out over the crowd. He looked very tired and like he was under a lot of strain. Then he started to speak. And his message, if not his words, will probably be remembered by the pilots to the end of their days.

"The boss sent me out to visit all the bases and talk to the pilots before this thing kicks off. . . . When I was a young captain flying F-4s in Vietnam in 1970, I remember this boneheaded general coming in to brief us on Linebacker, and it was just, 'Here are your targets; go hit 'em,' and that was it. There was nothing about the overall objectives and where we fit into the picture. I was just a mushroom, kept totally in the dark about the overall plan. I swore then that if I ever got to be a general, that would never happen to guys I commanded. So I'm here today to lay it all out for you—to tell you exactly what we're going to do on day one, day two and day three—what the 117s are going to do in Baghdad, what the F-15Es are going to do—what you are going to do in the campaign . . . gentlemen, you are going to make history. . . ."

The pilots were listening and hardly believing. Could it be true that a general was laying out all the pieces of his secret air campaign to a bunch of Hog drivers? Were we dreaming? Generals don't do that. That kind of stuff is always hush-hush, and for only those "with the need to know."

But that is what the general did and the pilots listened, awestruck at the magnitude of the plan. Then Glosson set some parameters for the risks they should take.

"Remember this," he said, his fiery, cheerleading personality now emerging from the depths of his fatigue, "when you get up there and see a target that's heavily defended, just back off and find another target or come home . . . right now there is absolutely nothing up there that is worth your life. . . . I repeat, we don't want to lose you. Fight hard but fight smart, and come back another day and see what that target is like—we'll send some more planes up later. Now when the ground war starts, when there are troops in contact and the good guys are dying, you go in low and you go under the weather and you do what you have to do to save them—your job is to help those guys, but until then, when it is not right, bring that plane and yourself back home."

The pilots walked tall after that meeting. And their feelings were all positive. Positive because the coach had treated them like the starters for the big game. Positive because they weren't expected to throw their "pink little bodies" against the Iraqi targets that were heavily defended. And most of all, positive because the leadership treated them as men with honor—men who could be trusted with the top-secret knowledge of the most massive air campaign plan ever conceived in the history of warfare.

They glued their ears to their radios as the countdown continued. They heard that the Soviets were now getting involved. That worried them. Were the Soviets going to create a problem on the Security Council? Was the Iraqi ambassador going to get a last-minute reprieve? Ugly visions of sitting in the desert for months while the diplomats did the lawyer routine of delaying through a succession of appeals made them frustrated and angry. *The judge has given the sentence; Saddam is guilty, damnit; now let's carry it out!* AND GO HOME!

Home weighed heavily on their minds. Before they had deployed they had filled out all the gloomy forms, with questions like, If you should be killed, who that your children would recognize could go to their schools and pick them up? It was one thing to live with death in the abstract, but filling out those forms—actually writing down names of persons who could pick up your children after you are dead—had been depressing.

And now they were being told by their squadron commanders that they had another somber duty. You had better write those last letters, guys. If you have last things you want to say to people, don't put it off. Sit down and write it out. For sure, you ought to have a last letter for your wife. And think about your children. Someday, when they grow up, they would treasure having your last thoughts. Then there are your parents and your friends . . . and just leave those letters in your room where we can find them. We'll make sure they get to where they belong.

Sobering stuff. Especially when one sits down and starts putting final thoughts on paper. And especially if you are a fighter pilot.

Fighter pilots shall never die when they are flying their airplane. That is the Eleventh Commandment invisibly etched on the backside of every fighter pilot's wings. That is religion. And any fighter pilot who strays from that religion—who thinks he is going to die—isn't worth a damn. Every air commander has said that forever. A pilot who thinks of dying is a danger to himself and a danger to everyone who is flying with him.

Now their high priests were telling them to take off those wings and place them in the drawer. Now, with their own hands, they were to bare their naked, vulnerable thoughts on glaring, white paper— and confess their vulnerability, and confess thoughts that most held tightly but knew they must now release.

Reluctantly, most did so. And in those moments they become acutely aware of what they really were; they were protoplasm, soft and fragile, and they were going head-to-head against searing hot steel. And at the real high noon, which looked like it was finally going to arrive, protoplasm never wins when the two of them meet. So they had to admit it. Yes, dear, I may die . . . and I want you to know . . .

Two nights after Glosson's speech, on the day of the deadline Saudi Arabian time, the colonels felt the need to lead their own pep assembly. This place is too gloomy; let's get their spirits up. Bring on the Vulture's band, the Lost Wingmen. Put them on the flatbed. Let them play rock-and-roll. And let's give speeches and fire these guys up. And then let's have some more music. Come on, guys, let's get fired up. Let's get ready to go up there and kick ass.

The pilots liked the colonels and respected them, and they genuinely wanted to do well for them. But the timing was wrong for the pep assembly. The guys had just written those last letters, and when they assembled they were not in a mood to cheer and stamp their feet. Said Eric Offill, one of the musicians, "We were up on that flatbed truck, the colonels were getting up and down telling how this was the deadline and how we were going up there and get them and that stuff. And out there were a thousand solemn people concentrating on their own thing. We tried to play our rock-and-roll and it was weird—it kind of tore our band apart [trying to play raucous music to people not in the mood to hear it]."

Then the countdown ended. On U.S. time the deadline had come and passed. The pilots debated. When will it be? But the commanders were not debating, nor were certain officers who were detailed to the Mission Planning Cell—the place in the wing where the ATO is broken down, allocated to squadrons, and where mission packs are assembled for the pilots—packs that include target information, TOTs, frequencies, call signs, secret code words, escape and evasion routes, tanker tracks, threat information, and intel photos, if available.

The air campaign was going to start on the seventeenth, Saudi time, and the sixteenth U.S. time—one day after the deadline in the United States. The main targets of the first strike packages were the military command and control centers and their communications network. The goal was to take away the Iraqi commanders' eyes, ears, and command capability. The attacks would start in the middle of the night with F-117s, F-15Es, F-16s—and many of the other assets.

And the Warthogs would not be far behind.

# 8

---

# The First Day

*". . . late afternoon the ATO came in [and] we found the A-10*
*part and we said, 'We are going where!? We are doing what!?'"*
—Capt. Todd Sheehy

The black-hole guys in Riyadh were the choreographers and they put the Warthogs in the Big Show. They didn't get bit parts nor were they to be mere walk-ons. They were not even destined to be minor characters. From the beginning they were cast in three major roles, along with all the big-name stars. Finally, the Warthogs had their chance for glory.

There was just one problem: They had never thought of rehearsing two of the roles they had won. Some of them were going to sit on CAS alert. This was a traditional role, a role they expected. With their planes cocked they were to be ready to attack Iraqi forces should they counterattack in retaliation for Coalition air strikes. Targets in Baghdad were destined to be destroyed. That would stir up a lot of national resentment, and planners thought Saddam might feel pressure to grab some headlines for himself. Also, revenge is spelled in capital letters in the Arab world.

One of the new roles was BAI, which, when spelled out in the tactics manuals, is Battlefield Air Interdiction. An aircraft that performs BAI flies behind enemy lines and destroys targets that could affect the outcome of a battle. The targets themselves are always nominated and given priority numbers by the ground forces. The distance the planes fly behind the lines depends upon where the highest priority targets are located.

The Coalition ground forces, or "Army," was most worried about the Iraqi artillery. It was massive in quantity; there were thousands

77

of "tubes" scattered all over Kuwait and eastern Iraq near the Saudi border. Also, much of that artillery was longer-ranged than that of the Army. In practical terms, to be outranged is to be outgunned. Since artillery is the real killer in ground campaigns, if friendlies are outgunned, a lot of friendlies are going to die. Nobody wanted friendlies to die, of course, so from the first day of the air campaign until it was over, destruction of enemy artillery was always given the highest priority.

Iraqi armor—tanks and armored personnel carriers (APCs)—was also present in massive quantities and was a great potential threat to the Army. However, despite the fact that it was the Warthogs' favorite target, it ranked second in priority. The Army felt that when they invaded Kuwait, their own armor could take care of that threat if it had to.

Some of the Warthog pilots—those tasked for BAI missions—were concerned. Never in their careers had they thought they would be flying such long, dangerous missions. That was work for the fast movers—ground attack hot rods like the Strike Eagles, Aardvarks, Stealths, and Intruders. BAI was their mission because they could get in fast, bomb their targets, and get out fast.

Why was the BAI mission considered so dangerous? Because the Iraqis were acutely aware of their battlefield assets and their value, and intelligence indicated that they would aggressively protect them with their deadly arsenal of ground-to-air weapons. So, poking around behind Iraqi lines looking for high-priority targets seemed like a good way to get killed. Certainly, the Warthog pilots who drew BAI tasking that first day knew that lumbering along behind the lines at 200+ knots with a heavy load of ordnance was a potential hazard to their health.

But their tasking looked like a Sunday picnic compared to what the third group of Warthog pilots drew for their assignment. Throughout Iraq the military had established a network of sophisticated air defense radar warning stations. Coalition intelligence analysts called them Early Warning Ground Control Intercept Stations; pilots ended up calling them GCI sites. In October, General Glosson had asked the wing commanders if they thought the Hogs could take out some of the GCI sites that were along the border. Their reply, "Hell, yes, throw us in the briar patch," along with their later pleadings for first-day tasking, got them a lot deeper into the briar patch than they expected.

As the planners in Riyadh looked at all the high-priority, first-day targets and began to match numbers of strike aircraft that could destroy them, they had come up short. There were too many targets and too few aircraft. In particular they were concerned about the

GCI sites; they had to be taken out so strike aircraft going after latter-day targets could reach them undetected. But who could do it? Most of the fast-movers were needed for targets of even higher priority.

Well, there are the Apaches and the Warthogs; the CAS helicopters and the CAS airplanes. Could they do it? Well, let's see . . . if we send the Apaches to the close targets just across the border, and if we send the Warthogs after the deep targets . . .

The afternoon of January 16 they opened their top secret packs and stared in awe at the magnitude of the first-day air campaign. "It was just what General Glosson said it would be," said Capt. Todd Sheehy, ". . . with 117s striking this, this and this in Baghdad and 111s . . ." Then they looked over the A-10 missions and they blanched. They were going where!? They were doing what!?

All the missions had been divided evenly among the squadrons. Each squadron commander, after consultations with his Ops officers, flight commanders, and weapons officers, decided who was going on what mission. Generally, the most experienced pilots were assigned the deep interdiction missions to the GCI sites, some of which were hundreds of miles into Iraq, near the Syrian and Jordanian borders.

The rest of the missions were divided up among the squadrons, which, in turn, assigned their most experienced pilots as flight leads and those with lesser experience as wingmen. In some squadrons, the pilots with the least experience were assigned non-flying chores. For those tasked for CAS alert there was little to do that they had not prepared for already.

For those with BAI tasking, few received anything more than latitude and longitude coordinates. Photos of the artillery sites, which were the primary targets, were generally not available. They would fly to a specific "kill box," roughly a 30-mile by 30-mile area designated alphanumerically on their maps. There they would use their eyeballs, perhaps with help from a FAC in the area, to search and find the artillery sites. From their intelligence briefings, they knew what most of the sites were going to look like. A few would have seven tubes in a V-shape, pointing south, with a command post/fire control center directly in the middle and behind them. Most, however, would have six tubes arranged in an arc with the same kind of command center. (After the pilots actually saw the latter sites, they would be known thereafter as "puppy-paws" because of their unique shape.) All of the anti-artillery missions were designated for kill boxes in southern Kuwait or in the tri-border area—the latter where the acute-angled border of western Kuwait joins the borders of Iraq and Saudi Arabia.

For those who were going deep after the GCI sites, a lot of the prep work had already been done. Some of the officers had been privy to the tasking for several days and they had assembled strike packets for each of the pilots. These packets included satellite photos, which would turn out to be a luxury they would rarely enjoy again. Intelligence data in general, and target photos in particular, were of poor quality or nonexistent throughout the war.

There was one thing, however, for which the pilots were not prepared. As a part of their ordnance they were to carry the G-Model Maverick, which differed from the Mavericks they had used for training. The G-Model was a new missile, with a 300-pound warhead, and an explosive charge designed for general demolition. (The Mavericks they normally used had 125-pound warheads and a "shaped charge"—a charge that concentrates the explosive force in one direction so that it is more effective against armor.) The pilots were told they could learn about the new missile from a videotape, but that turned out to be defective. Finally, someone located some photocopied instructions and they decided, after reading them, that the G-Model Maverick functioned the same as the other models they had been using.

Then some of the pilots got a new assignment. Those with search and rescue experience were tasked to sit "SAR" alert at King Khalid Military City (KKMC), an airport 245 miles northwest of King Fahd airport, and almost one hour closer to Kuwait. They were to be the "Sandys." Like their Southeast Asian War namesakes, they were to scramble if a friendly plane went down in enemy territory. Their job was to find the pilot, hold over him and fight off the enemy, and guide in rescue helicopters for a pick-up. Those selected were ominously aware that they would probably have a busy day.

While the pilots waited for their various missions, they did a lot of quiet thinking. Said Capt. Lee Wyatt, "You always wonder if you're going to be ready for the real test. I had just reread *Thud Ridge* and I thought about those guys that flew through hell in North Vietnam and I wondered if I was ready to be shot at. [Lieutenant Colonel Greg] Growth Wilson, one of the Cajuns who had been a Raven FAC in Laos, came down to the squadron and talked to us. He told us what it was like to be shot at, and how the different bullets and shells looked. And he said one thing that really helped. He said, 'You have doubts, but you are ready for it; you're prepared; you're trained for it and you'll do what you're supposed to do.' And he kept coming back to that, saying, 'You're doubting yourself, but don't worry, you are ready; you just don't know that you're ready.' It was a relief to hear that from one who had been there."

The countdown was on. But now it was in hours rather than days.

First Lieutenant Mike McGee, a young Falcon without tasking who only had to watch and wait, said, "Fighter pilots are a notoriously loud, talkative bunch, but as the hours passed it got quiet around the squadron. You could see that the guys were into their private thoughts. After midnight we broke out our chem gear and put it on, and we took the pills that were supposed to get our body defenses ready should he launch Scuds with gas warheads. None of us were happy about that, Besides causing intestinal cramps and gas problems, we thought, 'Oh, boy, we're going to have an Agent Orange problem when we're fifty from taking all this crap.'

"Few were sleeping. I know about twenty were in the squadron watching the president on the television that we had just gotten installed. It was funny; we looked like Michelin Men standing in that room with those bulky chem suits on. Finally, [Capt.] Dave Wappner and I went down to Ops, sat on top of the sand revetments and watched F-16s land and take off. Seeing them roar off with all their weapons really brought it home; we were going to war."

Captain Rob Givens was one of six Falcons tasked against GCI sites deep in Iraq. Said Givens, "We had been flying nights for a solid four months, then, suddenly, we had to get ourselves into the daylight mode for this mission. It was difficult for me. After spending the afternoon doing the final planning, I tried to sleep—I was supposed to get up about eleven—but I couldn't do it. I woke up about eight, tried to read, but was only seeing the words.

"Up till then I had avoided writing a last letter—it was like, if you write the last letter, it will be the last one. But finally I sat down and wrote some things about what I was feeling and what I thought it was going to be like. We look back on World War II and see the Battle of the Bulge and you just kind of glance right over it because you know how the war ended. But to the guys who fought that battle, when all of a sudden the Germans assaulted, they didn't know how things were going to end. Well, for us on the sixteenth of January, we had no idea what was going to happen. They had a very formidable force, lots of valuable and good equipment, planes like the most advanced MiG-29s to throw against us . . .

"Well, after a while the other five guys [who were going after GCI sites] were up and walking around. Everybody was nervous. We walked down to the squadron and at midnight we went to our higher chemical condition—we ripped open all the chemical suits and put them on . . . we brief again, we try to eat . . . now it is roughly three-thirty and CNN is on in the squadron—the first day we had it—then just before walking out to the plane, I happened to look in my mailbox and there is a letter from my wife. I took it out and I said, 'I'll read this,' but one thing after another happened and then Rolls

[Capt. Mark Roling] and I are on our way out to the planes and I still haven't read it. I stuck it in my flight suit—it was one of those things like, Gee, I'd hate to die not having read this letter.

"Just as we were leaving, the news reports were mayhem and we knew [from having seen the ATO] what was happening. Out on the line the crew chiefs were really pumped up and seemed nervous and I remember trying to be really calm and cool with them saying, 'Is this jet ready to go to war?' Then we got in. Rolls and I were to be the first A-10s to taxi and take off, then Major Jackson comes running out, 'Don't take off, don't take off,' and we're wondering what is happening. Then he climbs the ladder and says that the first strikes were a success, and he does the same to Rolls. I guess it was okay to know that but two guys from Alconbury got ahead of us and they were the first off instead of us."

Major Scott Hill, who, with an unlit cigar clamped in his teeth and the rolling, almost swaggering gait of a 145-pound linebacker, looks like everybody's image of the tough-guy fighter pilot, said, before his BAI mission into Kuwait, "I'm not normally a religious person. I believe in God but I'm not a church-goer. I go once a year to a Christmas service or something like that. . . . We walked out to the jet on the first morning—we were on the first go. I did a quick walk around . . . and the butterflies are going in the stomach. I do the preflight and walk around to the ladder ready to climb up and the crew chief is looking at me—there were two crew chiefs there and they are looking at me and they are like, do I wish him luck, do I shake his hand, whatever. You could see in their eyes [they were wishing] good luck and I turned around and looked at the ladder and dropped to one knee and prayed. Part of my brain is going, 'Oh, good, you are praying.' The other part of my brain is going, 'What are you doing? You don't do this!' I said to the other half, 'Oh shut up, let me do this.' I prayed and then it suddenly dawned on me that I was much more concerned with who I was about to kill than I was with my own safety because all our intelligence reports had told us that Hussein had put the young kids and old men on the front lines. That bothered me. These people were totally innocent and this was who I was going to attack. . . ."

There were many prayers said that morning, but most of them had the same opening line—a line known as the fighter pilot's prayer:

"Please dear God, don't let me screw up. . . ."

It was probably the young wingmen like 1st Lt. Brad Whitmire who worried the most and said that prayer with the most feeling. Said Whitmire, "Other than getting shot down and becoming a POW, my biggest fear was in not doing my job as a wingman. There were a lot of potential air threats that day and my job was to check six o'clock [to protect Lead's tail] and what if I missed a guy coming in? Another worry was the SAMs. I'd never seen one, so I was not sure what one would look like. Maybe I would miss it, or maybe I would be looking at the other side of the jet and all of a sudden [Lead] gets hit. I would always blame myself for that."

Their prayers were behind them now, and their fears and anxieties melted away from the heat of the tasks before them. Checklists, switches, weapon systems, communications frequencies, transponder squawks, identification procedures, escape and evasion codes and routes, target data, threat locations and data—their hands were busy and their heads were crammed, and even after they were airborne Capt. Rob Givens was ". . . so task-saturated I couldn't even begin to read the letter from my wife."

Captains Givens and Roling were the second pair off King Fahd, behind Vultures Lt. Col. Mike O'Connor and Maj. John Condon, but they beat them into KKMC where they refueled. Then they flew more than 300 miles on to the second FOL in western Saudi Arabia—Al Jouf. Said Givens, "We landed and they were starting to refuel us and finally we had sunlight. I'm sitting in the cockpit, nervous, because I know we are just fifteen or twenty minutes from the target. I pull out my letter from my wife and I'm sitting there reading it and I'm trying hard to concentrate on the letter. I'm kind of just looking at the words, then we get airborne and are droning along over the sand, heading into Iraq when I get an indication on the RWR [Radar Warning Receiver—pronounced RAW] that a MiG-29 has fired a radar missile. Every A-10 pilots reaction to an air threat is to get low so we went down to 500 feet. Then Rolls looks over his shoulder and sees this cruise missile going right over the top of us. It could have hit Rolls if we hadn't gone down."

Soon they were near the target, Givens continues, ". . . heading north as though we were going to go past them. The Iraqis were probably on the phone calling everybody and their brother saying that they've got two going past them. At the last second we turned left and dived out of the sun. I locked up my Maverick on a radar van but didn't fire because Rolls, who was slightly ahead of me, could have fired and broken the wrong way, right in the path of my missile. So I waited until he fired, then I fired, and in a few seconds two radar vans went up in a huge explosion of smoke and fire.

"We turned and locked on our secondary targets with our other Mavericks and within two-and-a-half or three minutes we had four good-sized fires burning in the compound. We were now down to about 4,500 feet, which was too low, actually, and we dropped our CBUs [cluster bomb units, which are canisters that open and release dozens of bomblets] on the command section and other priority buildings. We pulled off, ducked into the clouds, which were fairly low, then popped out and went at them repeatedly with the gun, pounding the snot out of anything we could see. We were in a frenzy; we were strafing everything. If it looked marginally undamaged, we were strafing it. The whole site was burning. Then we got a call from AWACS [airborne warning and control system] that MiGs were heading toward us. In our state of mind, if the CAP [F-15s flying protective cover] had not driven them away, we would have tried to shoot them down, too. We had our AIM-9s selected, and at our low altitude with all the weight gone, we could have turned into them and given them a hell of a battle. That's not just tough talk. We were pissed off after we'd spent five months sitting in the desert, away from our families."

There were a lot more Americans out there with the same attitude. Said Capt. Dave Tan, "I was with [Capt.] Dar Kemp and we couldn't wait to get out there—we wanted to pound hell out of them. We did the KKMC and Al Jouf fuel stops and went into Iraq with another six ships. Then the two of us broke off and headed for our site. Usually the Hogs don't have satellite imagery and that fancy stuff but this time we did and soon we picked up RWR indications right from where the radars should be. Then, we saw them—it was the same geometry as the pictures—we dived, fired two Mavericks, went around again, fired two more, and we obliterated two GCI radars and two tropo-scatter communications stations. Then we came around and dropped our twelve Mark-82s [500-pound iron bombs] on the support buildings and shacked them. We could see sparkles on the ground—they were shooting at us—but we had our fangs out. We went back with our guns and strafed hell out of the place—I shot about 900 rounds. There were no squeaks or squawks coming from that place when we finished. We beat the hell out of it."

The Warthogs beat the hell out of a lot of GCI sites that morning, and the five percent they didn't kill, they finished off the next day. Down in Riyadh, where the sites were plotted on a big map, they crossed off all twenty-six that were assigned, with a total of ninety-six radars destroyed. "The generals were pleased," said 1st Lt. Dan Dennis, one of the Alex pilots who had been detailed to Riyadh for the first days of the war. "But the 15E guys [Strike Eagles] were ecstatic because they could operate out there without the Iraqis knowing where they were."

"Ecstatic" was an overused word that day. So was "euphoria," according to Capt. Rob Givens, "When we landed at KKMC it was just euphoria—and I hate using that word because we got sick of hearing it on the radio. But the ground crews were just going crazy.

Then, when we landed at the Home Drome with clean jets—we were the first guys from the squadron to recover—the ground guys are just going wild. They're shaking our hands and handing us things from the plane—the bomb rings, Maverick missile couplings and a couple of shell casings—we had a whole pouch full of stuff to carry away. Getting out there and beating up on them relieved a lot of tensions, not only for us, but for the ground guys, too.

The long interdiction missions against GCI sites out into the interior of Iraq were totally effective. And all the planes came home. Several of the pilots had frightening moments when AWACS called out bogeys coming toward them, but in each case their CAP chased them away. Some also encountered light AAA (antiaircraft fire, pronounced "triple-A"), but none of the planes came home with battle damage. In short, the missions they thought would be the most dangerous turned out to be only long and tiring.

It was the other guys—those with BAI missions and some who were on CAS alert—that flew into the flames of the dragon. And it was the cautiousness of their commanders that saved them from the fire.

"You're going to cross the border at 20,000," they were told. "Then, when you get to the target area, descend to fifteen and do your searching. When you find your target, dive and  pickle at ten, and recover no lower than eight. And go easy with the gun—don't shoot any more than you have to. You got that?"

Those were not welcome words to most of the Hog drivers. Oh, they knew they were going to be using low-threat, high-altitude tactics—they had decided that months earlier. But search at fifteen and pickle at ten? And go easy with the gun? That was like telling a diehard pheasant hunter with a good bird dog to hunt cornfields without going in them. "Hell, we thought we should go on oxygen when we got above 500 feet," growled one pilot.

But they did what they had to. At about 46,000 pounds, loaded with six Mark-82s or six CBUs, two Mavericks, two Aim-9s, ECM pod, flare pods, 1,150 rounds of 30mm and full fuel, they labored up to 20,000 feet where they cruised just above the stall speed of the plane. And when they "crossed the fence," the traditional term for entering "bad guy country," they knew exactly when they were there because a huge berm, visible for miles, had been constructed along the length of the border by the Iraqis.

Said Capt. Blas Miyares who, with his wingman 1st Lt. Dave Ferguson, was the second two-ship to reach his assigned kill box, "We knew the frequencies of the guys in front of us and we talked to Colonel Sawyer and his wingman, Roger Clark, then with our squadron commander, Lieutenant Colonel Renuart and his wingman, Eric Miller. All of them were excited. They had found tons of stuff and they started telling us what the artillery sites looked like.

"When we reached the kill box we found lots of artillery and I rolled in first while Fergy covered. I did a 45-degree dive, dropped my CBU and then Fergy started hollering, 'AAA!' The adrenaline started to pump then and I pulled way too hard and G'd away all my energy. Bullets were flying by the canopy and there I was at 150 knots, practically standing still at 10,000 feet, everything quiet. That was stupid, losing my energy like that. I don't know how they missed me. Out of energy I couldn't jink; I just had to struggle on up to fifteen [thousand] and somehow I made it.

"Then Fergy rolled in and pickled his CBUs. Some of my bombs had hit north of the site because of the winds, and one of them opened too soon, making a big, wide doughnut that encircled the site. Fergy dropped short but his last two cans of CBUs covered the site. We didn't see anything burning but we didn't hang around, either. We went back and regassed, still carrying our Mavericks."

They went to KKMC where the pumped-up ground crews were setting records hot-pitting the planes. With engines running the pilots went from fuel station to ammo pit, and debriefed to an intelligence specialist who climbed the ladder. Then, after a quick drink of water or relief into a "piddle-pak," and perhaps a bite from something stashed in the cockpit, it was off again. They almost always hot-pitted in thirty minutes, but the zealots doing the work were never satisfied unless they could do it in twenty. The ground crews couldn't bomb and strafe, but they were doing the next best thing. And they knew that the sooner those pilots in the funny-looking airplanes did their job, the sooner they were going home.

After the Hogs were off and heading back toward Kuwait, the normal procedure was for Lead to check in with the Airborne Command and Control Center, known as "ABCCC" (pronounced: A-B-triple C). This was a C-130 loaded with communications gear that orbited in the area. It collected information from FACs and strikers about targets and threats, then, after authenticating each new contact with an exchange of secret code words, it issued tasking to new strikers coming into the area. When possible, the information was given in a format called a "nine-line brief." Rapidly, like copying a takeoff clearance, flight leads scrawled the information with wax pencil on their Perspex canopy: IP (initial point you navigate to first), heading from IP to target, distance from IP to target, elevation of target area, target description, target location by coordinates, positions of friendlies, egress direction for escape after damage or bailout, and other useful information such as how to avoid potential threats.

There were plenty of threats and they saw many of them that day, including missiles. But the Weasels were out in force, and when the missile radars went on, there was a good chance a HARM missile would soon be guiding toward it. After making acquaintance with some of those missiles, and despite their belief that Allah loved martyrs, the Iraqis seldom afterward used their missile radars for what they were designed to do. For the rest of the air campaign, they would occasionally "strobe"; they would turn them on for a few seconds to see what was out there, or to try and quickly lock-on a target. But often, they fired their missiles without radar guidance in barrage fire that had little hope of hitting anything.

Not all of the pilots tasked for BAI got in three sorties in what was known as the Kuwaiti Theater of Operations (KTO). Some did not even get in two. Weather was the problem. A moist flow of air from the southwest was bringing multiple layers of clouds over the region. They were high clouds—for the most part 6,000 to 8,000 feet high. But with the rules of engagement handed down by the commanders, it was impossible to acquire and destroy targets unless they could find a large enough hole in the clouds to dive through. Some did, particularly those who managed to get in three sorties. But that kind of attack was risky because, when pulling out, they were below the clouds and silhouetted nicely for the gunners against the cloud backdrop.

So they dribbled back home throughout the afternoon of that first day. Pilots who had been after the GCI sites climbed wearily out of their cockpits after nine or ten hours in the air. Those returning from the KTO had varied times, depending on the cloud cover over their assigned targets. But many of them had been in their cockpits for six to eight hours.

They were all tired but the post-adrenaline letdown was hours away. Perhaps reliving the agony of the B-17 crews who waited anxiously for stragglers during World War II, they were keeping tabs, waiting anxiously. Colonel Maim is in. Falcon One is in. Sunray is in. Wiley and EP are in. Snort and Rolls are in. Syph and Sweet Pea are in. Big Un and Bolt are in. Gumby and Mad Dog are in. Yobo and Chuck are in . . .

They watched and they waited. And when friends came down the ladder they shook hands and pounded backs. Then, together they waited for other friends—until the intel specialists caught up with them.

Those folks had only one question on their minds, which is the question their commanders had on their minds, which is the question the generals in Riyadh had on their minds, which is the question the chiefs in Washington had on their minds. What is your bomb damage assessment, or BDA? What did you kill out there today?

The Armed Services, in all branches and all levels, learned a lot of negative lessons in the Southeast Asia War. One that was guaranteed to arouse them passionately was the demand from McNamara's bureaucrats in the Pentagon for "counts" to feed their legions of computers. And of all those counts, the "body count" was the most egregious, for a variety of reasons, most of which are intuitive to any sensitive person.

And contrary to Oliphant and other cartoonists' caricatures of all generals as bloated, cigar-chomping ogres—an image well-programmed into the public's mind, the generals running this war were truly sensitive, deep-feeling and compassionate individuals. A wingman who flew with General Horner and who knows him well said, "This guy, if he were driving through the country 150 miles away and heard that one of his buddies was here and needed to see him, he would drive backwards through a blizzard to get here. He is that kind of a guy." And who needs to expound on the sensitivity of Schwarzkopf now that the public knows him so well? The man could rage like a bull when anything or anybody threatened his beloved grunts, but he could shed tears just hearing his country's anthem.

"So, hell no. There will not be any body counts. And that decision is backed by the chiefs and the secretary and the president. I don't give a damn what reporters scream and yell and threaten about wanting casualty figures. We're not going to get into the business of counting enemy casualties, and I don't want anybody in this command even thinking about doing that.

"But I'll tell you for damn sure what I *do* want. I want the numbers of the artillery tubes and armored vehicles that are left up there and capable of killing my guys. And I want accurate information—not like any of that inflated bullshit that was amplified through command levels in Vietnam. Someday, those ground troops are going to have to move in for an attack, and when they do, I don't want them experiencing any surprises. So when you collect your BDA, make damned sure it's accurate. And if you're in doubt, err on the side of those kids who are going up there. Don't say something is killed unless you're sure it's dead."

The Warthog commanders saluted smartly when they received those marching orders. They had flown lots of missions in Southeast Asia and they, too, were repelled by the body counts and the blatant amplification of BDA they saw commanders reporting for the purpose of career enhancement.

With those orders in their hands, they made certain every pilot knew the issue that was at stake—that the lives of the ground guys who would face that artillery and armor depended upon the accuracy of their BDA. But the commanders went beyond the human issue that was at stake. They also had the Warthog Factor on their side and they used it to the maximum.

"Hey, guys, we're not suggesting that anything inflated might come from the pointy-nose fraternity, but now that we're here and taking part in the Big Show, let's demonstrate to everybody that we're a real class act; let's convince those guys down at Riyadh that this community of pilots has integrity. Let's make our BDA believable right from the beginning. Let's show everybody that the Hogs don't need to puff up their image."

"Yes, sir! We'll do that, sir!" Their commanders' appeal went straight to their hearts. Schwarzkopf's love for the grunts down on the ground was no stronger than what the Hog drivers themselves felt. They had lived, breathed, trained and prepared themselves to die if necessary to protect those grunts. That was their life. That was their only reason for being—at least until the guys in the Black Hole in Riyadh began inventing new tasks for them. "So, hell yes, we'll give honest BDA. And frankly, sir, we don't give a damn about the Hog-driver integrity bit. We're going to report accurate BDA because we want those guys on the ground to get home to their families, too."

So at the end of their missions, they debriefed with intel specialists and they were adamant about what they reported.

*Intel specialist:* "You shot a tank at close range with the gun, right?"

*Hog driver:* "Yeah."

*Intel specialist:* "And you say it was getting dark and you could see sparkles where the bullets were hitting the tank, right?"

*Hog driver:* "Yeah."

*Intel specialist:* "But you're not claiming it as being destroyed. Why?"

*Hog driver:* "Because I didn't see any fire or secondary explosions."

*Intel specialist:* "But if the bullets were hitting it and you were at close range, the tank had to be Swiss cheese."

*Hog driver:* "Maybe, but I'm not sure."

*Intel specialist:* "So you're calling it a 'possible.'"

*Hog driver:* "Yeah."

*Intel specialist:* "And not even a probable?"

*Hog driver:* "No."

*Intel specialist:* "Why not?"

*Hog driver:* "I told you; I didn't see a fire or secondaries."

*Intel specialist:* "Then what would be a probable in your mind?"

*Hog driver:* "If I shot one with a Maverick, saw it hit, but there was no fire or secondaries."

*Intel specialist:* "And that would still only be a probable and not a kill."

*Hog driver:* "Yeah, it could have been a decoy."

And that is the way the debriefings went on the first day, the second day, and for the remainder of the air campaign. Of course, the intel specialists were never quite the Doubting Thomases the way they are depicted in the above dialogue. Interestingly, it turned out to be the generals who would be scratching their heads. But more about that later.

The first day was about over. Two by two the ugly birds came home to roost. And their pilots to laugh and smile and to shake hands and to yell their Sierra Hotels (Hotel stands for "hot")—and to go through the debriefs. Some of the CAS alert guys were called out during the morning and afternoon and they did their best trying to kill targets while diving through holes in the clouds. But the weather was turning against them and several landed with unexpended ordnance.

Then it happened. The last of the Hogs came in. None of them was lost. The SAR alert guys did not have to go looking for their buddies. And even battle damage was unbelievably minor, considering the abundance of AAA they saw.

Captain Rod Glass, one of the Vultures, had a hole in the top of his wing that they believe came from a falling bullet.

Captain John Whitney, the Falcon pilot who lost an engine on takeoff during the deployment back in August, was the first to experience bona fide battle damage. While rolling off a target and banked at 120 degrees, he took a round through the leading edge of his right wing, the bullet going through the top of the wing and out the bottom. He heard nothing and felt nothing, but when his master caution light came on, he quickly realized that a hydraulic line had been severed and he used switches on his panel to cut it off. After that, he motored normally out of the KTO, landed at KKMC uneventfully, but gave his friends a second reason to call him "Cloud" because of his bad luck. But he was happy and he would be the first who would thank the designers for the survivability that was built into the plane. He would not be the last.

# 9

# Scud Hunting

*". . . when the A-10s saved their butts, he loved them."*
*—1st Lt. Dan Dennis.*

On day one the strategic targets around Baghdad got pounded. The Iraqi Air Force was hurt so badly they decided to run or go into hiding. Armor and troops in the KTO received a painful introduction to the violence of war. Most of the GCI sites were blown away, blinding and silencing the Iraqi high command.

Thus day one turned out to be a good day for the Coalition, and it would have been even better if clouds had not moved in over the KTO. Then the man with the brush moustache and shifty eyes played his highest trump card. He started firing Scud missiles into Israel.

At the Tactical Air Command Center (TACC) in Riyadh they went crazy. It seemed that way even the day before, said 1st Lt. Dan Dennis, who had been sent down to work as an A-10 Fighter Duty Officer (FIDO). "The TACC was down one flight of stairs in the Saudi Air Force building. It was a big room, about 120 feet square, jammed with desks used by representatives from all the aircraft communities—tankers, F-15s, B-52s, A-10s, etc. Armed guards with machine guns stood outside in a sterile-looking hallway, but inside it was like the New York Stock Exchange. The war wasn't run by computer; it was run by little slips of paper. There were changes in the frag all the time—'Can you divert this package and send it here?' and 'How about switching the frag on those tankers and send them over there?' It was wild.

"Then Scuds started popping up all over the place and the question was, 'Who are we going to send after them?' There were already packages of F-16s airborne. Instantly they could divert some of them out to western Iraq where the Scuds were being launched. But the generals vetoed that. They didn't want F16s; they wanted A-10s out there. The F-16s would get out there and have a two-minute TOT—and they still wouldn't know where the Scuds were. They knew that the A-10s could get out there with at least a one-hour TOT—more with tanker support—and could do a lot of searching. So Capt. Dahl [another A-10 FIDO] and I got on the phone. . . ."

First Lieutenant Darren Hansen, a Vanguard, picks up the story: "I was the first guy out on the second day. My missions [with Lieutenant Colonel Vanderveen] were to go to the tri-border area for three sorties, turning at KKMC. Just before we walked out the door we got a priority call from Riyadh and they stopped us. They said we were going to Al Jouf. I had never even heard of it, nor had Vanderveen. Now we are sitting in our jets, holding, waiting for more information, and they come running out with a map. They unfolded it and said, 'Right here it is, see?' I'm saying, 'That's 500 miles to the west; what are we going to do way out there? I'm going to a place I've never even heard of; what does this place look like? Is there anybody even there? Who is going to meet us?'

"We leave, fly up to KKMC, stop for gas, and a captain came running up to my jet and handed me a note. It said: 'Coordinates such and such, talk to Cajun at Al Jouf. Scuds.' That's all it said. This is twenty-four hours after the war started.

"We flew out to Al Jouf and landed and there was nothing on the ground. No one is talking to us and we pull up and there are four Army guys with hoses for gas and they plug us up and we're like, 'Okay, now what.' Then, all of a sudden, like God, here comes this voice booming over the radio. I can't remember our exact call sign—it was Rifle something—all Hogs were guns for the whole war. Anyhow, this voice says, 'Rifle, whatever, Cajun Ops. Come up squadron common [frequency].' It was like God himself had just talked.

"We came up and talked to him—it was Colonel [Bob] Efferson. He gave us our little brief and said there were two ships ahead of us. Basically, he said, 'Here are some coordinates where you might find Scuds. Good luck and God speed.'

"We punched in the coordinates on the INS and we could see that we were going at least 70 miles into Iraq, without a map, without knowing exactly what a Scud or Scud launcher looks like, and we were doing that in an A-10. But we looked at each other and I said, 'Let's rock and roll, Dutch.' He said, 'Let's do it.' But I'll tell you, my seat cushion came up a little bit when we crossed that border."

Captain Mark Koechle and 1st Lt. Don Henry also got a surprise that morning. Said Koechle, "We took off early in the morning the second day, headed to KKMC, then to take out one of the GCI sites that we missed the day before. We landed at KKMC, got our gas, received warning that something else might be coming down, but were told to launch and continue with the original mission. At 0650 we were about 30 miles northwest when we got a call on Guard—that's the emergency frequency everyone monitors—telling us to contact one of the ASOCs [Air Support Operations Center—run by Army ground forces]. I talked to the guy—he had an emergency divert target for us. He passed me all the information—coordinates, target—which was three mobile Scud launchers. He said they had reports of them at those coordinates and wanted us to check them out.

"By this time the weather was really bad—we were IMC [instrument meteorological conditions—flying blind in clouds] and Don was hanging tight on my wing to keep me in sight. I was struggling, trying to copy all this information while flying the plane on instruments. When the controller finished, I authenticated him [with the proper codewords] and he was unable to give me the proper response. I thought, 'He sounds American and he was on the proper frequency,' then he told me to call back to KKMC if I didn't believe him. I did that, asked for a familiar voice, and got Capt. Jessie Morimoto, an intel officer whose voice I knew and she confirmed the tasking.

"I pulled out the map and tried to plot course but the weather was too heavy. I turned north, looking for some clear air space because I needed my wingman to plot and confirm the route. We finally broke out somewhere around 16K—it was kind of a milk bowl, in between layers. I put him back in wedge [behind and to one side] so we could do the planning, but then we got in some more weather and got split up. But we talked and both headed toward the target.

"I was continually looking down through the holes and when we got near the target, I held him up above while I dropped down for a look. When I popped out, I looked to the south—the visibility was about 5 miles—and I saw three launchers in a triangular shaped formation, 500 to 700 meters apart. I started arching toward the south and looked down at my INS. It was indicating right where they were supposed to be.

"I was excited, ready to attack right then, but without mutual support, that wasn't a good idea, especially since I didn't know what threat was down there. So I marked their location on the INS [more accurately] and went back up to where he was holding. It took us fifteen minutes to get together, then we came down through the clouds in formation and started our attack.

"We came in from the north—it was an equilateral triangle with the base at the south. I was 1-½ miles ahead so I took the southeast launcher and had him take the north one. I fired—we had the G-Model Maverick because of our original tasking—and all I saw was a puff of dust. It didn't explode—out of forty I shot in the war, this one had to be the dud. Then Don rolled in, locked on with his Maverick, and he couldn't get it off the rail—he had a bad battery in that Maverick.

"He had me in sight, so I circled back around west of the target and came back in with the second Maverick on the southwestern target. I fired, it guided and blew up, but it wasn't the explosion I expected—I found out later that they were erector launchers without missiles on them, and without a missile and warhead there would not be a big explosion.

"I pulled off, sighted Don, and cleared him for another pass on the north target. He rolled in, fired his other Maverick and his target blew up. Two targets were destroyed and one was left.

"The clouds were ragged and we again got split up by weather, so we climbed back to the clear air space at sixteen, found each other, but because of the very strong easterly winds that day, we drifted 7 or 8 miles west of the target. But we found a break in the clouds, dived down, got separated again, but I came right out over seven or eight other Scuds. I knew we had hit the jackpot then. I marked them on my INS, then went back up in the weather so we could get to clear air space and get together again.

"It was another ten minutes before I found him, then we headed for the original target. We went down, I had him hold north, and I rolled in on the southeast launcher and dropped my Mark 82s with airburst fuses. I rippled all six of them but messed up my mil settings [calibration for wind] and they hit short—the last one within one 100 meters, probably causing some damage because of the air burst. I was really mad. I was cussing myself because of my stupid mistake. I circled around to the northeast, rolled in and strafed. I was low and got in three trigger squeezes—200 rounds. I hit it—I saw the bullets going into it, but it didn't explode. I know its got some damage but I joined up with Don and we headed for the second site where his bombs could do more good.

"It was 10 miles west and he rolled in while I covered. But when he tried to call up his bombs, he got no ready lights—it was a malfunction and he spent five minutes running through the switches. He was a relatively new wingman with only a hundred or so hours in the A-10, so I wasn't sure what was happening. But I rolled in with the gun and made a strafe pass, then he rolled in and strafed twice. His shots were long—mine hit, but there were no explosions. By that time we were bingo—we had been airborne for two hours. We climbed back up into the weather, put him in trail, and as I flew, I drew formations on a card in my kneeboard and marked the map. Then I called ABCCC, gave a really detailed description, told them we hadn't seen any threats, and that there were at least a dozen more launchers in the area.

"When we landed at KKMC, I requested that Jessie come out—she was the chief intel person there. She climbed the ladder and I gave her the card, maps—everything. Then I tried to get them to launch us again but because of our weapons problems they refused."

Meanwhile, pundits from around the world were using the Scud attacks on Israel as a way to show off their hoard of insider's knowledge. With smug prescience they were writing and announcing what, for them, was a slam-dunk conclusion. "The fragile Coalition in the Gulf will soon be history. . . .When Israel launches retaliatory strikes against Baghdad, the tenuous thread binding Arab Muslims with Christians will break. . . .the seeds of World War III have been sown . . ."

Latter day sleuths will someday tell us how close those pundits were to the truth. Was Israel, in fact, about to launch retaliatory air strikes against Iraq? And, how were the Israelis influenced by General Schwarzkopf's television appearance that afternoon? He walked before the cameras and announced that Coalition aircraft had definitely destroyed two Scud launchers, definitely damaged two others, probably damaged another, and that strike aircraft were on their way to destroy up to a dozen more in a region where Scuds could be launched against Israel.

If in fact that announcement did help convince the Israelis that the Coalition was going all out to protect them from further Scud strikes, and if in fact that was, to some degree, a factor causing them to cancel retaliatory strikes, then there are two Hog drivers—Captain Koechle and Lieutenant Henry—who carved themselves a niche in history and who brought first glory to the Warthog community. For it was their report, accepted without question, that Schwarzkopf flashed to the world.

And that was just the beginning.

It has been stated many times that this was a war where the theater commanders ran the show. Unlike during the Southeast Asia War, when most targets were selected by bureaucrats in Washington, the target selection process in this war supposedly escaped those long tentacles.

In fact, there was tremendous pressure from Washington to find the Scuds attacking Israel and to destroy them. This was a political wrench thrown suddenly into the gears of an intricately planned air campaign. And it caused great headaches for the Riyadh commanders. Immediately, they faced a seemingly intractable problem: How the hell were they going to generate thirty to forty sorties a day to hunt Scuds when all of their strike forces and tankers were needed for the main air campaign?

Well, let's see . . . there are the A-10s and they've done a helluva job so far with interdiction missions, including Scud hunting. If we . . .

Captain Arden Dahl and 1st Lt. Dan Dennis were working as FIDOs in the TACC at Riyadh the second day of the war. Late that day, after the Scud bombshell had landed at the commanders' feet, and after Koechle and Henry hit their jackpot out in western Iraq, they listened as the commanders stood near the front of the large room and gave their routine evening briefing. The low-ranking generals spoke first, summarizing the day's accomplishments and adding their personal cheerleading touches to the presentations. Then the three-star, General Horner, walked to the front. He looked physically beat, as he often did during the war, but the achievements of the air campaign had been spectacular so far and he energized to the occasion with compliments to the aircraft communities represented in the room. When he came to the A-10s, he hesitated slightly, apparently searching for the right words. Then, in just ten seconds he made a comment that has literally reverberated around the world—a comment that virtually every Hog driver alive today—whether in Korea, Alaska, or in the cockpit of a Delta jet—can quote word for word. He said:

> "I take back all the bad things I have ever said about the A-10. I love them! They're saving our asses!"

Now, it is a shock of earthquake proportions when the guys at the dance openly state their admiration for the performance of the ugly girl. But it is a shock wave of about ten orders of magnitude greater when one of her vociferous critics openly confesses that love has blossomed. After all, this was the same man (so it is rumored) who said, jokingly, when his own son opted to fly the A-10 out of pilot training, "Oh, I don't think I have a son anymore; I think he died from brain damage."*

Immediately after the briefing, Captain Dahl raced to the telephone and breathlessly repeated Horner's comment to his A-10 com-

---

* It is also rumored that General Horner is extremely proud of his Hog driver son, who recently graduated from the prestigious A-10 Weapons School.

manders at King Fahd. And without realizing what the other had done, Lieutenant Dennis did the same thing. The word spread like wildfire. Pilots climbing wearily down from their planes, bleary-eyed from ten to twelve hours of Scud hunting, their faces imprinted like raccoons where their oxygen masks had pressed against their flesh for all those hours, listened with awe as their buds ran up to them with the news.

"Did you hear, did you hear?"

"Did I hear what?"

"What Horner said about the Hogs!"

"No. What?"

"He says he loves 'em . . . that we're saving their asses!"

"I don't believe it."

"Ardie Dahl was there. He was standing right in front of him when he said it!"

"No shit?"

"No shit. He said it right in front of God and everybody."

"Shit hot, man!"

The next morning the quote was reported in the A-10 *Battle Staff Directive*, the official publication put out by the commanders at King Fahd. And that night there was laughter everywhere. In tent city, the dog-tired maintenance and ordnance folks smiled and toasted the new lover with their illicit peach, apricot, and pear elixirs. In the trailers the pilots sacrificed from their precious store of Plax, Scope, and Listerine just to make sure their breaths weren't tainted for the occasion.

And the next day some of them headed out to "Cajun West."

Colonel Bob Efferson, who flew F-105 "Thuds" in Southeast Asia, was the group commander of the Cajuns. He flew over with them feeling that this was his responsibility as a commander—he had trained them for four years—but he was only to stay for ten days. However, the war was starting and he didn't want to miss it. So he began looking around, wondering where they might need a spare colonel. The problem was that they had four of them already at King Fahd—two commanders and two DOs. They didn't need another one there. Then he heard about Al Jouf. It was going to be a temporary FOL, used by A-10s in the first days when they were tasked for the GCI sites way out in western Iraq. Would he like to go out there and supervise that operation? Yes he would, thank you.

After the Scuds started hitting Israel, and after it was realized that Al Jouf was going to be needed as a western base for Scud hunters, Efferson's DO, Lt. Col. Greg Wilson convinced the Fahd commanders that Efferson needed an Ops officer. So, in a matter of days, Al Jouf was transformed from a remote, desert airstrip in western

Saudi Arabia (though used heavily by Special Forces operating clandestinely out of there into Iraq) to a major Scud-hunting base known to the pilots as "Cajun West."

Soon it became obvious to the A-10 commanders that the Scud-hunting missions were not going away—that Scud hunting was going to be an ongoing part of the A-10's work for the remainder of the war. However, the missions the pilots were flying—from King Fahd to KKMC to Al Jouf, then into Iraq for Scud hunting and back home again—were far too long and arduous, and did not make the best use of either the planes or the pilots. So it was decided that ten planes—five two-ship pairs—would be sent out to Al Jouf where they would remain for five days of operations. Then, they would be replaced by another ten planes, and the cycle would continue.

Colonel Efferson tells what happened next. "For three days I had been running a gas station, practically living in the tower because it had the only STU [secure telephone unit] on base. Then I got a call saying that tonight they're sending me fifty-two maintenance guys, tool boxes, crew chiefs, and munitions guys and tomorrow I'm going to get ten airplanes. I was to find a place to park them, and find a place for the guys to sleep.

"There were a lot of special forces working out of the base so I went to their support people. They said there was no place to park planes, nor was there any place for our guys to sleep. Finally, I was able to negotiate a few of the little hammerheads out there on the end of the runway for the planes. About ten thirty that night a C-141 came in with all of my guys. Some of them had sleeping bags and a couple of them had cots, and I put them in three little bungalows I commandeered in a compound just off the base. We put up a security force to guard them and most got two or three hours of sleep before I had to bring them out to start servicing A-10s.

"The ten A-10s arrived early. We fueled them and sent them off, then in the interim a C-130 came in with CBUs [Mavericks had come in during the night]. When they returned we were hanging Mavericks and CBUs, fueling, and doing complete combat turns.

"At the end of the day we parked them. Some of those guys had not been out of the cockpit for eleven, twelve, or thirteen hours. I went over to one of the buildings on base and commandeered this Saudi dayroom, moved their television out and moved in cots and borrowed blankets from the hospital. I gave each guy a cot and one blanket, but most of them had not known they were coming so they didn't have shave kits, nor any change of clothes. I grabbed the contracting guy and sent him into town and had him buy twelve toothbrushes, twelve razors, twelve sets of socks and underwear, and gave them to the guys. They stayed here for five days, lived in one flight suit and with just the toiletries we bought them.

"We didn't have a chow hall. We had nothing but MREs. After about twelve or fourteen days, we got the people back at Fahd to send us some cases of this meatlike substitute that they served, and some cans of peaches and green beans—things like that to supplement the MREs. Then I sent the contracting guy downtown again and he was able to get cases of potatoes, carrots, and onions. I took the meat substitute, chopped up onions, carrots, and potatoes, put it all in the biggest pot I could find, and then we had a stew for the evening meal. Eventually we got a stove, and the contracting guy was able to buy some garlic, rice and spices. Then, on the afternoons I didn't fly, I made beef jambalaya, which the guys liked."

Colonel Efferson spoke modestly about his contributions to the welfare of the Hog drivers detailed to Al Jouf. But they spoke effusively about him and all the ways he tried to improve their primitive living conditions. (Said one pilot, who had lived and trained with the Army, "Can you imagine an Army colonel cooking for a bunch of his lieutenants and captains?") Despite the primitive living conditions and the isolation, most of them enjoyed their five-day tours. The flying was low-threat, with little AAA.

And soon they would have exciting places to visit, such as Home Depot and Hicksville.

# 10

# Warthogs to the Rescue

*"We wanted to go up there and obliterate them so badly on the ground that they had no will to fight and no means to do it. We did that. We did that systematically and meticulously."*
—Capt. Mike Mangus

In October, when they saw their first cloud in the sky, they cheered. Now, in January, after two days of spectacular successes on missions they would not have dreamed of flying two weeks earlier, they were grounded by clouds. Only they were not cheering this time. They were angry. They had work to do and they wanted to finish it so they could go home.

On day three some of the planes were able to fly Scud-hunting missions in western Iraq and a few had success in the tri-border area. But that was about it; most of the KTO was socked in by low clouds flowing in from the southwest, the clouds ladened with moisture from the Red Sea and pulled northward by the subtropical jet stream.

On day four, as the clouds hung on, tempers began to rise, especially in Riyadh. Said 1st Lt. Dan Dennis who was at TACC, "I was on the phone constantly with the WOC [Wing Operations Center] at Fahd. Al Jouf, where ten airplanes were ready for Scud-hunting missions, was completely down. The visibility out there was ⅛ mile—way below minimums. The WOC at Fahd said they were not going to launch those guys because they might not be able to land and refuel. They also had the support of one of the generals at TACC. He said to keep them on the ground.

"General Horner, who was just a few desks away from me, heard about the situation and told me he didn't give a damn what the weather was out there—he wanted those airplanes launched, and he said he would support them with tankers. I called the WOC and they were adamantly opposed to that because another general had told them to hold. Also, the A-10s had not had any tanker support up to this time—they had all been tied up with higher priority strike packages. So they were probably skeptical about the tanker support.

"Now I was caught in the middle, taking shots from both sides. But I told General Horner what they said and he blew up and told me to get back on the phone and tell them to launch. I was starting to do that. I was sitting at my desk talking to them when I looked up and here comes Horner. He practically crawled over my desk, took the phone, and in very blunt terms told them what the three-star general running the show wanted to happen."

Lieutenant Colonel Chuck Fox, who was at the other end of the line, chuckles about the incident now, but concedes that he had a very angry general speaking into his ear. "I remember it as a short, very intense and very much a one-way conversation," he said. "And, yeah, we launched the planes right away."

The weather started breaking up a little bit on day five and a few missions were launched. Most were going to Kuwait and the tri-border area to continue pounding artillery sites and armor. Captains Paul Johnson and Randy Goff were disappointed that they couldn't join them. For Captain Goff this was the second day since the war started that he had been tasked to sit on SAR alert at KKMC—a boring job up to that time. Captain Johnson wasn't pleased because on day three he had flown seven hours on a fruitless Scud hunt and day four he had been grounded by the weather.

Said Captain Johnson, "We had only gotten about 2-½ hours of sleep the night before. We had had two or three Scud alerts during the night. It seemed like we would just get to sleep, then have to pile out, get in chem gear, go to the bunker and sit there in helmet, gloves and mask until it was over. So I figured we would get up to KKMC, cock the planes, and then we could go inside and take a nap. I knew we were just going to twiddle our thumbs all day . . .

"We were ready to launch early that morning but KKMC was down [below landing minimums]. We came back into the squadron and killed an hour or so, then we got word that the weather was lifting up there so we launched. About ten minutes before landing at KKMC I called to get an update on the weather—to see if we could land or if we had to fly back to Fahd. They said to stand-by to copy—that they had SAR tasking for us.

"Then they came on and told us that a Navy F-14 was down up in Iraq, that there was no contact with the weapons guy but a transmission from the pilot, call sign Slate 46, had been picked up. An Air Force helo [helicopter], call sign Moccasin 05, and a flight of two A-10s, call sign Enfield, were already up there looking. They gave us coordinates of where he might be and said that a tanker had been diverted for us.

"I hauled out the map, checked the position and saw that they were sending us way out into Iraq, out into the middle of nowhere. We headed west, staying over Saudi territory, planning to head north when we got abeam the location. AWACS was out there doing the coordinating and we began to get vectors from them to the tanker. Only it turned out that they had us confused with some others and we got bad vectors. It was close for awhile; thunderstorms were everywhere, and we were IMC, dodging in and out of them, trying to get to the tanker with what turned out to be bad vectors. We were right at the critical state, maybe five minutes away from having to turn back to KKMC for fuel, when we broke out into some clear air and spotted the tanker just two miles away. It was a KC-10. We hooked on, took our gas, then called AWACS to tell them we were continuing. Then they said that Moccasin and Enfield flight were still searching the area and that they wanted us now to check out a report on a possible Scud location. So we motored off to new coordinates, and found some Bedouin tents that somebody thought were hiding Scuds. We made a low pass, confirmed they were just tents, then called AWACS to see what they wanted us to do next. At this time we had already flown an hour and a half since refueling.

"They came up and said for us to continue with the original SAR—that Moccasin and Enfield were having no luck. We got gas again, followed the pipeline highway south of the Iraq border, then we headed north to a position about 120 miles west of Baghdad. We really wanted to find that guy, but there was the feeling that we might be on a wild goose chase. Also, it was frightening because at that stage of the war they still had plenty of fighters they could have sent after us. But we continued north and when we got close to the coordinates, I made several calls—I was Sandy 57 and Randy was Sandy 58.

"'Slate 46, this is Sandy 57; do you copy?' I repeated that over and over and there was no answer. Finally, when it was beginning to seem hopeless, I called again and this came right back: 'Sandy 57, Slate 46. How do you copy?'

"I turned the squelch off to improve reception and answered him. But I was bothered. He answered in a calm, collected voice. I thought at the time that if I had been in his position I would have been a lot more excited. He could have been an Iraqi pulling us into a trap—that's been done before. But I authenticated him, using personal data from AWACS—they keep that information for just such occasions, and all the time, while he was transmitting, I was trying to use the ADF to find him. [If his radio transmission was strong enough, it would cause the needle of the plane's Automatic Direction Finding (ADF) instrument to point to the bearing of the transmission, thus telling the pilot what direction to fly to find him.] But the signal was too weak. We drove east and the signal faded. We drove west and the same thing. Then we drove north and now the ADF needle swung north. It turned out that he was about 60 miles north of the coordinates where everybody was searching.

"The weather had mostly cleared out but there were little puffy clouds at about 3,500 feet—so many that we would never see him if we didn't drop down below them. AWACS had been listening and following us on radar. I told them we were going down and when we got below the clouds, I popped some of our self-protection flares and he saw us. He vectored us north, right over the top of him, but we couldn't see him. Then we had to give him the bad news. We were hurting for fuel; we had to leave, but I memorized the terrain features—he was in a clear area near a water tank and a patch of green that someone had tried to cultivate, and there were two dirt trails that crossed. I told him to hold tight, that we'd be back in thirty minutes."

Down on the ground, Lt. Devon Jones of the U.S. Navy had been surprised by the type of airplane that found him. "I had been down there about six hours," he said. "I had dug myself a hole in the hard ground with my survival knife. Then I started talking to this Sandy 57 and when they came over I was surprised when those big, ugly airplanes appeared. I didn't know the A-10 was used as a rescue asset and I was wondering what it was doing tooling around this far north. When he said he was going to get gas, I knew he'd be back. I just hunkered down in the little hole I'd dug, chopped at it some more with my knife and tried to stay camouflaged. I had seen a couple of trucks earlier that morning, but nothing since then. I felt fairly secure now that Sandy 57 knew where I was."

Just across the border, at an airfield called Ar'Ar, Moccasin 05, a "Super Jolly Green" helicopter piloted by Capt. Tom Trask, was on the ground being refueled, and he was monitoring Captain

Johnson's radio transmissions. He and his eight-man crew had departed earlier that morning in zero-zero weather, using terrain-following radar, flying at 140 knots 20 feet above the ground, heading for the coordinates where the downed F-14 pilot had been reported. Said Trask, "On the way up we inadvertently flew over a border post and immediately afterward our RWR began to light up, indicating that they were looking at us with SAMs. AWACS picked up all that and vectored us around some of them, then suddenly they gave us a snap vector south, saying that the Iraqis had launched a fighter out of Mudaysis [an Iraqi airfield] for us. Snap vectors are great for fighters but not for a big helo. We just got down low in a wadi [dry creek or river bed] and tried to stay hidden, but we continued pressing north. Finally the F-15s came and chased him away.

"We searched in vain until we ran low on fuel, then returned to Ar'Ar. When we heard Sandy 57 contact the pilot—we could only hear Sandy 57's side of the conversation—we launched again with another helo for coverage and pressed north."

In the meantime Sandy 57 and Sandy 58 were having difficulty. Because of the headwinds going south, they were lower on fuel than they expected. They called for the tanker to come north, to cross the border. The tanker replied and said they could not do that—at that stage of the war none of the tankers were allowed into Iraqi air space. "But, after I told them that we were getting critical," said Captain Johnson, "they came north and met us—and I'll say right now: I'll take my hat off to those guys; we were 20 miles into Iraq, heading north when we got on the boom."

"After we got gas our next problem was to rendezvous with Moccasin. We found him, but as he tried to fly to the coordinates I had given, we saw he was going in the wrong direction—that's because my INS had drifted and my position report was not accurate. It got all confused then, with AWACS and the CAP and everybody trying to talk, and finally I told everybody but Moccasin and Slate to keep quiet. Then, flying low, doing a daisy-chain weave over the helo [a moving, racetrack pattern by which a faster plane flies cover over a slower helo] to keep him in sight, we led the helo north. We crossed the two busy highways linking Baghdad and Amman, Jordan, then right toward a Roland SAM site."

Said Captain Trask piloting the helo, "AWACS was going crazy about this time, warning us about the Roland. They vectored us around it, but we weren't worried for our sake because at 15 feet they couldn't fire on us. Then Sandy 57 called and told Slate 46 to key his mike, which meant that he would hold it down for five seconds—long enough for us to get a DF fix on his bearing. But I was worried because the Iraqis were reported to have a DF station about 10 miles from us."

Said Johnson, "We got the bearing, then started talking to Slate 46 about 4 or 5 miles south of his position. He is vectoring us in and the helo is following, then he calls out that a truck is heading for him. Randy and I both look down and spot the truck, and as Randy starts to roll in I call him off. Not knowing where the survivor was, we didn't dare chance hitting him. We knew that the truck was south of him—he told us that—so we circled and attacked the truck from the north. Randy rolled in, shot and missed; I rolled in shot and missed; then Randy shot and hit the back of the truck and I rolled in and finished it on my second pass. The helo circled while we were shooting, then I can still see the next scene clearly. That truck was down there burning, orange flames and black smoke pouring out of it, and the helo comes in and lands. Then, just 100 yards away from the burning truck this guy jumps up out of his hole and runs to the helo. It was incredible luck that our timing worked out—we figured that the truck had been DFing on him, too. It was heading right for him and he was minutes away from being captured.

"We still had a problem after they picked him up. We had crossed those highways and they were loaded with military traffic. We had to come out low so the helo slowed down and waited for a gap in traffic before crossing them. We had CAP above us, of course, but we were a long way out in bad guy country and we didn't want a military truck to see us and report us. As it turned out, there were some military vehicles off the side of the road when we flew over but I don't think anybody shot at us.

"We got them across the highways and south about 40 miles, then we were running low on gas again. I talked to Moccasin and he said he felt okay going on alone—his wingman had held south of the highways and had joined him—so we called AWACS and told them we were heading for a tanker—it would be our fourth that day. Then, after getting gas, they asked us if we were ready for additional tasking. By that time the adrenaline was running low and I declined; we were a long way from home. When we did get home and crawled out of the cockpit, we had been in the air for eight hours and forty-five minutes."*

On day six a broken deck of clouds was still hanging over the KTO. But if the clouds are broken, that means there are holes. And if

---

* For this action Captain Johnson was awarded the Air Force Cross—one of the two that were awarded during the war, and Captain Goff won a Distinguished Flying Cross.

there are holes, that means targets can be spotted and attacks launched by diving through them. So on day six the Hogs were at it—not quite in full force, but with enough planes to get the full impact of what the weather-invoked hiatus had done for the Iraqis.

Said Capt. Dan Mulherin, a former F-111 navigator who went on to pilot training and who was now a low-time wingman, "The broken deck that day was at about 12,000 and there were massive winds out of the west, like at a hundred knots. On our first two missions we went up to where our INS said the target was, then hung out until a hole conveniently aligned itself. The clouds were moving fast, so that was not a big problem. Then, we dived down, smoked the targets and pulled off. We had been fired at, but it was nothing major league—probably small arms and 37mm.

"On the third mission it was near dusk when we got up there. We found a large hole over the target—the visibility wasn't too good, but we could look down and see a ton of vehicles. Rolling in you couldn't tell what they were, but looking in the TVM you could see they were hot military targets. Mitch [Maj. Dave Mitchell] and I both went down and made one pass to just confirm that they were no kidding viable Maverick targets. We pulled off, set up again, then Mitch rolled down and hosed off a Maverick and pressed down to the south. He got a good splash with a good secondary, then I started rolling down the chute. Then I got an indication of a missile launch. I called it out over the radio and started turning to put it on my beam [his RWR indicator was telling him the bearing of the missile]. I'm in a turn when Mitch, who is farther to the south, calls missiles in the air. I roll out and I see a missile coming—it looked initially like it was heading toward Mitch, then it came to my canopy level, but kept tracking. I started ramping down, getting some energy so I could turn into it. I could see then that it wasn't going to hit me; there was no way it was going to turn the corner when I broke into it. It was an enormous missile—they call them flying telephone poles. I broke into it so I'm looking through the top of my canopy as it explodes. It was a neat explosion. The way the charge is built it just kind of rippled along the same flight path instead of just a big, round explosion.

"Then Mitch hollers that there are more missiles. He said they were coming at me. I thought I had the site located because I'd seen the one come out of the clouds, so I broke to put it on my beam and in the turn I see two missiles going in between us. I don't know what happened to them but I started climbing for altitude. While I was climbing, I remember looking through a hole and it looked like everybody who had a pistol or anything else was shooting. It was dark down there and you could see every muzzle flash. Everywhere you looked there were literally hundreds of muzzle flashes. I kept climbing and Mitch had continued down towards the south, arcing the whole site and keeping an eye on me.

"I was still climbing when Mitch called out more missile launches—that they were on me and in a cloud. I kept climbing; I was fairly confident I could beat them if I could see them. But I picked the worst cloud to be near because two missiles came out of it just seconds apart. I called tally ho on them and started taking it down again. I was well out of chaff by then and I was getting full-up radar indications on the RWR so I knew they were in a full-up mode. The closest one was now staying at the same place on my canopy so I started bringing it further downhill—45 degrees or so, trying to get to corner velocity where I could make the quickest and tightest turn. Mitch is telling me he's out of chaff but that I should keep chaffing. But I know I'm out because I had been mashing the button nonstop.

"Now it's on a 30 degreeish wire from me, nose on and I'm continuing downhill. As it gets closer, it starts to rise on my canopy and I recognize that it's in its terminal guidance phases, locked on final phases of intercept. It's telling me that it's got me and then it gets to a place on my canopy where I know it's within four seconds or so of impact. That's when I laid in pretty much everything I've got with a turn into it, and it falls to my six and explodes in an enormous fireball. Then the other one, which was farther way, blew up. That made five missiles altogether, three of which blew up very near me.

"After that, we decided to call it a day and headed home. And in my mind I was thinking how amazing it was that I felt like it was just a training exercise. We were both using the correct terminology, doing the correct maneuvers—stuff we have read a thousand times and been tested on a million times. I was confident the whole time, and after it was over, I realized that in all of our training we had been doing something right."

The Iraqis had been caught by surprise on day one of the air campaign, and when they fired AAA or used their missile radars to lock on targets, many of them were blown away with bombs and with Maverick and HARM missiles. But after five days, while air operations in the KTO were severely restricted by weather, the Iraqi defenders were ready, and they aggressively tried to repulse air attacks in the region. The Soviet-designed S-60 57mm, fired in four-shell clips, which could be fused up to 22,000 feet, now seemed to be everywhere. And missiles, ranging from the telephone pole, radar-guided SA-2s that were fired at Mulherin and Mitchell, to the sneaky, smokeless, heat-seeking SA-16s that could be fired by almost any infantryman, were lurking everywhere in the region. The KTO was now a very dangerous place, and some of the Southeast Asia

An A-10 loaded for a mission. A Maverick missile can be seen second from the left. *Courtesy DOD*

The A-10's 70-rounds-per-second Gatling gun, shown here alongside a Volkswagen Beetle for perspective, is nearly 20 feet long and weighs two tons when loaded. *Courtesy Grumman Aerospace Corp.*

A pilot waits with engines running while being rearmed with 30mm ammo during Operation Desert Storm. Pilots often flew three missions without getting out of the cockpit. *Courtesy DOD*

An A-10 approaching a tanker for fuel. *Courtesy DOD*

Lt. Col. Greg ("Growth") Wilson, an O-1 forward air controller in Laos and the deputy commander at Al Jouf. Described as the "compleat warrior," he was universally admired by the younger pilots for his patience and concern as a flight leader.
*Courtesy G. Wilson*

Maj. Jeff Watterberg (left) and Lt. Rich Ferguson on the first day of the air campaign. Watterberg was killed after the war in a mid-air collision.
*Courtesy J. Watterberg*

The right wing of Capt. Paul Johnson's A-10. *Courtesy L. Korn*

Looking down the barrel of an Iraqi tank at night. This photo was taken through a Maverick missile's infrared guidance system. The tank's treads were warm and so appear dark. *Courtesy M. Koechle*

Capt. Steve Phillis just before his fatal mission against the Medina Division. *Courtesy L. Korn*

Capt. Dale Storr (right) before he was shot down, with his crew chief, Sgt. James Ard. *Courtesy D. Storr*

Capt. Todd Sheehy standing proudly beside the Iraqi flag painted on his Warthog for shooting down a Hip helicopter. *Courtesy DOD*

Best friends Lt. Darren Hansen (left) and Lt. Eric Miller before boarding their jets and returning home from the war. Miller was later killed in a mid-air collision. *Courtesy D. Hansen*

Capt. Bob Swain, who shot down an Iraqi helicopter, in front of the "Chopper Popper." *Courtesy DOD*

Lt. Pat Olson was killed on the last day of the war while attempting to land his severely damaged OA-10. *Courtesy A. Stanton*

Colonels Dave Sawyer (at microphone) and Sandy Sharpe briefing their pilots after the war. At this point, their goal was to get everyone home without a mishap. *Courtesy DOD*

After being released from Baghdad as a POW, 1st Lt. Rob Sweet (right) greets his friend Lt. Dan Kolota. *Courtesy L. Korn*

Lt. Col. Jeff Fox relaxing at home while recovering from surgery for injuries suffered as a POW. *Courtesy J. Fox*

A year after the war, Capt. Mark Koechle, Capt. Rob Givens, and Capt. Paul Johnson pose under a model of the A-10 at the USAF Fighter Weapons School, Nellis AFB, Nevada. *Courtesy M. Koechle*

The pilots believed their Warthogs could do it all. Capt. Erik Offill drew this version of the A-10 after it became known as the "RFOA-10G" — for Reconnaissance, Fighter, Observation, Attack, and a G for imitating the F-4G's electronic warfare capabilities.
*Courtesy E. Offill*

# THE DESERT STORM

COMBAT LOADED RFOA-10G

## HOG PILOT

MOTTO: YOU CALL? WE DO IT ALL !!

FAKE CAMEL HUMP

2 WINDOW A/C UNITS TO FOOL THE HOG ENGINES INTO THINKING IT'S COOL OUTSIDE

FOR DECEPTION

SWIVEL CAMCORDER SO WE CAN GET ON CNN

HARM MISSILES FOR WEASEL MISSIONS

HARM

HARM

SWIVEL TITANIUM SHIELD TO PROTECT BACK OF HOG FROM AAA / SAMS / AND EAGLES

VULTURE

AR FW

LOUD SPEAKERS FOR PLAYING ATTACK MUSIK

DESERT STORM

NEAR BEER

LIQUID REFRESHMENT

UGLY MRE FOR BRINGING ENEMY OUT OF FOX HOLES

6 OF 12 14 MAVERICKS

6 OF 12 MK-20 ROCKEYE

HOG LANTERN

HOG LANTERN POD (TRAVEL POD WITH PLEXIGLAS FRONT) (WITH 291 WITH NAV AND BINOS INSIDE)

FIRE EXT FOR PUTTING OUT OIL FIRES

## RFOA-10G

veterans who had seen some of the worst ground fire while flying there, believed the KTO to be more hazardous.

But the air campaign went on, and on day seven—a beautiful day when all of Kuwait was visible from the air—the Hogs were launched in full force. Their target priority remained the same: artillery sites first; armored targets second.

Mostly in two-ship combat pairs they went to kill boxes in southern Kuwait and the tri-border area, found their targets—often with the help of a single OA-10 FAC working the area—and proceeded to systematically destroy the Iraqi war machines.

They tried to get rid of their six bombs first, because of their drag and weight, and because they needed to be wings level when they dropped them. In those moments, when they were in stable flight and most vulnerable to enemy gunners, they wanted the element of surprise on their side.

The bombs were used mostly on the artillery puppy-paws, and usually they were employed by diving out of the sun at 45- to 60-degree dive angles. This often gave them the advantage of surprise, and even though they might be followed on their climb out with AAA fire, the fire was usually well behind them.

But the delivery tactics were up to the flight lead, and some of the pilots preferred other means of attacking. Monstrous winds, typically at 60 knots or more, made it very difficult to bomb accurately, and some of the pilots preferred to dive on the targets with the wind at an angle where they felt they could get the best results. Some preferred a downwind delivery; others favored diving into the wind; most seemed to prefer a crosswind component that they could compute with the "Kentucky windage," iron sight-type aiming calibrations in their heads up display (HUD). Also, some preferred to zoom off the target toward the sun, then break right or left—their rationale being that hand-held, heatseeking missiles fired at them would "bite off," or track toward the sun.

They alternated the bombs they used. On one mission they might carry Mark-82s—500-pound iron bombs, often with air-burst fuses. The next mission they might carry one or more types of CBUs which, when deployed, spread little bomblets over the target in a doughnut-shaped pattern. The CBUs seemed to be most effective on the artillery sites; quite often one string of bombs skillfully laid might destroy several tubes, or the centrally located fire-control center and one or more tubes. All of the pilots looked for secondary explosions, which meant that the stored ammo for the guns was exploding and compounding the destructive effect of the bombs.

After bomb delivery, some of the pilots also dived and strafed with the gun, hoping to create enough destruction to put the artillery pieces out of action. Later, as they began to share their after-mission experiences, some of them learned to detect the stores of ammo stacked near the tubes. Those ammo stores became favorite targets for the gun, and there were a lot of "Sierra Hotels" exclaimed as these stored munitions "cooked off like Roman candles."

With bombs gone and the obligatory first-priority targets conscientiously serviced, the Hog drivers were now free to "hang out" in the general area and look for secondary targets worthy of the two or four Mavericks they were carrying. This meant that they went tank hunting.

The tanks were parked in deep revetments throughout the KTO, and the lines were usually in military-precise straight lines. These were defensive formations and it made them quite formidable to attacking ground forces because they could climb up the revetment, fire, then back down and be almost totally hidden from view.

But in their revetments the tanks were juicy targets for the Hogs. At 45- to 60-degree dive angles, Lead would roll and fire a Maverick, then climb to altitude to cover Two who would repeat the process on another tank. Almost without exception, it would be BOOM, BOOM and two tanks would be destroyed and burning. Then they would repeat the process and two more tanks could be scratched from the inventory.

If they weren't carrying more Mavericks (most of the time they carried two because the multiple racks proved unreliable) and if there was little AAA threat, they started busting tanks with their guns, with a big advantage they never expected to have.

When training for the Central European Scenario, the tactic for using the gun against tanks was to stay low, below radar missile threats, and move to within 4,000 feet before engaging the tank. The armor-piercing bullets with their depleted uranium cores (uranium is denser than lead and thus gives the bullets more kinetic energy) would melt right through the tank's heavy armor in a head-on frontal attack. However, the Hog drivers did not have to do that in this war. Using their low-threat, high-altitude tactics, they were able to dive on the reveted tanks and fire from 8,000 to 10,000 feet knowing that their bullets would easily penetrate the relatively light armor on the top and rear of the tanks.

So, after expending their Mavericks, it was not uncommon for pilots to dive and shoot tanks with their guns. And while many of them felt they were actually killing the tanks, often they were not able to start the tank burning—or at least cause a fire that they could see. (Most of the tanks that were hit burned inside, but they didn't find that out until after the war.) And, of course, they were not likely to generate an explosion such as that caused by the impact of a

Maverick. So they came home, reported the tank kills where they saw fire or explosions, and the BDA estimators were left with many hundreds of other tanks listed in the "possible damage" category—tanks that had been fired on with the guns, but which did not reveal any obvious signs of destruction.

With the good weather continuing to hold, and with a combat pair of Hogs departing on average of about every fourteen minutes for the remainder of the air campaign, the latest and finest Iraqi artillery and armor were being methodically and systematically turned into scrap metal.

In addition, the Iraqi troops, which the Coalition Army would eventually have to confront, were suffering from the endless pounding. Except for the gunners who were attacked, and the troops foolish enough to stay close to armored vehicles, their suffering was not life threatening—at least enemy troops were not often fragged as targets for the A-10s. Their suffering came in the form of deprivation. They were being deprived of food by the interdiction missions of strike aircraft that went after the supply convoys. And they were being deprived of sleep by the action of the Night Hogs.

# 11

# Night Hogs in Action

*"At night it was the silent gun . . . all of a sudden the guy next to you would blow up and that's pretty demoralizing—you can't see or hear the airplane and your buddy is over there in a thousand pieces."*

—Lt. Col. Craig Mays

The Falcons from Myrtle Beach were the pioneers; under the leadership of Lt. Col. Rick McDow, they started training to be Night Hogs in October. In December, when it became obvious that another squadron was needed for night duty, Lt. Col. Jim Green's Flying Tigers from Alexandria quickly trained and were mission ready when the war started.

On days one and two, six of the Falcons flew daytime missions into Iraq after GCI sites. The others were on night alert, and the first night they flew sixty-four missions. After that the squadron never flew another daytime mission for the rest of the war.

The Flying Tigers, though ready for night tasking, flew daytime missions during the first two weeks of the war. Then, because the Falcons were overtasked and growing weary, and because the commanders wanted to increase the night pressure on the Iraqis, the Tigers were switched to night operations and that is how they finished the war.

Those who flew both kinds of missions expressed strong opinions about the difference between the two. Said Lt. Col. Jim Green, "Flying combat at night was a lot more difficult. It was much more intense because, without an autopilot, you had to concentrate and work harder just on the mechanics of flying. There was no way you could relax like you could in the daytime when you were out of the threat."

Added 1st Lt. Bryan Currier, "Flying at night was so much more demanding. And besides just flying the plane, which took total concentration, there were little problems that we didn't have during the day. Take map reading, for example. Reading a map in the daytime is no sweat—the first thing we learn is to fly with a folded map in front of us. But at night, with lights out, it's a hassle to get the red light focused, and distracting to go heads down. We learned from the Falcons to photocopy all our maps because black and white was more contrasty and easier to read. But most of us tried to memorize as much as we could to avoid having to use them. And that added to the workload."

The night tactics were also much different from those used in daytime missions. After takeoff, the wingman would go into a trail position about 3 miles behind lead. Up to the border, with lights on, the wingman could see lead and maintain visual separation. But when lights were out, they had to use their air-to-air TACAN to maintain distance. This instrument gives each pilot an ongoing distance readout of how far apart the two planes are.

They could also use instruments to find out the direction they were from each other. One pilot could key his microphone for five seconds and the other's ADF needle would swing and point to the direction of the transmission. However, the pilots tried to avoid unnecessary "DFing" because the enemy could also pick up those transmissions and use them for targeting.

When a two-ship flight launched, each pilot had sets of coordinates programmed into his INS. One of them would be a contact point somewhere near the kill box where they were going. Usually they would fly in Saudi territory for as long as they could, then cross the border and head directly to the contact point. Then they would navigate directly to coordinates at some point in the kill box. Often, two two-ship flights would be tasked to the same kill box, but they would agree before the launch on who would take which side—usually they split them on a north-south median line. Lt. Col. Jim Green describes what usually happened next.

"Generally, we would have target coordinates specified by the Army—usually an arty [artillery] site. We'd drive right toward those coordinates, but the hard part came when we started getting close. That's when we would have to put our heads down and start looking through our soda straw.

"Everybody uses the term 'soda straw' because looking through a Maverick is like closing one eye, taking a straw out of a drink and walking around trying to find something while sighting through that straw. We had two fields of view with the IR maverick. Going in, we would use the wide field of view, which was only a 3-degree field and which also gave us 3X magnification. Going into the target we had to use a little math to figure how much to pitch the plane down from our altitude in order to see things in the target area. Then, between 16 and 20 miles from the target, Lead would start a very slow descent, with head down looking through the screen and counting down the distance on the INS.

"You see heat sources—that's all. But you soon learn how the targets look—especially when you get closer and switch to the narrow field of view. This gives you 6X magnification and it was extremely easy to pick out the arty sites because of their distinctive half-moon shape. My tactics were, when I was ramping down on a target, I would drop a log when I was exactly 10 miles from the target. The log is a flare that goes off about 900 feet in the air and then burns on the ground for thirty minutes. It would become a ground reference we could then use in that pitch black desert.

"After dropping the log, I could continue on toward the target. I'd fly right over it, typically at 5,000 or 6,000 feet. If it was a tank in a revetment, great: it's not going anywhere and I'll come back and kill it on the next pass. But if I saw a mover, I'd lock on it and fire a Maverick on the first pass; we wanted to stop all of their movement at night. That was a high priority, and we achieved it after awhile.

"Anyhow, usually I'd fly over the target, mark it in my INS—invariably it would be off the target coordinates we were given—and drop another log. Now I could pull off and we would have two ground references burning about 10 miles apart. Then I could give my wingman a more accurate location of the target, and I could tell him to stay east of a line between the logs while I stayed to the west. The logs gave us an easy way to deconflict.

"Typically, then I would start climbing—a slow process with all that ordnance—six bombs, two or four Mavericks, two flare pods, an ECM pod, two Aim-9s, and a full load of ammo for the gun. In the climb I would also fly over the target and drop a LUU-2, which is a parachute flare that hangs up there and lights up the world. Then Two rolls in, drops his bombs, and then, if necessary, I do the same. And, depending on the target, we might just drop three of the bombs and save the others for another target, or we might drop the whole load.

"Then, if I still had good flare capability and a viable target, I would often go in and strafe with the gun. Lots of times you could set off the ammo storage in an arty site and get some awesome secondaries—much more beautiful fireworks than you see in the daytime.

"Early in the war the Iraqis almost always shot at the flares, which was a stupid thing to do because we could see where the fire was coming from and we could strafe them. We would also see AAA [from established sites rather than random fire] occasionally and that was an awesome sight at night. It wasn't all that dangerous for us, but it was often a deadly mistake for them because we could roll in and shoot them without them ever knowing where we were.

"After getting rid of our bombs we usually divided up our area and went searching for other targets. And during the early part of the war they were everywhere. Typically, we would launch our Mavericks on tanks or APCs and get four kills before we were bingo [with just enough fuel to get home] and headed back for gas. Then we would come back and do it again, and in one night we might destroy a complete artillery site, maybe a command center, and maybe eight or ten vehicles—including a mover or two, depending on our luck."

The learning curve was steep during the first night missions. When they pulled off a target in the daytime, it was routine for them to bank steeply and yank their head over their left or right shoulder to see what their weapons had done. At night they found that head-yanking was a quick way to induce vertigo, which they would then have to fight for the rest of the mission.

When they first started firing Mavericks at night, nearby flights sometimes thought they were SAM launches. Without a horizon for a ground reference perspective, they saw the brilliant flashes and immediately broke off whatever they were doing, released chaff and flares, and began to jink madly. Quickly, it became standard procedure for all the pilots to call out Maverick launches in order to prevent that confusion.

Deconfliction was a constant problem. Because of the very strong winds, it was easy for planes to drift out of their assigned area. Said Flying Tiger, 1st Lt. J. J. Krimmell, "It was real easy to get busy out there and get into somebody else's air space, especially when you're concentrating on getting away from AAA. One night we were out there and I was talking to these other guys and they said, 'We're down here in our area, where are you?' This other guy, who was a little disoriented, comes up and says, 'Well I'm right here, I think.' Well, I really don't want for this guy to do this, but I'm in need of a warm fuzzy right quick. So I call out to this last guy, 'Flash me, blow out a self-protection flare, then move.' I knew that they might shoot at the flare but if he moved right away, he would be safe. Well. I'm looking out and all of a sudden there it was, lighting just off the side of my jet. I almost got blinded from the ignition. This guy could easily have collided with me. I yelled for him to get back north—he had drifted way south of where he was supposed to be.

"We also had a problem with other aircraft coming into the area. We were controlled by ABCCC, but some of the F-16s were working with a new type of control called JSTARS. Sometimes I would be out there working my area and all of a sudden you would see some [after] burners a half-mile or mile off to your side—you'd see those streaming off in the sky and wonder where they came from. Then you'd see a couple of 2,000 pounders going off underneath you. After awhile we tried to stay on a common frequency and if they wanted to come in while we were still within our TOT, we would give them ingress and egress altitudes to provide deconfliction."

Doing battle with SAMs at night was a unique problem they never were able to solve. Captain Jim Cobb, one of the Falcons, describes their typical frustration. "What you need to do for missile defense is to be able to judge where it is in relation to you, and you need to time it. At night you can't do that, and it is just panic. You see it coming up, you see it then coming at you—it turns toward you but you don't know which way to go because now it is so disorienting—you don't know where the horizon is—you don't know if it is coming high, low, or straight at you. So essentially all you do is roll and split-S; maybe put a little turn into it.

"I was in cover on my wingman [Capt. Leon Elsarelli] one night and he was going in on a Maverick pass and I'm hawking him about 2 or 3 miles in trail, 5,000 feet above him, looking for missiles or AAA to call them off. Somebody in the kill box next to us yelled, 'SAMs to the south!' and I looked over and saw two SAMs coming up, one after another, and they both bent over and turned toward me. I don't know the distance of them and I yelled, 'We've got two SAMs!' I'm in chop tone [intermittent warning tone telling him that he is pulling too hard, losing energy rapidly] and what I'd done was roll 160 degrees of bank and pull for all I was worth, and was stalling the airplane. You can hear my wingman saying, 'Are you talking to me?' and you can hear him in chop tone, too, and we are both just pulling for all we can for the dirt. Then you say, 'It's got to be close' and you roll up and do the titanium bathtub number—you hunker down and just wait, with the bathtub between you and where you think it is and you say, 'Oh man, this is going to hurt.' You just sit there and wait and wait, and when you know it isn't going to hit you, you say, 'Hello wingman,' and he says, 'Yeah, I'm still here,' and you go, 'Yeah, right on.'

"What is scary at night is when you see one of them coming up—it looks just like a Saturn rocket launch. You can't see the missile but you can see the plume and as it comes up, you can see it bending. You can see the arc it takes; then you start laying the geometry on it and about that time, the boosters burn out and you lose it. Then you go downhill; you make it come downhill and bleed some of its energy. Then you come into it a little bit; you make it make a turn and deplete some more energy. You wait, and guess, and then you lay the best turn you can on it and hopefully it won't square the corner and get you."

Another problem the learning curve never really helped was the length of time often required in acquiring targets. Sometimes the coordinates where they were sent would be off a little, and when searching through a 3-degree soda straw, just a mile or two difference could mean extra passes and, perhaps, result in them never finding the target. INS drift was also a problem and it wasn't unusual for them to be off a mile or more by the time they got to the target area. Generally, they were allowed a thirty-minute TOT and twenty of those minutes might be taken up with just target acquisition. Since employment also took more time, with flare passes and confirmation passes, the Night Hogs continually felt a time pressure that was rarely experienced by the day fighters.

Flying at night required lots of patience. Many times a pilot would have his head down, searching for a viable target when he would spot something exciting like three tanks close together in revetments. He knows that they are viable because their tread marks show up as hot tracks in the desert, and he can see the even hotter skid marks where they slid as they turned into the revetment. Quickly, he marks his position with the INS because he is too close to fire on this first pass, then he begins calculating. "Let's see, with the look-down angle I have programmed in the Maverick and from my present altitude . . . I must be 4.3 miles and a bearing of one-nine-five degrees from the target. So, on my next pass, if I take the reciprocal of that bearing, ramp down from 9,000 feet and . . ."

Then he pulls off, circles and tries to find the target again. No luck. Then his wingman tries. No luck. And maybe that is it for the night. Maybe they are bingo on fuel. Or maybe the TOT is up. So they leave the area and never see those tanks again.

That's the way it went sometimes, and it was tough landing at home, taxiing up and seeing the disappointment in the faces of the ground crew when they look and see all the unexpended ordnance still hanging on your plane. One of the Flying Tigers, Capt. Ralph Hansen, kept a diary during the war and an excerpt, written after such a mission, bares this anguish. He wrote, "There is *nothing* worse to a fighter pilot than to bring home your ordnance. *Nothing.*

It is an awful, sickening feeling because it tells you that you did *not* do your job."

At times, however, they would get lucky out there and they wouldn't even need the soda straw, or even the LUU-2 flares. Said "Falcon One"—Lt. Col. Rick McDow, "It was really disturbing when you make a pass, find a good target, then can't replicate that pass and find it again. But you couldn't let yourself get mad. And, there were times when it worked the other way. One night I was out and I had four Mavericks—it was one of the few nights that those multiple racks worked like they were supposed to. We were searching in the area and found a row of tanks that were in a V-type formation. There were nine of them and I shot the ninth one with a Maverick, got it burning, then came around and shot the seventh and got it burning, then did the same for the fifth and third. My wingman had trouble with his Mavericks and couldn't get them off. Anyhow, I had four big fires burning down there and I didn't need my eyes [Maverick] any longer. I said to my wingman, 'You see those four fires down there—there's a tank between each of them. Roll in and fire at them with your gun. He did that and I did that, and before we left, I know for sure that we got six of those tanks."

In the beginning, most of the pilots dreaded the night missions. It was going to be difficult just flying the airplane. Finding the targets was going to be tough. There were all kinds of chances for midair collisions to occur. It would be difficult, if not impossible to avoid SAMs without ground references. These and other potential problems had loomed in their minds.

After two weeks of flying nights, few if any of the pilots wanted to fly any other kind of mission. The advantages of flying at night soon outweighed the problems they had anticipated.

The biggest advantage was their stealth. Because of their quiet, fanjet engines, they couldn't be heard above 5,000 feet, and they couldn't be seen at all unless they happened to be silhouetted against the moon. They were literally a silent gun, able to maneuver behind the lines wherever they wanted to go without being detected. Occasionally they would be strobed by radar, and occasionally radar-guided missiles were launched at them. But those were relatively rare occasions, and some of the pilots believe that the Iraqis were afraid to use their radars against them. They believe that after word got around on how active radars were destroyed by HARM missiles, the Iraqis were afraid to scope the A-10s because they feared that they might be carrying the HARMs.

So there was much less threat at night, and it didn't take the pilots long to realize that they were operating in a much safer environment. That was reassuring; in their jargon, the night was a warm-fuzzy.

When they did encounter AAA, they could see it easily, and they soon learned to identify the different types. The long-range S-60, which shot 57mm airburst shells, was fired in four-shell clips. The 37mm pieces—also firing air-burst shells—fired a five-shot clip. To differentiate between the two of them, they simply counted the shots. The 23mm fire was much easier to recognize. Anyone who saw the CNN scenes of AAA fire over Baghdad will remember the red hose-like streams of 23mm fire that were erupting over the city during the air strikes. Those red streams were a chilling sight for pilots because they knew that only one in five of the bullets was a tracer—that the other four in the bullet stream were invisible.

The general attitude of all the pilots in that war was, "You shoot at me, and I shoot back at you." That was a lot easier to do during the night missions because it was easy to see where the fire was coming from. Killing AAA sites was also easier because the guns could be firing in one direction and, unseen, a pilot could be diving to fire on them from another. So being an Iraqi gunner was not a healthy occupation, especially at night, and this awareness probably became widespread after a few weeks. At least, that's what the pilots think caused the gradual decline of night AAA fire as the air campaign continued.

There was one spectacular exception to that trend. Lieutenant Colonel Mike Wilkin, Ops Officer for the Flying Tigers, explains: "After awhile we got very predictable. One set of pilots would fly two goes [missions] before midnight and another set would take the last two goes from midnight till dawn. Well, I was flying up there with [1st Lt.] Eric Paul as wingman on the first go and all of us were having a little trouble with ABCCC over our tasking. This delayed us and while we were waiting south of the border, the whole sky suddenly lit up all over Kuwait. It looked like they were firing every AAA piece they had over there. It was barrage fire, straight up, and it was timed perfectly. They fired at exactly 1830 [6:30PM] which was the time that those of us on the first go should have been crossing over the border. It was the most impressive sight I have ever seen—we called it the 'Night of Fire.' It must have been a one-time experiment because I never heard of them doing that again."

The pilots who saw the least amount of AAA fire were those who flew the last two missions of the night—from midnight to dawn. Said Maj. John Bingaman, a Falcon, "Those guys up there were pounded around the clock, day after day, and I think they finally got to the point after midnight when they said, 'Hey, after eighteen hours of getting beaten, I don't care what happens; I'm going to bed.' It seemed like that was the case because all my night missions were flown after midnight and we rarely saw AAA fire."

When Lt. Col. Rick McDow stood up before his squadron back in October and told them he was volunteering them for night duty, he recited the advantages he had experienced as a night fighter in Southeast Asia. He also made some predictions about the advantages he expected them to experience in a war in the desert. After the first few weeks of combat, and after the Flying Tigers joined the night effort, all that McDow had predicted had come to pass. And of all those predictions, there was one that was of paramount importance: McDow predicted that those who flew at night would be much safer and stand a much better chance of surviving and returning to their families. At the mid-point of the war he was batting a thousand. Not a single one of the Night Hogs had been holed by a bullet or a piece of shrapnel.

The daytime pilots were not destined to be that lucky.

# 12

## Deep Interdiction

*"I was asked on several occasions to do missions that I thought, my God, why are you asking an A-10 to do this? You had to swallow hard and walk in and look those kids in the eye. . . . I have awe and admiration for every one of them—they have guts galore, I mean you talk about courage—my God!"*
*—Col. Sandy Sharpe*

"It was like going into cold water," said Col. Dave Sawyer. "You go in up to your ankles, you wait awhile, find out that's not too bad, then you wade out until you're knee deep. That's the way it was with us the first ten to twelve days of the war. We were doing things we never thought we would do, but we were having good success. We were on a roll, really doing some good work. We were kicking ass and taking names and we weren't getting our noses bloodied. But then we found out that the gradual stuff was over; we found out we were going to plunge into deep water."

On day eleven of the air campaign, Colonels Sawyer and Sharpe received some startling news from Riyadh. They would no longer just be attacking kill boxes across the border, where they had been successfully pounding Iraqi artillery and armor. The Army wasn't too worried about those forces now; intelligence showed that they had been well battered, and, of course, they were the conscripts—supposedly the old men and the kids.

What worried the Army was the three armored Republican Guard divisions stationed 75 to 125 miles north. They were the elite troops, equipped with the latest and best artillery and armor. "However," said Dave Sawyer, "the armor was not a big worry to the Army. They

123

figured that one versus one with the M-1A1 against the T-72, they could kill them all day. But that long-range artillery of the Guards—that scared the hell out them."

The word that came down on day eleven was that the Hogs were going to be sent against the southernmost division of the Guards, the Tawakalna Division. They were told that the actual tasking would be coming through in five or six days and that they should start planning now so they would be ready.

The Fahd commanders huddled with their deputies. They were all uneasy. They didn't like the idea of sending their "kids" so far behind the lines against the kinds of threats an elite unit like the Tawakalnas were sure to have. They really didn't have any choice, but they went back to Riyadh with a proposal. "Okay, we'll do it, but we want some imagery—if we're going to send those kids up there, we want the best damn photos and maps that the spooks have available." Except for day one, when they went against the GCI sites, the Hogs had been "out of the loop" when it came to receiving target imagery.

Then they called on two of their finest—Maj. Dan Swift, the Myrtle Beach Wing weapons officer, and Capt. Mike Isherwood, the Alex weapons officer who had almost singlehandedly sold the Flying Tigers on accepting their night-mission role.

Said Isherwood, "They called Dan and I in and said we have five or six days to get this all planned. They told us, 'Let's do it smart; let's use our air power but there's no requirement for us to stay around for a long time up there if we don't need to.' Then they gave us thirty-two beautiful 8 x 10 photos that covered the whole division, and a 1:50,000 Army map that was a Hog driver's dream.

"We then went to the Mission Planning Cell where we taped all the pictures together to make a big mosaic of the division. It must have been 8 or 9 feet long and 3 or 4 feet wide—it almost covered one whole wall and it was really detailed—it showed every tank and artillery position."

Major Swift picks up the story. "I wasn't happy when I first heard what we were going to do—that is not the A-10's mission. But we started working it out and then Mike [Isherwood] comes up with an eight-ship plan, where we put eight ships from each squadron in with a ten-minute TOT, and we do that six times, hitting them hard with a one-hour concentration of firepower. Then we come back and do it again and again—three times the first day, and we do that for three days in a row.

"At first, when Mike proposed this, I said it would never float. It was a new tactic and I was afraid the guys would not be too receptive to the idea of working that many planes together in one small area. But he convinced me that firepower concentration was what we needed, both for effectiveness and for safety—that we would get their heads down at the beginning, take out their major threats—the SA-6 that they had and the SA-2 co-located with it—and that we could then use our firepower to the maximum, and we could do it safely. So we got the plan together and went to the DO [Col. Hank Haden], briefed him, and he kind of lowered his glasses and looked over the top and said, 'Holy shit!'"

Then word came down from Riyadh that General Glosson, the proponent of the plan, wanted to implement it early—that the ATO was coming down for the twenty-ninth, which was two days after they had been told to start planning. "That really pissed me," said Isherwood. "I flew on the twenty-eighth and I was planning carefully so I would be available to fly and lead the first eight-ship flight. But, because my main job was running the night Mission Planning Cell, I had an agreement with Colonel [Tom] Lyon, my DO, that I would only fly every third day. So I ended up on the ground, watching the others taking off, and sweating them out."

Many of the pilots who went on that first mission over the Republican Guards wondered privately if they would be returning. Said Capt. Rick Turner, the Vultures weapons officer, "We expected the worst because of all the threats they told us about in our briefing. The night before the mission I wrote my wife and told her that tomorrow was not going to be a good day—that I may not be coming home. I told her quite a few things that I still remember, and I really thought I wouldn't be coming home from that one. As it turned out, I came close to getting it."

The day started out as planned, with every target assigned according to priorities. Captain Joe Rutkowski, call sign Savage 01, was leading the first flight (the one Isherwood wanted to lead) made up of Vanguards from Alexandria. He was to hit the SA-6 radar, which would take away the guidance for their most dangerous threat. He did that with a Maverick on his first pass. Savage 02, 1st Lt. Mike Greco, rolled in right behind him and took out the tropo-scatter antenna, which shut off their radio communications.

The third priority was a truck believed to be an SA-9 launcher, and just after Lieutenant Greco pulled off, it fired a heat-seeking missile. That was a choreographer's dream because Capt. Marty Brogli, call sign Pachmayr 03, saw it fire as he was rolling in on it from the other direction. He fired one Maverick and that was the end of the launcher. Then the other four, Maj. Steve Moffet, Capt. Rick Griffin, Capt. Dave Foelker, and Maj. Glen Weaver rolled in and blew away the priority artillery sites in their sector.

To this point everything had gone exactly as planned. "Then," said Isherwood, "Joe [Rutkowski], who had a TOT for his eight-ship of ten minutes—fifteen max—looked around, didn't see anybody coming in, and decided to hang around and destroy more targets. There were tanks and APCs massed up there, so he was doing what A-10 pilots do . . . "

Then Major Dan Swift came with his eight-ship flight from the Panther Squadron, but had to hold until the others cleared the area. Finally they got in, and after arcing the target in a series of two-ship attacks, they battered their targets and were able to keep the gunners' heads down throughout the whole attack.

Lieutenant Colonel Keith Bennett, who was in the third eight-ship flight of Vultures, had a different view when they came in. Said Bennett, "When we went in, we could see the target area from 60 miles away because of the black smoke [produced] from the strikes ahead of us. As we came off our strike I remember looking back and black smoke was coming off where we had hit and you could see bright flashes of things still exploding. When we came back on the turn, it was still smoking so bad we had trouble finding targets. When we came back the third time, pretty much everything had been burned out. We found some things to shoot [with the gun] but we had pretty much annihilated anything that was worth it in our area. When we finally shut down, I was one tired Jose. I got in the cockpit around five that morning, hot-pitted and rearmed without shutting down on the turns, and it was about sunset that evening when I crawled out of the airplane."

Captain Rick Turner, who was with Lieutenant Colonel Bennett, had the closest call during that first assault. Said Turner, "I was diving on an SA-9 and as I locked up on it, but just before I hit the pickle button, he launched on me. It was on my tape—two missiles were coming off the piece of armor that I had locked up. But I defeated them with flares and maneuvers and ended up surviving the three missions more tired than relieved after almost fourteen hours in the cockpit."

There were a lot of tired pilots that evening. The Vanguards went in first, followed by the Panthers, Vultures, Tigers, Cajuns, and a second eight-ship from the Vanguards. The Tawakalna Division got pounded for three solid hours; a total of 154 planes hit them with bombs, Mavericks, and 30mm bullets.

That night General Glosson called. "What did you guys get up there today?" he asked.

"Well, we dropped lots of rockeye [cluster bombs with armor-piercing bomblets], and fired lots of Mavericks, but we can't say for sure about things like artillery—you never know what you did without secondaries. . . ."

"But, geez, I've got to tell the Army something. . . ."

"Well. . ."

They went back the next day, but they felt the threat was diminished and that four-ship flights, with which the pilots were more experienced, would be adequate. They pounded the Tawakalnas again and they returned with no battle damage.

General Glosson called again that night. "We finally claimed about fifty tanks and I don't know how much artillery," said Colonel Sawyer, and he said, 'Is that all?' I said, 'Yes, sir. We just can't, with any degree of integrity, say we got a hundred—or three or four hundred—we shot a lot of them.' It was a real problem for Glosson; the Army wanted that division attrited by 50 percent and he wanted to tell them we'd done it. But we just couldn't say that for sure."

Then Saddam tried to get even. Or, perhaps as a shrewd tactic, he thought he could draw the Army into a ground battle prematurely, before his assets were destroyed. Whatever the motive, he crossed the border into Saudi Arabia at several points and began attacking with small forces. The resultant skirmishes became known as the Battle of Khafji because the strongest of the armored incursions occurred in that seaside resort city.

Air assets were immediately rushed to the area and two planes were lost during the battle: an Air Force AC-130 Spector, a gunship, and a Marine OV-10 piloted by a FAC. The Hogs also got involved.

Captain Dave Tan was on his way up to the Tawakalnas leading a four-ship flight when he received a message on Guard. Said Tan, "They told us to come back south, that they had some emergency tasking for us. I turned the four of us around and got back down by the border where I contacted a ground FAC, call sign Wildman something. There had just been a firefight down there and our guys were getting shot at across the border. Another flight also called out 'hairy' AAA so I had my three [Capt. Scott Alexander] and four [Capt. Mark Hedman] hold high while my wingman [Maj. Doug Richter] and I went down to check out the situation. We found two self-propelled guns [SPG] butted up against the berm—they were on the Baghdad side of the berm—and I hit one with a Maverick and came back around and both of us attacked the other with the gun. I'm not satisfied with either of our hits so I make one more strafe pass—there's no doubt this time as the sparkles of metal to metal contact erupt all over the SPG. Wildman is feeling a little better now and says, 'Holy cow, you guys are saving me today.' I was then about to tell him that he was clear when I looked up and saw a tank going eastbound. I tell him there is a tank out here and he comes back, 'You say he is going eastbound?' I say, 'That's affirm,' He is elated and says, 'Boy, you can light his ass up!' I go, 'All right, I heard that, I'm in.' As I roll in I'm looking at the best Maverick lock of the whole war. This guy was making these nice hot tracks and I had an IR Maverick. . . . The tank fills up the whole screen, I can see the gun sticking out. I popped him with the IR Maverick and the FAC was just elated. It was really rewarding to help those guys."

Other Hogs got into the action, destroying tanks, self-propelled guns and APCs. However, as the Iraqi forces began to withdraw, especially along the coastline south of Kuwait City, the AAA fire that knocked down the AC-130 and the OV-10 was murderous, and even the most intrepid Hog drivers had to turn away.

Said Night Hogs Capt. Rob Givens and 1st Lt. Mike McGee, who told their story together (and who are also close friends):

*McGee:* "It was my first mission—I hadn't even been in the cockpit for sixteen days—and I was nervous from the beginning. On the ground I kind of messed up my cockpit checks and the crew chief—a woman—said, 'Calm down, you're going to do just fine,' and I started laughing then. We launched and it got dark en route to southern Kuwait, and the first thing that struck me was from 60 to 80 miles away I could see fires everywhere—and smoke from the fires. It was a moonlit night so you could see smoke clouds coming from an oil rig fiercely burning about 3 miles off the coast. We were going to a target that was just about 10 miles up the coast of Kuwait and I was behind the airplane . . ."

*Givens:* "We have a way to check our distance with the air-to-air TACAN and I'm seeing the distance between us increase and I'm going, 'Come on man, where are you? Where the hell are you going?'"

*McGee:* "He was so excited . . . I could tell on the radio when he started blitzing off, and when I gave him the IP, he started going there and I said, 'You want me to hold?' He said, 'No, we're both enroute to the IP,' and I said, 'Well, shit, tell me.'

*Givens:* "Yeah, and about that time we are in contact with the Marines controlling the area and the radio traffic was wild. Then the Marines, they have to read out every threat that they ever assumed was anywhere nearby, but 75 percent of those either weren't in existence or weren't going off . . . they had a piece of paper and they were reading it . . .

*McGee:* "We were working with a Marine OV-10, Hostage something—he may have been the same one shot down later—he pressed into the target which was a FROG [rocket fired over the ground like artillery] and I'm behind, trying to fly instruments and punching coordinates into the INS like mad, then, suddenly, a real royal kind of bright light flashes and I'm thinking, 'Oh, God, here comes a missile up to kill me.' I start to swallow my tongue and then I hear another guy in our squadron, Maj. A. J. Jackson calling to his wingman, telling him that he has put out a flare. I laughed to myself and thought, 'Okay, you're still alive, calm down, you've seen a lot of strange things you've never seen before but obviously no one is shooting. As soon as I did that I realized I should be looking out for Lead and no sooner did I turn my head to the left to look for him when I saw what looked like popcorn kernels exploding with sparks coming out of them. When I first saw them it puzzled me and I thought, 'What the hell is that?' And very quickly it occurred to me that it was AAA fire. I called him and told him he was taking AAA at his twelve. He said, 'Roger, I see it.'"

*Givens:* "The thing that was driving me at that point was the fact that our Marines had been taking artillery and FROG fire from the Iraqis and I wanted to get in there and help them. They weren't going to withdraw—there's something in Marine honor—I guess withdraw is not in their vocabulary—so I know they're going to keep taking it until we can help them. We kept pressing in with AAA going off everywhere—I mean, no kidding, the entire length of the coast of Kuwait all the way up to Kuwait City, there was nothing but flak all along the coast. At that point I remember CNN reports saying they are putting up minimal air defense. Boy, if that was minimal air defense I would really hate to see heavy air defense. Imagine if somebody stood along the coastline, one person every quarter of a mile with a large hose with red colored water spraying it all out in the direction of the ocean, but up. It looked like fingers coming up over the water. Obviously they anticipated stuff coming across the coast. Unfortunately, the Marines were bringing us in up the coast so we were going beak to beak with the AAA . . . so when Mike called out AAA to my twelve, I thought, 'Yeah, all the way to Kuwait City.'"

*McGee:* "When they gave us the threats they said there were sixty 57mm guns on that coast. I was close to positive that every last one of them was firing."

*Givens:* "Hostage was trying to talk me in on the first pass and there was a thin scattered deck at 10,000. When I got below that, I was amazed that all the lights of Kuwait City were on and you could see the whole coastline as well. But I was having problems in the cockpit. The FAC was trying to describe the target based off a 1:50,000 map and I had a 1:250 in the cockpit. At that point in the war I wasn't proficient enough to do detailed map reading at night while flying the airplane—which was just as well, because turning the plane loose was the best way to counter the AAA—there was no way it would fly in a straight line and no way was a gunner going to predict where it was going."

*McGee:* "Do you remember what that FAC said about the target? 'Your target is a FROG rocket launcher. It's right next to a white building with a guy standing in the building and you can see him with the light,' and here you are at 8,000 feet. You gotta be kidding."

*Givens:* "Yeah, but I'm concentrating and I make the first run and I get down and I'm looking and looking and looking and I'm where my INS tells me it should be and I still haven't acquired anything yet. I came off that pass and at that point I really want to get that launcher, and also I know my squadron commander [Lt. Col. Rick McDow] is back across the border in a two-ship, just holding and waiting and I don't want him to have to come in and get it."

*McGee:* "I can't see him [Givens] but I can tell when he pulled off before he even came on the radio because the AAA slowed down. They had something down there that was picking us up."

*Givens:* "They were picking us up with something, but I wanted another pass so I asked the FAC if I could come in southwest to northeast so I could avoid the coastline where they were firing. At that point I got a needless lecture that my primary target was the FROG launcher and not the AAA and I didn't need that. I start back in and I'm thinking only of that launcher. But I didn't see anything on the second pass and I'm thinking about gas now, and about my squadron commander back there waiting. I told the FAC then that I was going to go in again and drop illumination flares because I thought that might help. I get cleared, I tell Mike to keep me covered, and he's watching and keeps telling me he's got me covered, then as I get wings level for the flare pass, he says—and I'll remember this radio sequence for the rest of my life, 'AAA to the north!' I see this stuff all the way to Kuwait City again. I go, 'Roger, I've got it.' And I think to myself why in the hell is he telling me about AAA; who could miss it; it's solid for 30 miles. I'm still going in and I'm about 2 miles from the target and I'm getting really set up, nice and level and finally he goes, 'Hey, man, you better be careful!' And the hair started standing up on the back of my neck and I just didn't feel right about something and the pitch of his voice was higher. I thought, 'What's wrong here?' and that's when I learned one of the most valuable lessons of the war, that is, how much space the nose of the A-10 actually blocks. I kind of raised up in my seat, sat up and looked over the end of the nose, and I saw, no kidding, it looked like fingers, really long red fingers just coming straight up for the nose of the airplane. It was coming straight up and I knew it was time to break."

*McGee:* "He couldn't see it but the stuff is getting bigger, and because it is coming closer to me, he's got to be right over it or in it. A few seconds later he very calmly said, 'Wings off to the left.' He pulled up and came back out. Before it was intense, but now it was, no kidding, you could have walked on it; it was that thick."

*Givens:* "We came out and we were too low on gas so I said, 'Okay, we have to get out of here.' In fact, we had to climb up really, really high to do a min fuel approach back home.* I got home later on that night—we flew another mission that night—and I felt really whipped. I felt, here was my chance to hit a really good target and do a lot of good and I turned around—and my squadron commander was right behind me and I know he's going to say something to me like, 'You could have worked around the AAA.' I felt really like I came home with my tail between my legs."

*McGee:* "I was just happy to be alive."

*Givens:* "McDow came in roughly a half hour after us that night and I was sitting there looking at the map. He walks in—he's a very stoic individual—he's definitely the wartime kind of guy. He sat there and looked at me and rubbed his face and said, 'Well, did you have fun out there tonight?'

"I said, 'Yes, sir, I really had fun, a lot of AAA.' He goes, 'I was behind you and I saw all that stuff to the north. I was trying to figure out roughly where you'd be and I figured you were right in it. I was just getting ready to call you off the flare pass when you called off. I almost came on the radio and said, "Good boy."'

"And that's where I learned probably my second valuable lesson from the war—that there's a time when it's okay to turn away—that sometimes that's the best course of action."

The Hog drivers also learned another lesson that night—a bitter lesson that would haunt them forever. Up to this point their confidence in the Maverick missile was total. It had seemed the perfect weapon; lock it on a target, fire it, and the target is history. Then, ominously, at about midnight on the thirteenth day of the air campaign, one of the pilots locked on a target with an IR Maverick and fired. But the Maverick broke the lock; in Hog driver's lingo it "went stupid." It dove straight down, right into a U.S. Marine APC that was engaged in the Battle of Khafji. Seven Marines died that night and two were hurt. It was a tragedy that greatly saddened the community. About thirty-six hours later they almost suffered another.

It was day fifteen of the air campaign when two of the Cajuns, Maj. Jim Rose (an American Airlines pilot) and Maj. Sonny Rasar (a pilot for Delta Airlines), were launched to hit the Tawakalnas. They were going to fly only one mission before recovering at KKMC for fuel because they were then going out to Al Jouf where they would remain and hunt Scuds.

---

* Generally, the higher an airplane flies, the less fuel it uses.

The day did not work out the way they planned. Major Jim Rose tells what happened.

"When the Iraqis came down [to Khafji] with so many tanks, it was a little embarrassing that they could mount an attack of such strength. They paid the price, of course, but we felt that we should have beat them up more. We were already having doubts about some of our actual BDA because we were dropping bombs from 10,000, an altitude where you really can't tell whether your target is intact, already destroyed, or even if it's a decoy—which we came to realize they were using a lot of. I felt, personally, that we were attacking many dead targets. There had been rumblings—talk among the pilots that we had a problem and that we needed to use lower-altitude tactics. I think the Khafji thing made everybody realize that, because on the morning we left, we got approval to go lower—to a minimum attack altitude of 4,000 feet.

"Sonny and I went to our planned target, which was more artillery positions. We found quite a few of them spaced out in revetments. We made one pass each, dropped our six Mark-82s close, and got nothing remarkable—no big secondaries. We did an orbit after coming off and at about 5 miles south of our original target I picked up a military vehicle with a canvas back driving high speed across the desert. I went ahead and called in with a gun attack and I left Rasar high to cover me. At that time I really wanted to get down lower to see what was there. I dived down on top of it at 400 knots plus and gunned it from the rear. It was the classic World War II thing; I just walked the bullets up the back and set it on fire. I came off of that pass and nothing was happening [no defensive fire]. I had a lot of energy and climbed to gain some altitude. I didn't feel threatened at the time; there was nothing on my RWR, nor any AAA. As I looked down to where my truck was heading, I could see a bunch of old trucks in disrepair that they were putting in revetments—I could see that somebody else would be wasting time dropping Mark-82s on decoys. I was thinking at the time, 'Okay, file that one.' Then I noticed an assembly of three or four vehicles in a kind of pattern, not random. I thought they might be something significant so I repositioned for an attack.

"My airplane had a problem with the SAS [stability augmentation system]. It kicked off during the gun attack; the plane wandered and I walked bullets everywhere. It wasn't a good pass. I was cursing the airplane and thinking that I needed to climb. I came inside [put my eyes in the cockpit], reengaged the SAS, and right at that time I felt and heard the impact of something hitting my airplane.

"It was a loud pop—nothing catastrophic—just a big pop and I felt something pulse the flight controls. The noise seemed to have originated from aft left, but I wasn't really that sure. It didn't jolt the aircraft; I just felt it through the flight control system. I said, 'Geez, what is that?' Immediately I got a master caution light on the warning panel. I looked down on the enunciator light panel and I'm trying to determine what was wrong. For some reason it didn't register that I had been hit by enemy fire. I was half thinking, 'Did a round blow up in the gun or did the airplane suffer some mechanical malfunction? I hadn't seen any fire come up, no threats, no warning. I still felt comfortable at that stage. I looked down and my left hydraulic reservoir low light was on. The pressure light was on as well and the SAS lights were on again. I had a lot of lights coming on. I thought, 'Oh, Jesus, I have to get out of here,' I checked my engines but they seemed okay. And right then a bunch more lights lit up. It was all my right hydraulic system going out. All this is within a couple of seconds—I hadn't even contacted my wingman yet. And I'm going, 'Holy geez, the airplane won't fly much longer with both hydraulic systems out.' Then I reached over real quickly and threw it into manual reversion.

"In manual reversion I had an unpowered rudder, which means it requires a heavier force to operate. I had pitch, but it's unpowered as well, very heavy. In the manual mode you are flying a control tab that is on the elevator; you are flying the tab that, in turn, flies the elevator. It is very susceptible to changes in your power setting. If you run the throttles up, it is really going to try and climb on you; if you pull the power back, the nose will drop like a rock. You have to force it around; you have to really fight with it. You don't do anything quickly—the aileron takes about four to ten seconds to shift over to the unpowered mode, so you don't have much lateral control during the transition, so you don't have much lateral control. For lateral control I always thought I could use the rudders, but I found out that it isn't as easy to do as it is with a swept-wing airplane [he had flown F-4s prior to joining the Air Force Reserve]. And at that time I didn't know that my left rudder was disconected—that I had only right rudder.

"I decided I was okay for the moment and called Sonny on Fox Mike radio. I told him I thought I had been hit and I'm trying to climb out and that he should go cover. I didn't get a positive response; he was giving me some superfluous information about coming south and this and that. I'm going, 'Look, I've been hit; I'm getting it worked out,' and he again seemed to respond somewhat casually. Finally, I came on the Uniform radio and said, 'I'm in manual reversion, heading east, climbing out and have two good engines.' And he finally goes, 'Roger!' What had happened was my Fox Mike transmitter cable had been cut with shrapnel; I could hear him fine but I wasn't transmitting.

"I was heading east northeast at that point, getting the airplane in a good positive climb—I had been at about 5,500 when I was hit.

Sonny knew something was wrong because I stayed down there too long, and he had seen some puffy, white smoke underneath my airplane, however no missile trail or pattern of AAA.

"He turned me south and I climbed to 15,000, feeling more comfortable but the plane would yaw as I built up airspeed so I held it down to a blistering 200 knots. I was beginning to get a lot of RWR indications but luckily nothing came up, and after we crossed the border, Sonny came up and gave me a full debrief on the damage. The left rudder was just fluttering in the airstream and the left horizontal stabilizer leading edge was messed up—that was causing drag and yaw. Also the whole bottom section of the left aft fuselage was shot up pretty bad, with skin torn off, and there were shrapnel holes in the left engine cowling. He also saw fluid streaming from the right wing and we started worrying about a fuel leak, but then it seemed that internal fuel indicators were normal.

"We flew directly to KKMC and the SOF [Supervisor of Flying] in the tower read the checklist for a manual reversion landing. The one thing that stuck in my mind—and I'm glad he made a big point of it—was that the nose will drop abruptly as the aircraft enters ground effect [when there is an air cushion between the wings and the ground] and that I should fly a flat approach. You don't want to come in steep; you want to drag it in with the nose already in more of a flared position so you don't have to worry about the lack of pitch authority.

"I did a right base to final, turning for the west runway, and I was thankful that the 20-knot wind was straight on because a crosswind would have been a disaster. With the sluggish controls I could not have handled crosswind gusts—it would have been like trying to handle one of those four-wheel luggage carts where all four wheels want to go in a different direction.

"I put it on a long 10-mile final, did one last control check, lowered the gear manually, got three green lights, checked the tires—they looked okay. Then they asked me if I wanted to jettison my Mavericks. It certainly would have been appropriate to do and maybe in hindsight I probably should have—the Maverick could have been dangerous if the gear malfunctioned. But I felt comfortable, the airplane is flying solid, my gear is down, the wind is good, the weather is good. Also, I was feeling badly about the airplane—I was the first one to experience major damage and that was notoriety that I didn't want. Anyhow, I kept the Mavericks, continued the approach at the appropriate single-engine speed—160 knots—came in over the threshold and right at the flare the nose really wanted to drop. I pulled back on the stick and the nose still hit solidly. It was a major effort on my part to get the stick back and if I hadn't been keyed to that by the SOF, the nose would have really bounced hard and could have led to much worse things. Now I was rolling, rolling, rolling down the runway, no regular brakes—just an emergency brake accumulator which is good for one shot—you can't pump the brakes because you'll deplete the pressure. I began to lose patience so I said, 'Okay, let's stop this thing,' and hit the emergency brakes and stopped after about 5,000 feet—not much longer than our normal roll.

"When I got out and we checked the plane, we felt sure that a heat-seeking missile—an SA-16 or SA-13 or even an SA-9 had impacted and exploded under the left empennage just under the tail section. It ripped up the leading edge of the left horizontal stabilizer, threw a lot of shrapnel into the fuselage directly under the engines, cut both hydraulic lines and had even frayed the elevator cables, although they held together. Also a piece of shrapnel had hit the right Maverick next to the warhead—that would have been cute if it had cooked—and the bottom part of the left rudder was badly damaged and the actuator rod that connects it was gone.

"The design of the A-10 saved me. The dual rudders, the backup manual reversion system, the armor shielding around the engine, the spacing of the cables for the flight controls, the way the gear falls down into the airstream and locks, the big straight wing that flies solid at 160 knots—all those things made the difference. But even with all that, that landing in manual reversion was the hardest thing I've ever done in an airplane."

Major Jim Rose was the first A-10 pilot to make a manual reversion landing under combat conditions. There were others to follow, and one would die in the process.

# 13

## Luck Runs Out

*"Out of all my missions I only flew one that the plane was designed for and I was trained to do. Flexibility was the key to our success."*

—*Capt. Eric Offill*

General Glosson kept after them. "I need that division 50 percent combat ineffective."

The Colonels kept replying. "Sir, we can't say for sure what we have done. We think we have killed a lot of things up there but they are clever. They're using a lot of decoys and they may have a lot of stuff camouflaged."

Finally, after the Tawakalna Division had been pounded for three days, General Glosson was fed up. The images from the fancy satellites were not adequate. And the RF-4s he sent screaming over the division came back with photo evidence that was inconclusive. What he needed were some eyeballs over the target. He needed eyeballs from pilots who were used to using them. He needed some Hog drivers.

"I replied, 'You want us to do what?'" said Colonel Sharpe when he received the call. "They wanted us to do armed recce [reconnaissance] missions like they flew behind the lines in World War II. I hated to send those kids up there, but I understood Glosson's problem. He had the Army breathing down his neck; that division had to be attrited before they could move in. So all we could do was salute smartly and say, 'We'll do it.'"

Colonel Sawyer was equally disturbed by the idea, but he was cautiously optimistic because, "We had done a lot of reading about the enemy—all those studies that came out on the Iran-Iraq War. And one thing that was clear was that once the Iraqis experienced something new—something they didn't expect to happen—they would stop whatever they were doing. There didn't appear to be any initiative in that army; everything seemed to be controlled at the top. So what I was hoping was that when our guys came in low over them that it would surprise them, and that it would take them a while to get their act together."

The next morning, February first, the pilots of two four-ship flights of Flying Tigers went in to brief at three fifteen. Captain Ralph Hansen, who flew as number three in one of the four-ships, wrote in his diary later that day, "We had to go to the Wing Headquarters . . . to be briefed by Colonel Lyon and Colonel Sawyer about our 'special' mission today. So I knew something was up . . . It would appear that we're not getting the kind of information we need from the RF-4s and other recce planes and satellites . . . so with all of our fancy equipment, it comes down to A-10 pilots flying low altitude using nothing but their eyeballs to identify what is what . . . that kind of goes against common sense, and didn't make us feel too comfortable—but it was our mission for today. I could tell our leadership wasn't very comfortable about sending us out on this mission, but they had their marching orders, too. So off we went. Some of the guys were *really* upset about all this . . . there were a *lot* of negative waves in the van on the way to the squadron . . ."

But they went and they did the job. Captain Scott Kelly, who led the first four-ship that was to recce the southern section of the division, describes their action.

"I was leading; [1st Lt.] Steve Olmos was number two; numbers three and four were [Capt.] Ralph Hansen and [1st Lt.] Eric Stoll. On the way up we got diverted to the MarCent [Marine Central Command] area where we held while other fighters were working one of their targets. Finally, after telling them we had an important mission, they released us and we flew on up to our target. Numbers three and four were briefed to hold high while Steve and I were going down low—to 4,000 feet, or even a little lower, which was right in the heart of the AAA. When we got there, Steve was flying wedge on me, and we dived down from high altitude, built up all the speed that we could and flew over them. What we found was that they had a lot of targets down there, but they also had old beat up pickup trucks and other junk in some of the revetments, and they had camouflaged a lot of stuff. From higher altitudes you would think they had a lot of stuff in there. We did one pass, caught a little bit of AAA, and then went back and did another pass and that's when we started getting a lot of it. There was stuff coming out everywhere.

I remember looking back and it was like a snake [coming up]. With the A-10 you're trying to get away and gain altitude at the same time, but if you jink, you are really going to lose your energy. That wouldn't be bad if it was a normal front-line type of thing where we could bug out low and get back out of the threat. But when you're 85 miles deep into enemy territory . . . "

Captain Mark Koechle, who led the other four-ship flight said, "Because [Capt.] Phil Fichthorn was a former FAC, and because [Capt.] Jim Glasgow has a real good eye, it was briefed that they would fly at 3,000 feet over the northern part of the division while [Capt.] Pete Edgar and I were to stay high and cover them. The way it turned out, we got diverted to the MarCent area and held there for quite a while before they released us. Then, when we finally got up there and when Phil and Jim went in—they actually got down to 2,000 feet—it was fifteen minutes before we saw any AAA. They S-turned over the division and found that about half the stuff down there was good targets. The other stuff included old farm equipment, plywood decoys, old pickups and barrels of oil. Then Jim saw a truck moving and rolled in on it with the gun. He hit it but three guys piled out and dove into the ditch, and just as he was pulling off, Phil yelled that he was taking fire. From above we could see his jet completely surrounded by flashes and smoke from AAA. Then they shot an SA-7 at him and he yelled, 'I've got a missile coming at me, somebody take them out.' But we were not in a position to roll in on them and we just watched as he released a couple of flares and saw the missile decoy on them. Then Phil rolled back around and strafed where the missile came from. Then Pete and I dove down and dropped our Mark-82s on some other AAA that had opened on Jim. After that, we destroyed some more stuff with our Mavericks."

Because both flights had been delayed by the diversion to the MarCent area, neither one of them had enough fuel to do what they felt was a thorough job of reconnoitering. So they went back, although 1st Lt. Steve Olmos in Captain Kelly's flight had to abort his takeoff on the return flight. Both flights made repeated passes over the division, dodged AAA, and Captain Hansen, who decided to put a Maverick into one of the camouflaged bunkers, got spectacular secondary explosions and assumed that he made his first tank kill of the war.

That afternoon, back at King Fahd, the pilots of the two recce flights reported to Wing Headquarters again and briefed Colonel Sharpe and his DO, Colonel Haden. They spread out their 1:50,000 map and described in detail all of the junk and burned-out hulks they had found, and they tried to pinpoint the camouflaged targets that needed to be hit. Finally, after several minutes of discussion,

Colonel Sharpe, who had flown one of the missions over the Tawakalna, asked each of them to estimate the percentage of attrition based upon what they had seen. Some said 50 percent; others said more; none said less. Trying to reach a consensus, Sharpe got them to agree that 50 percent was the safest and most probable estimate, and that was what was reported to Riyadh.

The Warthogs were really on a roll now. They had gone through sixteen days of combat, flying dangerous, behind-the-lines missions—missions that the plane was never intended to do, and after every one of them, the planes all came home. At this stage in the war the pilots weren't celebrating their good luck, but they were beginning to think that maybe combat flying wasn't that dangerous after all.

Then their luck ran out, and the shock of their loss sent sobering tremors throughout the community.

It was February second, day seventeen of the war, and two Vanguards, Capt. Dale Storr and 1st Lt. Eric Miller, were tasked as a two-ship flight to a kill box near Al Jaber airfield in southern Kuwait. They launched before dawn and as they crossed into Kuwait, they were unable to contact ABCCC. Hearing that Nail 36 (Capt. Sean Kavanaugh) had viable targets, they contacted him and, with his guidance, expended their bombs and Mavericks on artillery and armor. While in the area Storr spotted a large, vehicle assembly area that he would keep in mind if they ran out of other targets.

They returned to KKMC, refueled and rearmed, then were sent on alert up to the MarCent area and told to contact Combat 11, a Marine FAC flying an F/A-18. Storr called the FAC, couldn't reach him, then called AWACS and ABCCC, neither of whom had heard from him, either. After ten minutes of waiting, Storr called ABCCC, asked for another target, and was sent to a suspected Scud location near Al Jaber airfield.

They didn't find the Scud, but were in sight of the target area they had hit on their first mission. Storr called ABCCC, got permission to go on to that area, and both of them unloaded bombs and Mavericks on some warehouse-type buildings. The AAA increased dramatically after that, and remembering the truck park he had seen on the first mission, Storr went over there, rolled in and strafed the trucks. As he pulled off to the left, he saw his bullets hit long. He told Miller to stay high and cover him, that he was going to take a "penalty lap" to the north and roll in on them again. Miller watched, saw him roll in from the north and saw his bullets tear into the parked trucks. "Good hits, good secondaries," Miller yelled enthusiastically.

Storr pulled off to the left again, and when Miller took his eyes off the exploding trucks, he saw what looked like a cloud of dirt under Storr's airplane. Then, in agony he watched as it began a rolling, out-of-control descent. Miller called repeatedly, first trying to get a response, then, after hearing nothing, and as the plane spiraled into a steep descent, he yelled repeatedly, "Storrman [Storr's nickname]; eject, eject, eject!"

But there was no response and Miller watched, horrified, as the plane struck the ground and erupted into a fireball. Though watching closely, he saw no chute, and as he dropped down to fly cover over the crash site, he tried repeatedly to contact Storr on Guard, which Storr would have used on his survival radio if he had been alive. But he heard nothing and saw nothing but the huge fireball that continued to erupt below him. He then called ABCCC and AWACS, continued to fly cover, and when he saw some trucks heading toward the site, he went down and strafed them. By that time, Nail 55, Capt. Mike Beard, who was working some nearby targets, came over to search and fly cover, and Capt. Eric Salomonson and 1st Lt. John Marks, sitting on SAR alert at KKMC, had been scrambled by AWACS and were heading for the scene. In the meantime, Miller, who was running low on fuel, went for a tanker, then came back and flew over the area until he had to refuel again, then was ordered home.

Eric Miller was killed after the war in a midair collision, so the rest of the story is told by Lt. Darren Hansen, Miller's roommate and closest friend in the squadron.

"Eric flew back alone, and he had to be in hell. He was extremely sincere, honest, sensitive, kind, and straightforward—just a great person. As a wingman your total goal is to protect your lead—to watch out for him and make sure nothing gets in. It had to be a horrible feeling, flying home alone, and I know from our later talks, that he felt guilty—that he felt that somehow he had let Storrman down.

"He flew in late that afternoon—he had to be ordered away from the scene—but before he landed we only knew that one of them, call sign UZI 11 or UZI 12, had been shot down. We all waited anxiously for more word. Roger Clark was Storrman's closest friend and I was Eric's, and it was difficult when we found out that Storrman and not Eric was the one. I breathed a sigh of relief, but then felt badly when I realized what Roger was going through.

"They met Eric at the plane, whisked him off to the WOC to talk to the colonels, then to the special Ops folks who needed information to plan a rescue if it was needed. In the meantime, Fish [Captain Salomonson] and Karl [First Lieutenant Marks] who had been sent up on the SAR, came in and said that all they could see was the engine pods sticking up—that the plane went in nose first, and that there had been no sign of Storrman—no sign of a chute, and no communications.

"I waited in the squadron and when Eric came in, I gave him a big hug. And I think, if I hadn't held him he might have fallen to the floor. That's how badly he was hurting. [Capt.] Tim Saffold, his flight commander [who had been his wing commander at the Air Force Academy], and the squadron commander, Lieutenant Colonel Renuart, were also there and we did our best to comfort him. He was tough and hung in there, and it is incredible the amount of support he got from everybody. That night we all got together and talked about it—said things about Storrman. Colonel Sawyer came by the hootch and wept as he told about losing his own son and how losing Storrman was like losing another one. Then we went over to the chapel tent about ten, said a few prayers and had some quiet time, then went back to the hootch. So many people came in to shake Eric's hand and to reassure him that it was not his fault. One guy had even written a note and left it on his bed while we were gone.

"We didn't talk about the accident for quite a while—we just tried to let him relax. The next couple of days they had me stay with him and then he opened up and let it all out. Then, when nothing more was heard about Storrman, we had a memorial service out in front of the squadron. The chaplain gave a talk, a couple of nurses and a flight doc sang some hymns, Renuart spoke, then Sawyer gave a wonderful talk, emphasizing that we should never give up hope. It was really sad for all of us because we didn't see any reason to hope. Storrman was gone and he was really missed in the squadron—he was a tall guy, six-four, a fun-loving bachelor, drove a Corvette—just a great fighter pilot and a friend of everybody."

Storrman, when he hears that story today, just winces and shakes his head because it is a poignant experience to be considered dead and then brought back to life, and it is especially painful now that his devoted wingman, who grieved so deeply, is dead. But that was in the future; let Storrman now tell his side of the story.*

"I came off that strafing pass and as I was pulling, I heard Eric saying, 'Good hits! Good secondaries!' As I looked back I could see trucks blowing off and I could see secondary explosions and smoke coming from the trucks. But when I pulled off—being the stupid pilot that I am, I pulled off again to the left, as I had just done

---

* Colonel Sawyer had urged them all to maintain hope during the memorial service because of a highly classified report he had received that day that a "tall A-10 pilot had been captured and taken to Baghdad." However, because of the classification, he could not share the report with the rest of the troops.

before. I was in a climbing left turn, about 30 degrees of bank, 5 degrees nose high, passing through about 10,000 feet. I had some pretty good energy and I was looking for Eric when something hit the airplane. I never saw it and Eric never saw it. It felt like a 50,000-pound sledge hammer just came up and hit the bottom of the plane. It was a real sharp, violent type of impact. The airplane didn't depart; it just kept on flying but it transitioned to a smooth right-hand turn, just like all the flight control surfaces had streamlined but were trimmed for a right-hand turn. The stick wouldn't do anything. There was no resistance in the stick—it was really loose like there was nothing left. I looked inside. I still had two good engines and I saw the hydraulic pressure and I thought, 'Man, what's wrong, what's wrong?' As I noticed the airplane rolling over I made a radio call on Fox Mike. I said, 'Hey Bolt [Eric's nickname], I'm hit and I'm hit bad.' He didn't say anything to me that I heard. The airplane rolled over and the first thing I did was to reach for the manual reversion switch. By this time the airplane was almost upside down and I was kind of hanging by the straps so I had a hard time fighting my way over to the emergency flight control panel. I did eventually get it into manual reversion and I sat there and waited for it to work. Before I did that I remember looking out to my left—I was looking for Eric and I slammed the stick to the left to stop the roll and I saw that the aileron didn't move. I knew then that this was really bad.

"The airplane kept going down and down. I gave the manual reversion as long as I could, but it just kept on rolling and doing barrel rolls all the way toward the ground. Eric thought I was doing wing flashes going after another target. But what it was . . . the airplane was rolling over and over . . . whatever hit me just severed all the flight control cables—at least, I lost my aileron and elevator response and I don't know if I had rudder authority, although it wouldn't have done me any good. As the airplane continued spiraling to the ground, I did the bold face [flight manual emergency control procedure] for out-of-control recovery, brought the throttles back to idle, neutralized the controls, and that did nothing. The airplane continued to spiral down.

"During the time all this was going on, I heard Eric call on Uniform. He said, 'Storrman, recover, recover, recover!' He thought I was going after another target. Then he yelled, 'Storrman, eject, eject, eject!' I was still too high I didn't want to eject yet. I was still trying the out-of-control procedure—trying to isolate the speed brakes from the flaps, from the hydraulic systems. I was trying anything I could think of but nothing did any good. Finally, I just happened to glance up and the ground was getting really close and so I decided to jump out of it. I got hit above 10,000 and probably took it below 2,000 because I was only in the chute maybe twenty seconds.

"It was really, really quick. I was upside down and pinned to one side when I saw the ground coming up. I fought the negative G's, forced myself into a good seat position and pulled the handles. It went real smooth after that. The canopy blew off and white smoke came up between my knees. My head got kicked down as I went up the rail and I saw my kneeboard get blown off by the blast of air. The canopy went tumbling end over end. I saw the stuff that I had written on it and I remember thinking, 'Oh, gee, if they find that they will know everything.' I went tumbling end over end, and heard the parachute punch out behind me and heard it open. I forced my head back and saw the last half of it fill up and inflate and thought, 'Oh, geez, sweet.' I never thought a seat would work for me but this one worked flawlessly.

"The first thing I realized when I was hanging in the chute was how loud the war was. You never hear it from inside the airplane; the war is pretty quiet, pretty sterile. Hanging in that chute it sounded like every single gun in Kuwait was pointed at me and I could hear them all going off. I could hear bombs exploding, guns going off and then the next thing I heard was the airplane blow up underneath me. It was like, 'Oh, no.' I looked down and there was this huge fireball coming up at me. I started climbing up the risers, my right riser, just pulling it as hard as I could. Fortunately, it started to work and I went through the smoke cloud.

"I didn't go through the fireball. I was in the smoke for about five seconds. It was really warm and really thick, and I couldn't see anything. Then, all of a sudden, I popped right out of it and looked down and I was about ten seconds from hitting the ground. I let go of the riser and it gave me a little jerk. I started doing the drill—feet together, eyes on the horizon, don't look at the ground, don't look at the ground, then, 'Oh, shit, I looked at the ground.' I got real lucky. My landing was terrible but it was in the only sand dune within 50 yards of me. The wind was blowing pretty good and I kind of spun myself around, got out of the parachute, but got it tangled in my mask so I threw my helmet off and started running to get my hit-and-run bag [of emergency supplies]. I couldn't believe I wasn't hurt, that there was nothing wrong with me. I picked up my hit-and-run bag—I knew the Iraqis were coming to get me. While I was hanging in the chute, I could see a truck coming from the truck park that I had just strafed—it was coming to get me. I grabbed the bag and tried to get the radio out but realized that the closest one I had was the one in my survival vest. I grabbed that one and started trying to talk Bolt down to get me or to put bullets on this truck. I made three calls to Bolt, 'I need some bullets on this truck; I need them right now!' Got nothing. There was static on the radio but I didn't hear him say anything to me. I thought, 'Geez, he's turned Guard off.' I said, 'Bolt, I need some bullets right now! They are coming to get me. Too late, Bolt, they got me.' Just as they were walking up I threw the radio on the ground.

"What happened was that it was the yellow radio used for training and it was on a training frequency, not 243.0 which is the Guard frequency. So no one ever heard me. If he had heard me and could have gotten that truck, there may have been a chance because there wasn't anyone else around for a long ways. I thought about that a bunch. He would have had to kill everyone in that truck, and there were six of them, all with submachine guns. If any of them had lived, it would have been me with my six-shooter against that Iraqi with a submachine gun.

"They got out of the truck and roughed me up. Some of them spoke English. I couldn't believe they didn't just kill me right there. They slammed me on the ground and they slapped me. They hit me with a gun in the back of my head and in the gut. They slapped me around and pushed me into things, but I don't really consider that being beat up. That's just harassment.

"The first place they took me was to a bunker. They frisked me down and took my gun. The first thing they asked me for was some food—'Hey, you got any food, mister, you have any food?' I said, 'No, I don't have any food.' I did have a roll of Life Savers on me that they took, and later, on the way up to Baghdad, they offered me one.

"While they were sitting there frisking me down, I was only about 200 feet from my airplane. I could feel the heat, and I could hear the 30mm cooking off and it was like, 'Holy shit, you guys know what this stuff is?' Didn't bother them. It sounded like the rest of the war. It was bam, bam, just cooking off. I was getting worried, especially if one of those HEI [high explosive incendiary] rounds came around. God, you guys don't know what the hell this is. Then, all of a sudden a Maverick cooks off with the LAU-117 [mounting rail] still on it. It was the one I had left. Luckily the damned thing arced up and away from us, and when it impacted the ground it didn't detonate. When they saw that thing it was like, 'Okay, pick me up, put me in the truck and we were out of there.

"I still wonder why they didn't kill me. I had just strafed them; I had just put some bullets down where they had their truck park. I can't believe they didn't just come up to me and say, 'You son of a bitch,' and then kill me. One of them was really pissed. He beat me up more than any of them. He was the one who finally, when we got to the truck—I wasn't being the most cooperative guy in the world—got mad and hit me in the back of the head. I fell down, then he got me in the stomach. They basically loaded me up and threw me in the truck, but he got yelled at. I wasn't paying a whole lot of attention but it sounded like there was a lot of yelling going on after that and I think he was getting most of it. They were conscripts. They had no rank insignia and their boots seemed to be civilian, like, 'Hey, you're going to the desert, bring something to wear.'

"The first place they took me was an infantry bunker right in the front lines. It was like a company headquarters. Then they took me farther back to a quonset-type building and I got my first interrogation. It wasn't much—name, rank, serial number, airplane you were flying—and they wanted my home address. That's the first time I really had a gun put to my head and it was from a screaming colonel. I didn't want to give him my home address and the interrogator kept asking me and asking me. I said, no, then I said the 'Geneva Convention says I don't have to do that.' They just came unglued when I told them that. One of the colonels who was sitting behind the desk started talking back and forth to the interrogator and all of a sudden the colonel just went crazy. He came jumping up—the interrogator probably told some lies about what I had been saying. The colonel comes screaming over and starts slapping me and slapping me. 'I'm not going to tell you my home address for that,' I said to myself. Then he takes his pistol out of his holster—I remember it was a nickel-plated Colt—he takes the pistol out and beats me over the side of the head with it, then cocks it and just starts screaming and screaming and screaming and shoves it right against my head. The interrogator looks at me and says, 'What is your home address—better tell me before he kills you.' It was like, 'Nine-twenty Twin Bridges Road, Alexandria, Louisiana.' I was pretty scared. I wasn't really ready for that. It was just sudden, out of the blue. But that was it. That was all he wanted to know and that was all he asked me. And I was thinking, 'You morons, I probably would have told you a ton of stuff, but you quit. Okay, I can play this game.' But I quit using the John Wayne technique from there on."

Captain Storr was hustled off to Baghdad and the interrogation he has described was child's play compared to the agony he was destined to suffer. However, that story will be related later, when he is joined by another unlucky Hog driver. In the meantime it is time to move the story 300 miles westward, to Cajun West.

# 14

# The Wild West Show

*"The way Colonel Efferson ran the operation out there . . . it was like going back to fighter days. All of us who went out there begged and begged to be left out there."*

—Capt. Tim Saffold

They woke them at four in the morning and, despite the unknown flora prospering on the floor and walls of their tiny shower, they reluctantly performed the American's ritual morning tribute to cleanliness.

After forcing down a cold MRE and getting a quick intel brief, they launched into the sunrise to begin their first mission into the desolate, far reaches of western Iraq. When they returned after three plus hours, they sat in the cockpit with engines running while being refueled and rearmed. During this time they would switch used piddle packs for fresh ones, take on another MRE and a new bottle of water, and swap intel information. Then they launched again, headed back up into Iraq, did whatever they were tasked to do, and returned for another engines-running combat turn. Then they would do it again, and as the sun was setting—but sometimes after dark— they would land and crawl stiffly out of the plane, their feet asleep, their bottoms sore, their backs aching and their brains somnolent.

Said Col. Bob Efferson, the CO at Al Jouf, "Those guys were beat when they got out of that cockpit in the evening. I got so I would do an eyeball check on them and there was nobody there sometimes. But we'd feed them another MRE, lay them down on a cot, and wake them up at four the next morning and out the door they would go. It was a lot tougher conditions than we ever experienced in

Southeast Asia and I began to worry that their fatigue was going to catch up with them and cause somebody to get hurt or killed."

From the standpoint of the pilots, Colonel Efferson was right; it was tough flying. But the pilots loved it, absolutely loved it, and more than one of them asked their commanders to leave them out there. "I'll do a better job; I know where everything is; I know where they're likely to hide the Scuds; I can tell if they've moved so much as a barrel; I'll be a lot more effective than some new guy you send out here—some guy who'll take two or three days just learning the territory."

Certainly it wasn't the accommodations that attracted them. For a long while they slept on hard cots, without a pillow, and, on the days when Colonel Efferson flew a late afternoon mission and couldn't cook stew or jambalaya, they dined on MREs three times a day.

And even though their friends and commanders joshed them and accused them of wanting to stay out west because of the reduced threat from AAA in that region, they maintained that that had little to do with their motivation.

"It was like a family out there," said Capt. Tim Saffold. To Colonel Efferson and [Lieutenant] Colonel Wilson, we were their 'boys.' They really cared about us—they showed so much concern. Both of them had what you might call 'magnetic personalities.' And they had a wealth of experience. Efferson flew Thuds in Southeast Asia and Growth [Greg] Wilson was a Raven FAC flying O-1s in Laos. They were always calm and cool and they had, I guess what you would call a fatherly image for us. They did everything they could to make us comfortable out there. And at the end of the day we would all sit down together, often over something like Efferson's Cajun cabbage stew, and swap stories of what we had done that day, what tactics we had used, what we might do tomorrow—those kinds of things. There was just a unique camaraderie out there that made it seem like we were a part of an elite group. Definitely those guys made us feel like we wanted to do 200 percent for them."

Their primary job out at Al Jouf was to fly into western Iraq and search for Scuds that were being fired into Israel. The Scuds were doing very little actual damage, but the political consequences of *any* missile striking Israeli territory were enormous. So they went out, day after day, and searched diligently for them.

Finding the Scuds was a difficult problem because of the vastness of the area that was within range of Israel. However, the Scud and its truck launcher were too heavy to travel just anywhere in the desert. So the search problem was somewhat simplified because the Scuds were mostly confined to roadside locations—and there weren't all that many roads out in western Iraq.

The major road out there was the four-lane, Baghdad to Amman, Jordan, highway. Various intelligence sources, including American and British Special Forces teams inserted into the area, had identified certain stretches of that highway as the main location of the launches. The problem was that the missiles were fueled and launched at night, then the launcher was driven off the highway into any of the hundreds of huge culverts under the highway—culverts large enough to handle massive flows of water that resulted from occasional monsoonlike rains.

The pilots found some of the Scuds near the highway in the early days of the war. Later, as they started to return without results, they were ordered to fire into the culverts. Some did that with EO Mavericks. Those missiles could lock on targets that were heavily contrasted—in this case the black shadow inside the culvert contrasted against the bright, outside background. Out of frustration a few of them also swooped low enough to fire their gun into some of the culverts. But they soon gave up on both of these tactics. The problem was that when they did fire a Maverick or their gun into one of the culverts, they would not see any evidence of a kill even if they hit something. The Scud missiles themselves were just hollow tubes before they were fueled. And, unless the pilots hit the gas tank of the truck launcher, there was no way of knowing if one had been struck.

Another trick of the Iraqis was to hide the Scuds under Bedouin tents. Said Lt. Col. Greg Wilson, "The Bedouins used these, long brown tents, with white and beige stripes on them. They were about 30 feet long and that just happens to be the length of a Scud missile. This ended up being a problem for us because we didn't want to harm those people. But we learned that when they [the tents] were used to hide Scuds they would be organized and arrayed in a geometric pattern—in a kind of circle. Also, there would be pickups and tow vehicles, and when you looked real closely—I used binoculars— you could often see that they had dug some gun pits down there.

"The real Bedouin tents would not be like that. The real Bedouins would typically also have little truck gardens and you could see other signs of agriculture—water holes, livestock, water trucks, etc. Even then, knowing all that, it was hard to go in and destroy them thinking that you might be killing friendly people. One day Hulk [Lt. Col. Larry McCaskill] and I found just such an array and took it out. Later, we looked at the film, frame by frame, and confirmed what we had hit; we saw real good imagery of Scud missiles. We took out six of them that were in that one array."

But the Scud attacks on Israel continued, and although there were fewer of them and the Israelis now had American Patriot missile defense teams on their soil, the pilots remained under tremendous pressure to find and destroy Iraq's remaining Scuds. And, in general, they were successful, especially after they started ranging north of the Amman-Baghdad highway, up near the Syrian border. But Scud hunting was hard, frustrating work. It required long, long hours of tedious searching. Many pilots had begun using binoculars, which increased their fatigue because the vibration of the enlarged images caused eyestrain. Still, on an individual basis, the rewards for all of those hours of searching were few and far between. Several of the pilots flew fifteen to eighteen missions on their tour out there without ever seeing a Scud.

It wasn't all tedium, however, thanks to pilots like the Cajun, Maj. Greg Durio, who in peacetime is a Delta pilot, and who, before that, was in the first operational squadron of A-10s. Durio made a discovery that eased the frustration of all the pilots.

Said Durio, "I was tasked, along with wingman [Capt.] Ed Kinney, to fly way up into northwest Iraq to destroy a radar site that the Iraqis had rebuilt. We launched, and without tankering, struggled up to 30,000 feet so we would have enough fuel to get there and back. At that altitude and with the weight we carried, we were hanging up there just above stall speed, but we got to the target coordinates okay. The only problem was that there was an almost solid undercast from 10 to 14,000 feet and we could not see the target when our INS showed that we were over it. But we orbited and finally found a hole we could dive through. And as we were descending, we immediately saw what looked like dozens and dozens of bunkers beneath us. They were surrounded by fencing with towers interspersed along the fencing. We did not see any gun pits or any missile sites, and we were receiving no electronic threats from that area. We saw all this, but we immediately left and headed northwest, out toward our primary target area. When we got there, we scoured the area and found absolutely nothing. Finally, it was time to go home, and we decided to take another look at the bunkered area we had seen.

"As we approached, it became obvious that this was something very major—there were dozens of bunkers. It was a very dense area like a labyrinth of interconnected bunkers. They had tried to camouflage some and others had a metallic covering over the top. We could see that several of them had what looked like armored vehicles in them, and because of that, we deemed that it was a military target and started attacking. Immediately, we started seeing secondary explosions, and as we continued attacking, we thought we were receiving ground fire because the secondary explosions were causing projectiles and flaming pieces of material to shoot out toward us.

It was a heavy, overcast day, sort of dark, and it was easy to imagine that we were receiving AAA fire. But we expended our ordnance until fuel became critical, then we started motoring home.

"As we egressed to the south—at medium altitude because we didn't want to get highlighted near the cloud bases—we learned that what we had attacked was only the very northern part of what was a massive bunkered area. The whole thing was at least a mile wide from east to west, and was 7 or 8 miles long from north to south. There were various types of fencing, and various types of guard towers. Also there were many types of bunkers—some had lots of earth over them, and some were very expensive-looking, like the nuclear storage bunkers that you see in the States. I would guess that there were thirty to forty of the expensive-looking bunkers and maybe a hundred of the smaller types. In addition, there was a matrix of thirty to forty beige-colored metallic warehouses, not camouflaged or bermed or protected in any way. And as it turned out, on that mission we only saw less than half of the total stuff that was stored in that area.

"When we got south of the highway [Baghdad-Amman] we started climbing to save fuel and we were on the radio talking to other guys heading up on Scud hunts. Probably from our tone of voice they could tell we were in awe of how big and how lucrative the target was in a military sense. Those guys also hit the area when they quit hunting Scuds and we, ourselves, returned to attack it at the end of two more Scud-hunting missions we flew that day. We told intelligence when we first landed that we had found a target that would be ideal for B-52 strikes, but as far as I know, they were never used on it.

"That night we sat around talking about that big area with the commanders and the pilots who had hit it that day. Fighter pilots always have to give something a name, and as we joked about the area having anything that anybody could want for a target—just something for everybody—the name "Home Depot" just came up. I don't remember who first used that name, but it stayed with us. For the rest of the war, Home Depot was a place to hit on the way home if you had any ordnance left after your Scud hunt."

Captains Paul Rastas and Brad Whitmire, two Vultures who had been sent to Al Jouf for the week, were the first two to hit Home Depot the next day. Said Rastas, "We went for the north part where all the revetments were and it was like somebody had taken a big sewing needle and made a huge tapestry—there were just hundreds of these revetments, all interconnected, and they all had something in them. It was probably a 10-square-mile area just of revetments. There were no threats that we saw in the area, so we started attacking, dropping bombs, firing Mavericks, and at the end, down to 4,000 feet, we emptied our guns. The explosions were amazing. Every squeeze [on the gun trigger] created an explosion. You shoot something that even looked innocent and it would start to burn, then it would explode and create a concussion like a 2,000-pound bomb.

"Later that day we were coming back north across the border of Iraq, which was about 120 miles from Home Depot, and we saw this huge explosion up there. It was incredible. Later we found out that one of the Cajuns [Capt. Bob Swain] was looking through his EO Maverick and saw the doors to this big bunker being opened. He locked on to the dark entrance, fired and the Maverick flew inside and triggered a chain of explosions. He [Saddam] really had some powerful stuff in there."

Home Depot was the first concentration of armor and explosives they found. Then they found East Tac and West Tac, two concentrations of armor near the town of Nukhayb, where the 55th Infantry Brigade was dug in to defend an important highway junction. They took those names from the East and West Tac ranges out of Nellis Air Force Base, Nevada—two of their favorite gunnery ranges.

After that, they found the "Villas" just north of Home Depot, which was a concentration of buildings with stored munitions. Then they made another huge find—a stored mass of armor and munitions larger than Home Depot. It was found by Capt. Al "Gator" Hicks and 1st Lt. Jim Schmick. Said the two of them, who were interviewed together:

*Schmick:* Gator and I were up north of Scud Alley on a special mission to help the Army but nothing came of that so we were just tooling along, looking for targets of opportunity, when we found this huge military storage site. It had two or three hundred huge trailers full of ammo, and south of that about 500 revetments, half of them full of trucks and tanks. They were in this big wash and they thought they were hidden. They were hidden from the ground, but not from us. We went over and dropped a little CBU on the ammo storage bins. It didn't take but one little bomblet to light the whole thing off—I mean, the smoke goes up to 15,000 feet.

*Hicks:* "Yeah, and it was real sporty to try and get three of them with one bomb. If you were lucky the doughnut spread of the bomblets would get one in each of them and then all you did was wait until they started lighting off.

*Schmick:* "You would watch and if one of the bomblets hit a building you would see just a little smoke or a little sparkle. You keep watching and you could see the building kind of shake, and then something cooking off inside would cause the whole thing to erupt in this gigantic explosion. You could see the smoke from those explosions from miles away.

*Hicks:* "On the way out I reported the target and there was some kidding about my name being associated with it, and after that, everybody just started calling it Hicksville."

Now they had something to look forward to each day. First they would search for Scuds until their eyes were bleary, obeying their tasking order scrupulously. But for the trip home they always tried to save some ordnance and a few hundred pounds of fuel for a stopover at one of the secondary targets. Rarely did they complete a mission without leaving something burning in Hicksville, Home Depot, East or West Tac, or the Villas.

Later, as their success in finding Scuds diminished and the relative value of the secondary targets increased, some would hit those targets first with their bombs. That way they could get rid of 3,000 pounds of weight and eliminate a lot of drag that slowed them down. Then they could go after the Scuds more efficiently with their Mavericks.

Of course, everybody wondered why Saddam had these massive storage areas out in that region. That question was never answered, although it was asked of the intel folks many times. Were they stored out there to be used in an invasion of Syria or Israel? That was the most common speculation that the pilots heard.

The Special Forces, both American and British, were actively patrolling western Iraq. They were collecting intelligence, evaluating military targets, and also searching for Scuds. One evening Capt. Dave Duncan, a Cajun and peacetime Delta pilot, had to land at Ar'Ar, a Special Forces base near the Iraqi border because Al Jouf was weathered in. Said Duncan, "Over an MRE that evening these American Special Forces guys dragged me into one of their back rooms and showed me a lot of their video. Much of that stuff is classified, but I can say that it was very impressive what kinds of things they were able to do in the dark. Then they told me how they were finding most of their Scuds.

"Basically, they said to look under power lines—that the Iraqis put them there so the Special Forces guys going in at night would tangle in the wires with their helicopters. Well, in a three-ship with [Capt.] Willie Shepard, a Cajun, and [Capt.] Greg Benjamin, a Vulture, we went clear up near the Syrian border where the Euphrates passes from Syria into Iraq. I saw on the ground a wooded area that was just like the nursery I had seen on the film the Special Forces guys had shown me. And it was just beyond a power line, so we got on the power line and started working east to west.

After following the line for 4 or 5 miles we found two Scuds and destroyed them. Then, the next day, in a three-ship with [Lt. Col. Greg] Growth Wilson and a Vulture, Capt. Colin Moffat, we got three more in that area using the same technique. So the forced stopover with the Special Forces ended up paying off big."

After the first mission, when Duncan, Shepard, and Benjamin found and destroyed the first two Scuds, Colonel Efferson relieved Shepard to give him a rest and went with the other two on the second mission, which was to take out a GCI site that had been rebuilt. As they were heading north, they got a call from AWACS that eventually allowed them to pay back the Special Forces for the good information they had received.

Said Duncan, "They had briefed us that morning that the Brit Special Forces [SAS] had put in a convoy to resupply their troops in the field, deep in Iraq. We knew this convoy was going to try and get out of there that day, that they would be following this particular wadi, and if they got in trouble, they would be calling us.

"On the way north to our assigned target we got this call from AWACS saying we were to proceed to coordinates such and such and contact a guy on the ground on a certain frequency. We knew, as soon as we heard the guy's call sign, that it was the Brits and that they were in trouble.

"We proceeded to the coordinates and started talking to a FAC and sure enough their fourteen-vehicle convoy was pinned down by an Iraqi force. They were taking automatic weapons fire, grenades, and mortar.

"From our perspective at 18,000 feet and the way the FAC was describing it, they were behind a stone wall of a destroyed building. 'They are shooting at us; can't you see them?' he asked. I'm looking around and there are a lot of buildings that are just the way he has described them, and I saw the convoy. Then, after talking the other guys' eyes on that [telling them where to look], I saw the bad guys. I could see them firing, and their position fit what this FAC on the ground was telling us.

"But I was worried," said Colonel Efferson, because those buildings weren't too far from the border and we could have made a mistake and killed some innocents. I knew the British FAC—I recognized his voice—and I asked him if he had his laser designator. He replied that he did. Then I asked him if he remembered the four-digit number we had used during a practice session back at the field. He affirmed that and said that he would put that code in his designator. I did the same for my Pave Penny, and then he aimed the laser at the buildings. It was just like aiming a flashlight, only the reflected laser energy was picked up by my Pave Penny and a green diamond on my

HUD moved over and enclosed the spot he had lased. Thus we were able to confirm that the bad guys were behind those buildings, and after that, we set up a wheel, Duncan to the west, Benjamin to the north and me to the east. Then we took turns rolling in as the FAC called the targets. We dropped Mark-82s and CBUs and the FAC is real pleased. Then he asked us to come down and strafe—only he doesn't ask for strafe, he says, 'Use the cannon, mates.' After that Benjamin and I rolled in and hammered those guys."

Captain Duncan, who was in his western orbit waiting his turn to go in, said, "I was ready to dive when I saw three vehicles coming across the desert at high speed, throwing up big rooster tails of dust behind them. Those suckers were moving.

"I go, 'Hey, Lead, you have some guys coming from the west at high speed; they look like trucks.' Efferson passes the information on and comes back telling us to keep him posted. We were down to four or five thousand feet on the gun passes and I wanted to get lower because the FAC has no idea who those guys are in the vehicles that are coming. I talked Colonel Efferson's eyes on them and they were closing the gap now pretty rapidly. Meanwhile, the Brits have their convoy moving again and they are on the east side of a ridge while the trucks coming toward them are on the west side and heading for a perfect intercept. I say, 'Colonel Efferson, I think I'll drop down and take a look at those guys; maybe I can tell if they are good or bad.' He says, 'Fine,' so I drop down out of my orbit and zoom by the first two, looking to see if they are Land Rovers or if they have the inverted 'V' or orange panels [of friendlies]. I blow by those guys, don't recognize the type of truck and Colonel Efferson is calling, 'Hey, pull off; those guys are unloading on you.' Out of the corner of my eye I see what looks like a Ford F-250 four-wheel drive pickup with a machine gun in the back shooting at me like no tomorrow.

"I pull off and tell the FAC that I don't recognize the vehicles and that they are shooting at me. The FAC said, 'Okay, we don't know who they are either, you better take them out.' Colonel Efferson rolled in from the east at that point and took the lead guy in the convoy. It was pure magic. He came in low and made sure that everything was lined up right so the bullets wouldn't ricochet toward the Brits, and as the 30mm settled on him there was this huge ball of dust enveloping the truck and a split second later it was a flaming, rolling vehicle, with a fireball coming out the top and black smoke rolling off of it.

"At that time I was lined up with the next two guys in line when the guy in the middle comes to a screeching halt just as my bullets hit his truck. There is no sign of life from him and I see that the guy in the pickup truck with the machine gun starts hauling out of there.

I start to get in on him and squeeze the gun off as he hits the accelerator and this truck starts fishtailing as my bullets cut right across the back end. I missed him but he had seen enough at that point. He went another fifty yards, stopped and I'm pulling off and looking back and see four doors open—it was a king cab-type truck—and four guys get out and start running for the hills. They didn't want any part of what they had seen and they were smart.

"We got the trucks and the Brits still had to drive out of there. But they had no further trouble and they really appreciated us saving them. After the war the regimental commander flew down to Fahd and presented Colonel Efferson with a unit plaque, which is a very rare award, and he personally thanked the guys who flew cover for them out there, and especially those who saved that convoy. So my three days of flying out of Al Jouf were very satisfying."

They were on a roll out at Al Jouf. They were destroying Scuds, which was their primary mission. They were flying effective cover missions for a variety of Special Forces incursions inside Iraq. And they were slowly and steadily destroying Saddam's massive stockpiles of armor and ammunition in Hicksville, Home Depot, East and West Tac, and the Villas. As the days went by and the Al Jouf commanders saw the extreme fatigue of the pilots after three-mission days, they, themselves, began relieving the young pilots periodically and flying their missions for them. That is how Colonel Efferson happened to be on the mission that saved the British convoy. And that is how Colonel Efferson came very close to getting killed the next day.

Colonel Efferson tells the story: "We had just gotten some new guys in and I decided to take a four-ship flight out for a combination orientation/Scud-hunting mission. On the way north I took them to Home Depot and showed them one of our major secondary targets. While there I had them drop their bombs, which cleaned up our airframes and lightened us up. We had some air-burst Mark-82s, which we only had when somebody new flew in from KKMC, and we dropped those on a concentration of bunkers and vans that looked like it might be a command and control center. However, my wingman, [Lt. Col.] Lee Brundage—one of my Cajuns—saved one of his bombs and I had two hung bombs—bombs that I couldn't release.

"Then we headed toward an intersection in Scud Alley, which was supposed to be a high-traffic area for Scud equipment. Just before we got there, about 8 miles from the intersection, some dummy opened up on us with a 23mm. We are up at 18,000 feet and there was no way he could have hit us. We saw him shooting, and I rolled in and tried to jettison my two hung bombs on him but couldn't.

Then I high-angle strafed him and pulled off. We moved on down to the intersection and three of us orbited high while one of the Alconbury guys [Capt. Rick Turner] dropped lower and eyeballed the area with his binoculars. He didn't see anything and the rest of us couldn't see anything so I decided to drop down and make one recce pass. I rolled in from 17,000 feet, shallow—30-degree dive, and bottomed out at about 9,000 feet. I rolled the wing up and looked down to try and pick up any kind of equipment at the intersection, but didn't see anything. I got the wings level, pulled hard in the vertical and then started a left jink. I was about 11,000 feet above the ground when I heard a big thunk and felt a huge jolt. And just then a missile goes tearing by and that scared the hell out of me. I started kicking out flares thinking I had been hit by a heat-seeking missile and that there were others coming at me. Later I realized that fragments from the hit I took caused one of my Aim-9s to cook off and when it fired, I thought it was a missile that had just missed me.

"I then looked out at my right wing and it was just full of holes, with fluid oozing everywhere, and then a lot of master caution lights came on in the cockpit. I came into the cockpit and saw that the right hydraulic reservoir warning light and the right hydraulic pressure light were on. Also the pitch SAS and yaw SAS lights were on and some of the windscreen looked like a car windshield looks like after it gets hit by a big rock. I looked back out at the right wing again, saw that I had the wings level and was climbing, then came in and yelled Mayday over the radio.

"I kept the airplane climbing and headed south, but I must have made those guys down there real mad at me because they must have seen the hit, but here I was still flying. I got lots of RWR indications, like they knew they had a cripple and everybody in the world was locking onto me. I thought about trying to jettison the hung bombs and Mavericks, but with all the fuel and stuff oozing out of the wing, I didn't want to take the chance of them causing an explosion. Soon we contacted AWACS and they scrambled a tanker so they could support a SAR if I had to jump.

"But the old airplane just kept right on cooking, and even though I lost the fuel in the right wing tank, I had enough left in the fuselage tank to make it back without tankering. I didn't move it any more than I had to—I did a lot of straight and level flying. As I got close in, I did a controllability check, isolated some systems and was able to get the gear down with the emergency system. I had no flaps or speed brakes but I came in, touched down nicely, but the left tire blew because it had been damaged. I used my emergency brakes but at about 150 knots I couldn't keep it on the runway. Fortunately, it was good, hard ground and the gear held while it skidded to a stop. I turned off the inverter and the battery, unstrapped, raised the canopy, jumped over the side and ran like hell.

"The blown tire was smoking but the fire crews put that out. Then we started inspecting the airplane. Later, they counted 378 holes in it. According to the frag lodged in the plane, we deduced that all four shells from a four-round clip of 57mm hit me. Two exploded and hit just behind the plane—that got the tail feathers and the right engine, which had forty-five holes in it—it wasn't developing full power but it was still running when I landed.

"The third round exploded underneath the right wing, which sustained the major part of the damage and cooked off the Aim-9. The fourth round probably exploded right in front, up by the nose.

"If it hadn't been for the titanium bathtub, I probably wouldn't be here. The right side below the cockpit had seventeen major holes in it and the bathtub had a lot of chinks in it. Think of that; seventeen major holes just below the cockpit and I didn't get a scratch! It has to be a rugged airplane to sustain that kind of damage. And five days later they had patched it with speed tape, changed the right flaps, aileron and speed brakes, and Lee [Brundage] flew it back to Fahd. Then, after some more work, they got it in shape and we flew it home. It's in the hangar now—they call it 'Patches' and eventually it will go on static display at the base in New Orleans."

After giving this account, Colonel Efferson twisted in his chair, frowned, then said almost apologetically, "There is one other thing I should also tell. When I was getting shot, Capt. Rick Turner saw the muzzle flashes coming out of an orchard up there. He and his wingman, Capt. Mark Hedman, went back the next day to get that gun, but only after I cautioned them to be extremely careful of civilians who might be near that orchard—we always tried to be nice to the Iraqi people themselves. They took the gun out. They wanted to do that."

A pilot who had been one of Efferson's "boys" out at Al Jouf and who heard about that comment, just smiled and said, "I wonder why?"

# 15

# The RFOA-10G

*"When I think of the threats I flew against as a Raven in Southeast Asia and compare them to what we saw during Desert Storm, I think the latter was hands down the more high threat of the two."*

—*Lt. Col. Greg Wilson*

First it was an "R" that they added to its name. It got that because of the recce missions the pilots had been flying deep behind the lines—missions that were normally the job for the RF-4s. What started as an A-10 had already become an OA-10 when the FACs started using it. Now it had become an ROA-10. And soon it would add a "G" and a whole new name.

The F-4G was the Air Force plane that was given the task of taking out the Iraqi radar-guided SAMs. They were called the Wild Weasels and they carried HARMs, which are anti-radiation missiles. Their task was to accompany strike aircraft, and when the enemy turned on the radars that would guide the SAMs against them, the Weasels would fire the HARMS, which would guide in on the radar and destroy it.

That worked for awhile. Then the Iraqis got smart, or chickened out, depending on the perspective. After the first few days, when turning on the radar proved to be a sure way to invite death from a HARM, they shut down normal use of their radars. Occasionally they would turn them on quickly and "strobe" attacking planes—get a quick fix on their position—then turn them off before a HARM could guide in on them. Sometimes they would turn them on briefly when they thought they could safely lock on a target and launch the missile before a HARM could find them.

Therefore, one key part of the air campaign had not been accomplished. Radar SAMs that were supposed to have been destroyed in the first days of the campaign still existed. Each day, as the pilots briefed for their missions, they carefully studied the big intel map showing their locations. As they ingressed and egressed from their target area, they wanted to be sure to avoid those missile sites whenever they could.

Those same intel maps were bugging hell out of the Riyadh commanders. They were a constant reminder that an otherwise magnificent air campaign had a serious flaw—a part of it that was not working. Another factor increasing their anxiety was the impending ground war. If those radar missile sites were still operative when the ground battle started, planes flying CAS over the battlefield would be seriously threatened. And if the planes could not carry out their CAS missions and prevent friendlies from being killed. . . well, there was a big, tough, commander in Riyadh who had the reputation for having a world-class temper when anything or anybody threatened his beloved grunts on the ground. . . .

So the tasking came down from Riyadh and the Fahd commanders had another occasion to look over the tops of their glasses and shake their heads in amazement. And they were to mutter again, "We are going to do what?"

Then they got on the phone to Riyadh and heard, "Yes, fellas, that's what you're gonna do."

"But that's not a job for the A-10s. That's for the fast movers, the strike guys."

"It's a job for the A-10s now."

"But our kids are going to get killed doing that. You're talking SA-6s and 8s."

"Don't worry, you'll have Weasel and Sparkvark [EF111—electronic countermeasure] support. If they come up on radar to get your guys, they're dead."

"But what about the heat missiles and AAA protecting those sites. That stuff is deadly."

"Colonel, your orders are. . ."

"Yes, sir. I understand them, sir."

Captain Eric Sobol, a Panther, was in the first four-ship (with Capts. James Baldwin, Eric Salomonson, and Jim Schmick) "SAM suppression team" that was sent out on those hazardous missions. Said Sobol, "We were tasked to go up just west of Ali Al Salem Air Base, which is west of Kuwait City. That place was extremely well protected by SAMs and AAA, and I'll tell you, without being embarrassed about it, that it was very difficult climbing up that ladder after you've been to a brief and seen the kinds of stuff they had up there. On these kinds of missions James Baldwin and I would look at each other when we got the tasking and say, 'Well, this is about a 50-50 mission. We thought there was about a 50 percent probability that we would make it back.

"We were specifically tasked against an SA-3 site, but we learned at the intel briefing that we were going to be near four SA-8s and two Rolands at Ali Al Salem, that we were going to be inside an SA-2 ring [within its range] and kissing the edge of an SA-6 ring—plus being vulnerable to all the AAA they had in the area.

"They really started shooting AAA at us when we got in the area, and as we searched, it was tough not getting blown over Ali Al Salem by the 100-knot winds. Actually, I did find myself at one time hovering at 20,000 feet over Ali Al Salem, looking into the face of those SA-8s and the two Rolands. My impression of why I survived is that here I am, with the radar cross-section the size of Mount Rushmore, and here are these Iraqi SAM missile operators going, 'Cease fire, cease fire, don't shoot! Here's two dumb Mike Foxes [Mike stands for mother] at 20,000 feet and 200 knots—you know, must be Iraqi, hold fire, hold fire!' I think that's the only thing that saved us.

"As it turned out, the SA-3 Low-Blow radar—the target tracker for the SA-3—was in the center of a site that had three launchers. We had G-Model Mavericks, which had explosive warheads instead of the shaped-type charge we had in our other Mavericks. I rolled in and killed the westernmost launcher and the radar, and James took out the other two launchers. The AAA was vicious but so far as we know they never shot at us with a missile and our mission was successful. However, in a way that was bad, because it just encouraged those guys in Riyadh to say, 'Hey, guys, go on up north in Kuwait and strike those SA-6s.'"

That is what they did, of course. Captains Tom Dean and Don Fann of the Panther Squadron were in the first flight to do that. Said Dean and Fann:

*Dean:* "I was leading a four-ship way up by Basrah against an SA-6 site of the Republican Guard. Don was my wingman, [Capt.] Steve Phillis was leading the other two-ship and [1st Lt.] Rob Sweet was his wingman. I was really concerned about this mission because the SA-6 can take out an A-10 any time it wants to come up. I was very nervous. I didn't sleep the night before."

*Fann:* "We got up there just as the first rays of the sun were coming up in the morning, but there was a haze down there from things burning and we could barely see anything.

*Dean:* "I had a decent photo of the site, which was rare for us, and I knew exactly what it looked like. But I didn't see it until I was directly overhead at about 15,000. . . ."

*Fann:* "Which was no place to be—I was very uncomfortable sitting up there."

*Dean:* "I looked straight down and saw it and called out to the other three that I had the target in sight. No one else saw it so I elected to use the gun and strafe the target—mark it so the others could see it. I rolled in and as I was strafing the target I started taking AAA—heavy AAA. I was diving at about a 60-degree dive angle—and this was my near-death experience. I saw what appeared to me to be a fireball come by my canopy. It was either heavy AAA going by or it was a missile and it scared me just as I was strafing the straight-flush radar that controls the site."

*Fann:* "It was the first time I had actually seen tracers because usually in the daytime we couldn't see them. But it was going by as he was strafing and when he pulled off, he was so excited he left his finger on the trigger and he had bullets going clear into Iraq."

*Dean:* "Later, I listened to the video and my voice went up about six octaves. . . ."

*Fann:* "His voice went clear off the scale. But it was a nice mark and I could see it [the site], but he was very frustrated because Syph [Phillis] and Sweet Pea [Sweet] were now flying over it and hadn't seen where his bullets hit."

*Dean:* "Don and I pulled around, I rolled in but couldn't get my Maverick off.

*Fann:* "He finally just made a radio call, 'Anyone who has the target in sight, you are cleared—just take a shot—someone hit it.' Syph, who is always very calm, looked over and said, 'Two, do you have it in sight? ' I said, 'Yeah, I have it in sight.' Syph then says, 'Okay, I have your six, you're cleared.' By then I had lost sight of it but I rolled back and down and there it was. The first thing I could think to do was to shoot the missiles that were pointing at me, so I shot the southern TEL [transporter erector launcher] with a G-Model Maverick. I locked on quickly because I wanted to shoot it before it shot me. My missile hit and there were secondaries that were unbelievable; the whole site just exploded, scattering molten debris over the whole site—so I was pretty sure they had some rocket fuel down there. Deano tried to get another missile in and again, it failed to launch. So I said, 'I'm here and I'm ready,' and this time I went for the straight-flush radar site and hit that. Syph and Sweet Pea finally got in there to start taking some shots and we completely destroyed the launchers, vans, everything. All the time we were taking AAA but we never could identify where it was coming from—which is odd because we usually see the muzzle flashes first."

Now they were ROA-10Gs, and they had their videos showing SAM destruction and the hideous AAA they went through to prove it. But that wasn't enough. They had to have a name for the guys who flew against the SAMs.

"Well, what name shall we give them?"

"They're Weasels, right?"

"Yeah, in a way."

"And they were Warthogs, right?"

"Yeah."

"Then let's call them Wartweasels."

"Sierra Hotel!"

So much for the graveyard humor—for that was what it was. They were young men, scared to death, Sierra Hoteling by the cemetery as they dove down in nose to nose confrontations with the deadliest missiles on earth. So far, they had been incredibly lucky. It was just a matter of time before that luck would run out for someone. For Capt. Paul Johnson it almost did.

They were on a SAM suppression mission to southern Kuwait. It was an SA-2 site about eight miles south of Kuwait City, and when they attacked it, they could easily drift within range of SA-6s and SA-8s. And, like all of the sites they were sent against, it was heavily defended by a variety of AAA.

Captain Johnson was the media cowboy among the pilots, having received lots of publicity for the rescue flight he led that saved Navy flier Lieutenant Devon Jones from certain capture by the Iraqis. And, according to his wingman on this mission against the SA-2 site, Capt. John Whitney, "PJ [his nickname] is a top-rank pilot, one of the top-rank pilots in the Air Force—not just our squadron, but in the whole Air Force. He is by far the best flight lead I've ever seen and I've been a wingman for quite awhile. So when we talk about this one mission that should be understood above all else. Because on this one mission, PJ made some big mistakes."

"We flew up there," continues Whitney, and we had good intel—a good photo—but the weather was Delta Sierra [Delta stands for "dog".]. We had a real strong four-ship, with Captain [Greg] Weidekamp and Captain [Larry] Butler flying three and four. But the base of the clouds was down about 6,000 feet and the tops varied from 14,000 to 18,000. It was broken to overcast—not the kind of conditions you want when you are attacking a SAM site.

"PJ tried to attack the site first with his Mavericks but couldn't get them off [because of the lack of contrast]. Then we hung out above the clouds for awhile. The winds were 80 knots and the stuff coming in was heavier. There was no way we should have been trying to attack that target under those conditions."

Captain Johnson agreed. He said, "We had been messing around on top of the clouds for ten minutes or so and I should have made the call as the flight lead that this isn't going to work and that we should leave. But I got my fangs out and I was determined that I was going to put something on this target, which was a pretty serious error on my part. What I was thinking was that I could put some Mark-82s on it, but that wasn't a good option because, if we used Mavericks, we could say for sure that the target was destroyed—that the BDA was positive. But if we put bombs on it, we'd have to say that maybe it was hit and maybe it was damaged, then somebody else would have to come in to finish the job. I made an error.

"I was starting to roll in on a Mark-82 pass, weather worse than before, but with my fangs out. I'm diving down, dodging clouds, and I get down to ten thousand and can't meet parameters for a bomb release. So I pushed over a little bit and let fly with 30mm, which is pretty useless—all I'm doing is aggravating them down there. I shot about a hundred rounds, and at this point it's even obvious to me that we're finished, a conclusion I should have reached five minutes earlier. GQ [Weidekamp] and Spock [Butler] are on top and Whit [Whitney] is somewhere in the clouds following me down. However, he lost sight of me and called that out, but I missed the call. Later, I heard it when we reviewed the tape, so I had made another mistake; I should have heard him and aborted the pass right there because you never attack without somebody watching your six [o'clock].

"Anyhow, I told those guys to head back southwest and I started climbing back up. I was climbing through seventy-five hundred feet, heading to the southwest when I got nailed. I didn't see anything coming—I was looking for Whit, not the ground, but I took a pretty good hit and the plane rolled to the right in about 120 degrees of bank [30 degrees past vertical]. I looked out the cockpit to the right and got a cold chill—I could see hydraulic lines sticking up out of the right wing, a little bit of flame over the top of the wing and a big gaping hole in the leading edge, with some of the top wing skin gone and the housing of the right [landing] gear shot away. It was an ugly sight.

"I tried to roll back level but it wouldn't respond and the nose started to slice down. Now I'm tromping on the left rudder, and finally the stick responds and I get back to level flight at 6,000. I have no idea of the airspeed because the pitot tube on the right wing is shot away. But the engine instruments are good, and the only thing showing wrong was the right hydraulics—I had lost that system.

Sometime about then I yelled that One's been hit and that I need cover. Whit comes zipping down out of the clouds, gets me in sight and starts to escort me out—we were about 12 miles north of the border. Now everybody is firing at me and Whit is diving on the AAA, doing his best to suppress it, and I'm hunkering down in the bathtub. I can't jink—any turn had to be to the right; I'm standing on the left rudder and with almost full left stick just to keep it straight and level. My only thought was to get across the border so I could jump. The wing was flexing up and down and the pylon holding the Maverick was moving. I could have dumped the Maverick and the Mark-82s and got rid of some weight but I was afraid they might be messed up and releasing them could create more problems.

"Finally we crossed the border and Whit came up, looked me over and said I was doing one-ninety knots. It seemed like the plane was flying okay, that maybe I wouldn't have to jump. But then I had the decision of whether to go to KKMC which was closer but into 60 knots of headwind and would require a right turn [or a left 270], or try to go to King Fahd which was straight ahead and would give me a little tailwind. I decided to try for home, then I called GQ down to look me over—he was a functional test pilot with lots of experience—and I sent Spock and Whit on home to alert them that I was coming in.

"But now I was really burning up the fuel, running at maximum power and at low altitude, and my gauges weren't matching my totalizer. So I had another problem and I immediately called Bulldog [the AWACS controlling the area] and told them I was hit and needed emergency fuel. Then this tanker guy closed his eyes and clinched his teeth and came spiraling down through weather and traffic to save me."

Salmon 71, a KC-10 tanker piloted by Capt. Tony Huelin and co-piloted by Capt. Brian Lukanich was in Lemon Track, a 50-mile long and 10-mile wide racetrack pattern at 25,000 feet just south of the border. They had already had a "leg-shaking" close call; four F-1 French Mirages had blasted out of the top of the clouds and had just missed colliding with them by only 150 feet. Now they got a call from AWACS. There was a battle damaged aircraft coming south, down at 6,000, badly needing fuel. Could they go down and help him?

"Without even thinking about it," said Capt. Tony Heulin, "we said, 'Sure.' Then they cleared us to descend and it was wild. I rolled in anywhere from 60 to 90 degrees of bank and spiraled down at more than 6,000 feet per minute. The hairy part was that there were other tankers at twenty-two, twenty, eighteen and sixteen—I have no idea why they weren't given the job—and we were descending through the weather, blind, with AWACS calling targets—some as close as three miles. Finally, we popped out and started slowing up so we wouldn't overshoot. At 260 I threw down the gear, got down to 200, put slats out and the gear back up, but we were still going too fast. They said we'd have to slow down. But 187 was our stall speed and we finally stabilized at 190. But the elevator vibration was causing the yoke to shake in my hand.

"The wingman came on and got a couple of thousand pounds, then the damaged plane tried to come on. And for what happened then, it would be better for [S. Sgt.] Jim Protzmann, the boom operator to tell the story. He was the guy who did all the work on this—the real guy who got the job done."

Staff Sergeant Protzmann continues the account, "After the first plane moved off, the guy with the damage slid in and I said, 'Holy shit, pilot, you ought to see this guy, we've got to get him home.' I had seen the movie *Memphis Belle* just before we went over and his wing looked like something out of that movie. It was flopping up and down and barely on the aircraft. It looked like it was going to break off at any time, and I was afraid it would flip over and hit our jet and we would be too low to recover. I was also thinking that this was war and I wished people back at the compound—the paper pushers that gripe about everything—could see this. It would have opened their eyes.

"We were nose high and I was pointing down, which made it impossible for the computer that runs the boom to operate normally. Also, the damaged aircraft was extremely nose high and the right wing was banked off in maybe 10 degrees of roll—cocked off the side quite a bit. But he came in, and because his hydraulics were out, he couldn't lock on so it was a stiff-arm engagement—he had to fly and maneuver to keep the boom on, which, under those circumstances, was an amazing feat of airmanship. Even then I lost him six or eight times, but I was able to get him back, fighting the computer each time, until he had taken about fifteen hundred pounds, which was enough to get him home."

Captain Johnson continues, "It was just brute force that I used to stay on that boom—I was standing on the left rudder trying to keep the right wing level. When I came off I was right over the airport at Al Jubayl [a city on the Saudi coast] and it was tempting to try and land there. But I would have had to maneuver to do it, and at the time I was on a 50-mile final for Fahd. I wouldn't have to bank to get in there; I could just drive straight in, so I decided to push on. I had cleaned the ordnance off the wings and so I was able to get up to 230 knots, and was feeling better about the plane. My last major worry was the gear; whatever hit me had detonated at the joint where the outer wing fastens to the center wing, and I was afraid that when the gear went down, that force, or the drag after it was down, would cause the wing to come unglued. But when I cycled the gear, it went down as advertised: clunk, clunk, clunk; I had three green lights and the wing was still on. After that it was just a matter of standing on the left rudder as I eased off power and I flew a no-flap approach down with GQ chasing and calling my airspeed. It was one of my smoother touchdowns, and even though the right main tire was shredded and collapsed, I was able to keep it on the runway until it stopped.

"I shut down and scrambled out. Fluids were dripping all over the runway, but I wasn't thinking about the plane any longer. I was absolutely furious with myself. Colonel [Tom] Lyon, the DO drove up in his car, but I didn't care. I was so livid I tore my helmet off and threw it on the ground. It was all my fault; I did what I shouldn't have done. I stayed in the target area too long and I had messed with the weather.

"About that time Eric Staniland, the assistant crew chief—the crew chief was at KKMC—heard that I was down and he said that when he had to come look at my plane he felt like somebody going to the morgue to identify a member of the family. But they changed the tire, towed it off, and later they found that of the three wing spars, both the front and middle spar were completely blown through and that the aft spar was damaged. So it was only the damaged aft spar and the lower wing skin that was holding the wing on. They also found, by running the tape of the engine analyzer through the computer, that the reason I couldn't immediately roll level after being hit was because the right engine had ingested all the debris blown off the wing and that it had compressor-stalled for a few seconds. But, thanks to good old GE and a tough engine, it just spit the stuff out the back, spooled back up and kept running. Coincidentally, it was my airplane I was flying—the first time I had flown it during the war—and after they put on a new center and outer wing, I was able to fly it back home."

Captain Johnson and the other gutsy Hog drivers who flew into enemy territory on SAM suppression missions certainly earned the "G" that the Warthogs had now added to their numerical designation. Now it was time to add a new letter—the letter "F"—and Captain Bob Swain, a Cajun, and a USAir 767 pilot in peacetime, had the distinction of being the first one to earn it.

Said Captain Swain, "[1st Lt.] Mark White was my wingman and we were on our third BAI mission of the day up in Kuwait. It was hazy, with visibility only about 3 miles, and we were in a kill box just west of Ali Al Salem, an airbase just west of Kuwait City. We had found a row of tanks and I put my Mavericks into them but Mark was having trouble getting his off. We were planning on strafing them but then one of the OA-10 FACs, Capt. John Engle, checked in and asked if he could come into our kill box and look around. I said, 'Please do, the more eyes the better.' Then Capt. [Larry] Merington [another Cajun] called and asked if he could come up—that he and his partner [Capt. Jim Callaway] had some Mavericks but no targets. I said, 'Sure.'

"As he was coming into the target area, we were climbing up to watch their six o'clock and work a coordinated two-ship on the target. About that time I happened to look down on the ground due west of the target area and I saw two fleeting objects. It was like two water bugs on a pond, skipping along, but they were going a lot faster than tanks or trucks or anything else we had seen, and they weren't leaving a dust trail. At that point I was at fourteen or fifteen thousand, in a climb and I said on Uniform, 'Hey, I think I've got some helicopters here.' Everybody went silent because we had never seen one, nor heard of anybody seeing one. At that time the other guys couldn't see them because it was so hazy and smokey, so I said, 'I'm padlocked on them [I can't take my eyes off them or I'll lose them] and I'm following them; don't hit me.' Then to Mark, I said, 'Keep your eyes on me and clear my six because I'm going to stay padlocked on these guys.'

"I'm following them now, not looking at anything else. They are helicopters, two of them, and I'm trying to get the FAC's eyes on them—he has binoculars. We didn't have AWACS coverage right then, and I was afraid it might be some of our Special Forces guys in there because I knew that some of them were coming northbound that afternoon. Finally, I decided that I'd let these guys see me. But when I got down to about 11,000 they split, and since I'd been talking on Uniform, they should have heard us and gotten back to us on Guard [frequency]. Just then the FAC said, 'Let me put a couple of smokes out there to see if we are looking in the same general area.' He shot a couple of rockets and I said, 'Yeah, that's the lead and he's heading south right for your smoke,' and he said, 'I got him.' Then he put his binoculars on him and at that point I decided, 'Well, we'll take this guy out since they aren't talking to us.

"I went down and was thinking that no one had ever shot an air-to-air missile at anything off the A-10 so I thought I would try that. We had been at Fort Hood the summer before and I knew that helicopters were tough [to lock from above with heat-seeking missiles because the rotor blades dissipate the engine heat]. But, I called up the Aim-9s, rolled in and also turned on my gun and armed it. Twice I tried to lock him up with the diamond [HUD display for Aim-9]— the Aim-9 makes a little growl when it locks on. It kept breaking lock and by that time I was at 60 degrees [dive] doing about 400 knots, going downhill fast and I couldn't keep lock—the diamond kept breaking away. Frustrated then, I decided to run a string of bullets and try to shoot him. I put about seventy-five bullets down, but thought I'd missed. John Engle, the FAC, told me later that he was watching and that some of the bullets must have hit him because he started to wobble. I pulled off and went over the helicopter at about 5,000 feet and Mark White had seen it—he had seen my bullets, but he was 2 or 3 miles away and no way could he have killed it.

"By that time I was over it again. I shot a hundred rounds and as I was about to fire again, it made a hard right turn and I hit him with another hundred rounds. After that I could see the fuel tank erupt, then a fireball, and then it cartwheeled down the desert floor. When the Army guys went in after the war, they found the wreckage but there wasn't enough left of it to even identify the type."

After that mission one of the Hog drivers, Capt. Cliff Grafton, who was working as a FIDO in the TACC at Riyadh, decided it was time for the world to know the truth about his airplane. Said Grafton, "Here we were, a big, slow, strictly low-tech CAS airplane that would have been heading for the boneyard if the war hadn't broken out—and now we're doing BAI, armed recce, SAM suppression, and then Swain shoots down a helicopter. We were talking about all this one day, going over the different letters that we could add to the A-10, and I brought up the idea of making a sign and putting it up on our computer terminal. This major who was working the desk with me said, 'Make it happen,' so I went to the graphics computer and laser printer and made a real nice, double-sided sign, with an A-10 on it and saying in big letters: RFOA-10G. It became an instant hit, with guys coming by and saying, 'Yeah, you guys are doing a great job.' Then people wanted to add more letters. Since some guys had dropped bombs from above a total undercast on INS coordinates, they thought I should add a 'B' for bomber. I thought about making it an RFOAB-10G, but that didn't sound right. Later, someone else wanted to add a 'C' for cargo because we were carrying mail out to KKMC and Al Jouf, but that didn't sound good either. So as far as I know, after I left Riyadh it remained an RFOA-10G."

A few days later Capt. Todd Sheehy, a Vulture flying out of Al Jouf, proved to everybody that the "F" designation was legitimate—that it wasn't acquired as the result of a one-time fluke.

Sheehy explains, "It was February 15th, my last day out at Al Jouf, and the second mission of the day. I was flying my wingman's plane because mine was broken, and my wingman was [1st Lt.] Jay Keller, an Alex guy whose flight lead also had a broken plane. We took off at 1045 and were going to Mudaysis Air Field about 45 miles into Iraq. Keller had been in a formation the day before that had attacked some Soviet-made SU-7 Fitters that had been taken off the field and dispersed north of there. They had destroyed two of them and there was at least one that was still intact, so we were going to get it. There is a road that goes northeast of the airfield, a paved road, and they had towed the planes about a mile up that road and dispersed them to the side, partly burying them in sand revetments. We found the one that had not been hit, dropped CBU on it, but it didn't explode so we couldn't tell if it had been damaged. So I made one last pass with the gun and put a few hundred bullets into it and as I pulled off, Jay said it started to burn. Then a big cloud of black smoke came up as we egressed the area.

"We are climbing back up to about 20,000 feet and we are almost at the area called East Tac, in the vicinity of Nukhayb, where there had been a lot of tanks and APCs. There were two other flights of A-10s already working that area, but as we arrived, one of them left. The other flight was not taking any fire that we could see, and it was a beautiful clear day—you could see forever, and especially we could see about 30 miles southeast where smoke was still rising from the Fitter we had killed.

"About that time I got a call from AWACS for the flight that has just left—call sign Marlin. They didn't answer so I replied, telling AWACS that Marlin flight was headed home, that I was Springfield two-seven, and what did they need. They said, 'Well, we have a low, slow contact on our radar at zero-six-zero for twenty-seven [miles],' and I said, ' We have three-zero minutes of gas and we can check it out if you like.' 'Roger that,' they said, so now I'm starting to get just a little bit excited because it sounds like a helicopter. We started descending, heading zero-six-zero and it starts taking us toward Baghdad. We armed up our AIM-9s to cool them down, then I queried AWACS. I said, 'Confirm that you have positive radar contact on me and zero-six-zero is the vector.' There was a pause, then he came back and said, 'Springfield two-seven, look two-seven-zero for two [miles].' Basically I am right on top of the contact now. I make this big left turn, descending quickly with Jay in cover.

"I'm descending now, looking at the roads that come out of Nukhayb. Jay is reminding me of the 23mm, I roger that call, then call AWACS for an update. They come back, 'Contact has faded,' and just as he was getting that out I saw out of the corner of my eye off my left wing a black dot moving across the desert with dust behind it. It's right down at ground level, no more than 50 feet off the desert. Instantly—I didn't even think to select my missiles—I just rolled over on my back and pulled down for a guns pass. It was a steep dive, and I took aim and started firing at about 10,000 feet. I got off about 300 rounds. I jinked the airplane around to avoid some 23mm Jay called out, and climbed back up. Jay said that I had hit him but he couldn't tell if it had gone into a hover or landed. I was at about 8,000 feet and I rolled in this time and got off about 250 more rounds before the helicopter exploded. As I pulled off the second time at about fifty-five hundred, I could see that it was definitely a gunship—a Puma or a Hip. Later, after looking at photos, I positively identified it as a Soviet-made Mi-8 Hip, because of its boxy shape and the weapons rack on the side. It also had something hanging from it like rocket pods, which was typical of the Hip."

Captain Sheehy and his wingman were excited because the Hogs had made their second air-to-air kill. Exclamations of Sierra Hotel started reverberating throughout the community. And in Riyadh, where Capt. Don Fann had just been detailed, it was also big news.

Said Fann, "It was my first day down there when Sheehy got his kill and it was fun to see the reactions and to see that everybody knew the job we were doing. At the A-10 desk we had seven phones, and between me and two others, we were kept busy answering them—it seemed like they were ringing all the time. But you look around—the F-16 setup was just off to my left and the F-15 guys sat next to them—their phones never rang. They just sat there and played Nintendo and Game Boys. Then, after news of Sheehy's kill came in, an O-6 [colonel] walked up and said, 'So tell me, how many air-to-air kills does the A-10 have now?' I replied, 'Two.' And really loud, he said, 'What? Two?' Then he turned around and asked the F-16 guys, just as loud as he could, 'How many air kills do you have now?' They just looked at him and shook their heads. They hadn't shot down anything."

That was the fun part of Don Fann's first day in Riyadh.

Later in the afternoon he had the sad duty of announcing that Syph and Sweet Pea, two close friends in his Panther Squadron, were down in Iraq and that Colonel Sawyer, one of the wing commanders, had limped home with his tail practically shot off.

So, February 15, 1991, which started as a good day—a day for breaking out some of their precious stores of Listerine and Scope—ended up being the worst day of the whole war for the Hog drivers.

# 16

# Tragedy Over the Medina Guard

*". . . the Iraqis launched eight IR SAMS at us yesterday,
bagging two A-10s and damaging one, which I happened to be
flying. . . loneliness is climbing at 200 knots with the nearest
friendlies 55 miles away. . ."*
*—Col. Dave Sawyer in a letter to Lt. Gen. Charles Horner*

On February 15 they increased the ante. Basically, they said,
"Okay, Warthogs and Wartweasels, you have done a great job so far.
You have taken out the western GCI sites, found and killed Scuds,
obliterated artillery and armor in the KTO kill boxes, destroyed
SAMs that would have been a threat in the ground war, made an air-
to-air kill (Sheehy had not killed the second one yet—that came later
in the day), and attrited the Tawakalna Division of the Republican
Guard by at least 50 percent. Congratulations. Now we have new
tasking for you.

"We want you to go 80 miles behind the lines, past the Tawakalnas,
to the Medina [Luminous] Division of the Republican Guard. They
have lots of arty and armor up there and we need to start attriting
them before the ground guys move in. You'll have to tanker going in
so you'll have some playtime. Good luck and check six."

When the pilots heard this, it was the same old refrain. "We are
going where? We are doing what?"

The author has spent several years with the Basques in Spain,
researching the battles they fought in the Spanish Civil War. When

listening to and watching the faces of the A-10 pilots who told of increasingly hazardous tasking they received in their war, he was reminded of the actions of the Basque *gudariak* as they told of the head-on charges they were ordered to make into deadly machine-gun fire. First, their faces would take on the look of abject loneliness—as though God had reached down and picked their lonely souls to march straight into hell. But then, with their jaws set, they would stand up, spit on their hands and rub them together, hike up their trousers and unsling an imaginary rifle from their shoulder, then proceed to describe how they marched, line abreast, into the guns, their heads down like fending off aggravating hailstones, but with all the courage and stubbornness bred into their ancient race.

No soldier in his right mind looks forward to going into a battle regardless of the chances of dying. But every soldier has to answer the call, and good soldiers do it with poise and the knowledge that it is a duty they are honor-bound to perform.

Certainly the Hog drivers who flew past the north border of Kuwait, almost into the Euphrates Valley of Iraq, to attack the Medina Division of the Republican Guard, were good soldiers. Some griped, of course. And others probably said unkind things about some of the Riyadh commanders' ancestors. But when it was time to go, they spit on their hands, hiked their trousers, unslung their guns, and went with their poise intact, their minds focused on their duty to take out the artillery and armor waiting to kill their comrades when they wheeled north. They didn't like it, but most would probably have agreed with one of the salty old pilots who commented on that tasking after the war. He said, simply, "It was a shitty job, but it needed to be done."

Two of the first ones to head north on that day were Col. Dave Sawyer, known in the air as "Colonel Maim" because of his aggressive flying, and one of the Vanguards, Capt. Karl Buchberger. They flew to the south edge of the Medina Division where they were tasked against some reveted armor. "But we were carrying CBU-58s this day," said Sawyer, "and they're pretty useless against armor so we looked around for some soft targets where we could put those before attacking the armor with our Mavericks. We flew around for awhile, found some reveted trucks, some containers that looked like sea-land shipping containers, and a metal building that might have been a command center. I went in first and dropped on them, then Buchberger continued the string and we pulled off. We got some secondaries, but nothing spectacular.

"Then we went over to the coordinates where the tanks were supposed to be. We found the revetments and I checked them out with the binoculars. What was in there were boxy shaped—they were tanks or APCs. I rolled in from the west and tried to get a lock on one of them with my EO Maverick. But the sun angle early in the morning was bad; I had to have contrast to lock it up and I didn't have it. We swung around so I could attack from the northeast. I did that, got a lock and blew up a tank or an APC, pulled off, and through my yellow, high-contrast visor, I saw, when I looked back over my shoulder, three guys running toward some more vehicles. I immediately rolled in from the southeast—I had been in a climbing left turn around 8,000 feet—and strafed the vehicles, and as I pulled off I guess I didn't flare as aggressively as I should have. I had my tail pointed right at those guys, but nothing but vacant desert ahead of me.

"Suddenly, I heard a clank and felt a thud in the rudder pedals. Then it got quiet, but of course I was slow and climbing, and there wasn't as much air moving past the canopy. I looked anxiously at my engine instruments—they were all right, then I checked the master caution panel. Hydraulics were okay—everything was okay but the SAS lights—they were on. I looked at the SAS switches and both pitch and yaw were off. I flipped them on, continued to climb, then looked at my INS and figured I had 55 miles to go to get to friendly territory. I had already talked to Buchberger—he was in trail clearing my six."

Captain Buchberger was a worried young man at that point. "Here I am, supposed to be covering the wing commander, and he takes a hit. But there was no way I could have warned him. He was at least a mile lower than I was and the missile that hit him—we believe it was an SA-13—was smokeless because I had my eye on him all the time and I didn't see a thing until a big, white puff of smoke appeared under his tail. He came on the radio and he was real mellow about it. He goes, 'Okay. I've taken a hit.'

"He does all the checks, finds that the plane is flying okay, and after we cross the border, I moved up and gave him a damage check. He was shot to pieces; this jet had five or six hundred holes in it. The right rudder was completely bent over. The right elevator is completely gone, the left elevator about 20 percent gone, and the tail cone—what was left of it—was flapping in the wind with wires hanging out. And he had holes all over the airplane all the way up to the right gear pod.

"But the plane was flying almost normally," said Sawyer. It was just a little heavy on the pitch control [because of the damaged elevators] and the SAS kept kicking off. But that's it. It flew fine. I didn't put any demands on the plane, of course. I just flew nice, straight, and level directly to Fahd. I did the controllability check about 50 miles out; everything was fine. Then 40 miles out I put the gear down and got three green lights. I just flew straight in and landed.* And I was going to get in another airplane and go back for the second mission but the word had come down that Saddam had agreed to pull out of Kuwait. So I went to Sandy Sharpe's trailer and we conferred because we thought the war might be over. As it turned out, he [Saddam] had a whole bunch of unacceptable conditions attached to his offer. But if that hadn't happened, we would have been heading back up to the kill box over the Medina Division where Syph [Steve Phillis] and [Rob] Sweet got hit."

Captain Steve Phillis was leading the flight and 1st Lt. Rob Sweet was his wingman. They were in the Panther Squadron and they launched that afternoon, taking planes that had already flown two missions over the Medinas earlier that day. From all the information they had received, the situation looked better than they ever expected.

Said Capt. Dan Mulherin, "Mitch [Maj. David Mitchell] and I had already flown two missions up there with excellent success. There were targets everywhere. We killed lots of tanks, got good secondaries, and strafed a lot of arty pits. We even got some secondaries where you could definitely see colored gas coming from the explosions—we thought they might have been chemical rounds, but they could also have been marking rounds.

"We actually briefed Syph and Sweet on the ladder. We had been Enfield three-seven and three-eight for the Alpha and Bravo missions. They were taking the Charlie mission—Sweet in my plane and Syph in Mitch's. We told them we hadn't seen any AAA fire all day. Nothing. We briefed them that it was lucrative up there and that we took absolutely no fire. We told them that as they were climbing in."

"We hit a tanker going north," said Rob Sweet, and even though the word about threats was comforting, we had also heard that a guy got hit up there that morning so we had some anxiety about that. It was 60 or 70 miles from the closest border and that's a long way for an A-10 that putts along at 200 knots when you're over 20,000 and with the heavy load we had. And we were going against the southern part of the division—some of the guys went even farther north than where we were going—and they had taken a lot of fire. In fact, when

---

* Colonel Sawyer's airplane was back flying combat ten days later with the tail from Colonel Efferson's plane, prompting lots of jokes about a Flying Tiger with teeth and a Cajun tail.

we got up there, we could hear the guys talking with a FAC and we could hear them calling out the fire they were taking.*

"Syph led us to our fragged area and there was stuff everywhere on both sides of a hardball road running through the area. Syph rolled in and dropped his CBUs and started taking pretty heavy AAA from north of his target. So we decided to go south of the road where there were a lot of targets but no shooting going on.

"At this time we saw a mover going down the road, driving to an encampment of trucks. Syph rolled in and tried to strafe it and missed. The truck drove into a compound of trucks and then he told me to go ahead and drop my CBU on the trucks so I did that. One detonated right in the center of the trucks and I had another two that covered about half the encampment. I was happy that I got some of them.

"Then we decided, since we were pretty far up there, that we should vary our targeting so we moved about 5 miles over. That way we wouldn't be staying over the same area, letting some guy draw a bead on us. Now, we found some tanks that looked pretty good but it was late in the afternoon and we were having some problems locking up our EO Mavericks because of the lack of contrast. We each made a pass but neither of us locked up, then we went back and each of us made a strafe pass. As I was coming off circling clockwise from the northeast, my flare program going, I looked and saw a SAM coming at me from two o'clock low. No RWR indications—it was an IR SAM. It was a tracker. It was guiding on me. I jammed on the flares and pulled a little bit and it missed me, barely. Now I'm really pissed off. That would have been our last pass; we would have been heading home by now, but this guy had almost shot me down so we were mad. We had seen a little smoke trail coming from where the missile had launched so we were going to hammer this guy. Syph rolls in and strafes the tank next to it. He hit it and comes off. I said, 'You had some good hits but I think it [the missile] came from the truck next to it. He said, 'Okay, you are cleared in for one more pass and then we are out of here.'

"I was just about ready to roll in. I was northeast of the target and the sun was low, which means that I'm easy to see. I was just about ready to roll in when there was a boom behind the airplane and at that time I heard Syph call out two SAMs, but they had already hit

---

* Another pilot heading up there heard the same thing and said that it reminded him of when he was a kid sitting outside the principal's office hearing his friend getting spanked and dreading having to follow him in.

me. I looked back—I had been at about 30 degrees of bank, and the hit rolled me wings level—and I saw some pretty extensive damage. The aileron was gone. . . . The whole trailing edge of the right wing was gone and there was a fire—there were little tubes and wires sticking up with flames on the end of them. I didn't bother looking back any farther. I didn't even check the engines; I unconsciously firewalled the throttles and headed south. I was thinking that it was a long way to the border.

"Then I settled down for a second and decided to figure out what was wrong. I looked down and had a bunch of lights on my caution panel, and the ones that stuck out were the hydraulic lights on the left side. I isolated them, then I made a call to Syph telling him I was hit and hit bad and heading south. He said, 'Okay, I copy that you're heading south. You look all right.'

"About then I came back inside and was looking at my engine instruments to see how they were doing and the plane started rolling off to the right. I put full left stick in but it continued. Then I started using my rudder, but nothing worked; I just kept rolling to the right. At that time I went to manual reversion, thinking my hydraulics were gone. I was now at 130 degrees of bank, trying to neutralize the stick laterally so the manual reversion would kick in. Then I pulled on the stick and that was doing nothing—it was like the stick wasn't connected to anything. It just kept rolling in a steep spiral— not a spin—but a 60- or 70-degree nose-low spiral and I'm trying to recover; I got hit at about 12,500 feet and when I saw 6,500, I decided to eject.

"The steep spiral had me forward in the seat so I had to force myself back. About that time Syph was calling me, telling me to roll my wings level and I answered him telling him that I couldn't. Then I told him, 'I'm out, I'm out,' and I ejected."

Captain Dave Hanaway was in a two-ship flight north of them and his flight lead, who prefers anonymity, had talked to Syph when they first came into the area. Said Hanaway, "Lead overheard Syph and Sweet coming up—they had just gotten off the tanker—and Syph was asking us what it was like up where we were. Lead said that it didn't look too good. There were big bomb craters from Buffs [B-52s], and we didn't see anything worth hitting. As it turned out, we were wrong. We just hadn't seen all their stuff up there yet. Then we started working with a FastFAC, an F-16, and he was more toward Basrah. He said, 'I've got some good targets over here if you Hogs want to drop on them. I wasn't feeling too comfortable over this army but we went over and Lead saw what the FAC was looking at and went in. He drops and starts getting shot at real bad. I yelled at him—there were white clouds going off all around his airplane—and he started back west over the Medina. He put me out front, I rolled in on some arty, ripped off my six Mark-82s and just as I was recovering Syph starts talking to us.

"First he said—he called Lead by his call sign, Pachmayr zero-three; he knew where we would be because we briefed together before the mission. Lead answered and Syph said, 'My wingman is bag.' That was the codeword of the day; it meant that his wingman was battle damaged. Then he told us that he needed us to come over for escort help.

"Right away we knew exactly what was wrong. We headed due south—we knew they were 5 or 10 miles away. We were trying to get visual with them and Syph, very calmly was talking to us, giving us ground references, telling us that they were over where there is a 'V' in the road. We didn't see it, and before we can get visual, Syph says, 'This is Enfield three-seven, I'm bag at this time also.' His voice was very calm, extremely calm—incredibly calm, but that was Syph. He could have been saying, 'I'm happy to see you.' He had a distinctive voice. He always came across very calm and controlled on the radio. You could definitely tell his voice—I had flown wingman with him in peacetime. But that was the last he said.

"We heard a faint wobble tone on Guard beacon—we would hear it and not hear it. In the plane it goes off when you eject, except that we don't let it do that in wartime. So we know it is not Sweet and not Syph, and that it had to be one of the Iraqis playing with one of their radios. We never saw either one of the airplanes. We thought one of two things; both were down or both were limping out by themselves and couldn't talk. Syph said he's bag so he could have lost his radios.

"We held overhead looking for planes on the ground or for parachutes. Then Lead went to SAR frequency and I called AWACS and asked them if they were painting another flight. They said they had nobody and two more Hogs came on frequency asking to help. Then Lead gets shot at by an IR SAM. I saw it and told him to break. He breaks and punches flares, and it misses him. Then we're out of gas and have to head south to get on a tanker. When we come back, others have been looking and it is getting dark. We got shot at some more, then had to head home. [Lieutenant] Colonel Shatzel [the Panther Squadron Commander] met us at the ramp and we knew something was wrong then. He takes us to the command post to debrief to the commanders and intel. By that time we were feeling horrible. We still had hope because we deduced that Sweet had talked to Syph after he was bag and we had heard Syph tell us he was hit.

Nothing more was ever heard from Steve Phillis, and after the war, when the wreckage was found, it was confirmed that he went in with the plane. No clue was found to indicate why he did not eject.

Rob Sweet survived to tell his part of the story. Said Sweet, "I was in the chute about four minutes—no injuries—I had a little whiplash but that was nothing. When I ejected I was north of the tanks Syph had been shooting at and I thought I'd try to stay north of them and land in no-man's land—that way I would definitely have time to make a radio call. In fact, I thought about taking my radio out while I was in the chute, but I was afraid I would lose it. But the wind was blowing hard and it was taking me toward the tanks. I tried to steer and stay north but it blew me right into them. I landed about 30 yards away from a T-72. There were about sixty guys there—guys that we had been shooting at; they were in their holes until I got real close to the ground, then they rushed out after me. I landed hard, tore a tendon in my leg, and then they all ran up and started beating the shit out of me with rifle butts to the head and all over. I acted like I was unconscious or dead but that didn't deter them any. Half the guys were trying to take my gear off and the other half were beating me. I thought, "Well, this is it, I'm history now.' I figured they were going to beat me—do whatever they wanted to do for awhile—then they were going to shoot me. Then I got dragged off by some officers and interrogated.

"The soldiers themselves went to great pains to show me they weren't suffering. They brought me a bowl of food—some kind of rice and bean mixture that I couldn't have eaten if I was starving. 'See, we have food; see, we have medicine,' they kept saying. They didn't look like they were starving, either, but you have to realize, they were up north a long ways and they hadn't been hit hard at that time.

"Then they took me to Baghdad and turned me over to the Security Police—the goons. The army guys didn't treat me too badly, except for those first guys—they were just pissed off. But the goons—they beat the shit out me. . . ."

Rob Sweet arrived in Baghdad and met the goons on February 17, on the second day after he was shot down. But Capt. Dale Storr, the pilot everyone believed was dead, had already been with the goons for fourteen days and we should first catch up with what happened to him before continuing with Rob Sweet's story.

Right after Storr was captured, in the bunker where the Iraqi officer had held a cocked pistol to his head and screamed that he was going to kill him, Storr made the mistake of drinking some of their water. "I was really thirsty and probably in a little bit of shock," said Storr, "so I drank some of their water even though it was kind of brown and looked pretty gross. I started paying the price later that night when they took me to a place in Baghdad called the 'Bunker.' I got really sick. I was puking and I was in bad shape, but that's when they started beating me up. They beat the shit out of me.

"While I was handcuffed, they beat me with big round sticks. Basically, they concentrated on my shoulders, my knees and the back of my neck. I'd try to lean into the punches, just lean one way or the other, and this one guy would come by and grab my arm and jerk it, pulling it out of the joint, then they would beat me on that arm and it would pop back in. One time they hit it really, really hard and it felt like it popped in and back out, and when they did that, I rolled off the chair because it was really hurting. Then they started kicking me when I was on the floor and I started screaming at them. That didn't do me any good because they started screaming at me then. They were still trying to get me to tell them things and I was still being stupid. I didn't want to tell them anything. Eventually, they ended up breaking my nose, separating my shoulder and screwing up my knee.

"Back in my cell, all alone, I got sicker than a dog. Everything I ate came out both ends. I puked in my food bowl and I messed up my cell because of the diarrhea. At one point I had to live in that mess for three days before a guard finally gave me a bucket that I could use for a toilet—and that took a lot of convincing. It was really gross, and it would have been a lot worse mentally if I'd known that everybody considered me dead. Later, when I found that out [from another prisoner], I was afraid the Iraqis would discover it and I wouldn't be worth squat to them—that they'd feel like they had free rein to do whatever they wanted to do with me."

The goons also began beating Rob Sweet as soon as he arrived. "I guess it was their way of softening us up before interrogating us," said Sweet. "They started right off just beating the shit out of me with kind of a rubber hose. They concentrated on my legs—one was already swollen badly because of the torn tendon—and that hurt like hell. But they kept at it. Then the next day they did what I guess is one of their favorite tricks; they hit me on the ear to deliberately burst my eardrum. That hurt.

"Later I found out that I was kind of in the middle as far as the beating was concerned. Some guys got it a little worse; some guys got a little less. I didn't get any of the electrical treatments—the car-battery stuff that some of them got. Partly it was the luck of the draw, but I think it was partly how you carried yourself. If you were too arrogant they beat you and if you were too wimpy that beat you. There seemed to be a fine line there. At the beginning I think I was a little too wimpy and then I got too arrogant."

While the prisoners in Baghdad were suffering physically, the commanders in King Fahd were enduring another type of misery.

After seeing the hazards of their taskings increase dramatically over the past two weeks, they received a query from Riyadh basically saying, "You lost three planes yesterday; what can be done to cut future losses?"

Good soldiers do not answer their superiors with replies like, "Why the hell do you think we lost those planes, you dumb asses? You sent us up there; you should have known that we might get clobbered."

Colonels Sharpe and Sawyer kept their cool and their private thoughts to themselves (and from the author) but the pilots around them report that the atmosphere was tense for awhile—until Colonel Sawyer drafted a letter of reply.

In the letter he described the history of the tasking to increasingly hazardous targets. In that letter he added a sentence that caught the eye of General Horner, who later quoted it in a congressional hearing after the war. Said Sawyer, after describing the hit he had taken on the fifteenth and the subsequent flight out of enemy territory, "Believe it or not, on the way home I flew over a flight of F-16s working a target approximately 15 miles north of the Saudi border! A-10s over the Republican Guard [up north] and F-16s in the southern KTO doesn't compute."

At this time four A-10s had received severe battle damage and two had been shot down. But actually, this loss rate wasn't nearly as bad as everybody had expected, considering the threats they were going against. With 144 planes flying thousands of sorties—with a two-ship flight taking off about every fourteen minutes around the clock and flying against the kinds of AAA and missile fire they were experiencing, the loss rate was phenomenally low.

But that really didn't matter. There was a ground war about to be launched and the Air Force had a heavy responsibility to be right there, day and night, with CAS support for the troops. That was the reason for bringing the A-10s into the theater in the first place. So it didn't really matter if the loss rate was lower than expected. There had been losses, and those planes damaged and destroyed would not be available to support the friendlies. And there was a big, tough, commander in Riyadh who . . .

So the Hogs were put on a shorter leash. They were no longer going to do deep BAI in the KTO. (However, they would continue their deep Scud-hunting missions out of Al Jouf into western Iraq.) The pilots didn't mind the shorter leash. In fact, they breathed a sigh of relief when they heard about it.

The Fahd commanders also took one more step to cut losses, and it was not popular at all. "We have," wrote Colonel Sawyer, "prohibited A-10 daytime strafe for the present, except in true CAS, SAR, or TIC [troops in contact] situations. With OA-10 FAC spotters, flight leads using binoculars, or a high (relative) speed recce pass in the 4,000- to 7,000-foot range, we should be able to determine worthwhile armor targets; then stand off and kill them with Mavericks. We'll save the gun (and our aircraft) for the ground offensive."

Later, when Colonel Sawyer commented on this directive, he said, "I know it bothered the guys, made them mad, but we had to do something to stop the losses. We looked back and figured that most of the hits we had taken were after the guys had made a strafe pass. We didn't want anybody doing that until the ground war kicked off—unless, of course, somebody on the ground really needed help. We had Mavericks. They were proving to be an outstanding stand-off weapon. We could still kill Iraqi arty and armor. No sweat. We weren't diminishing our effectiveness. Not at all. Besides, with the ground war coming, we knew we were going to have to get down low and do whatever it took to help those guys. We knew our guys were going to get plenty of opportunities to use the gun."

The pilots were still grumbling after the war when they talked with the author. They didn't like fighting without the gun. Yes, the Maverick was an outstanding weapon. And, yes, they could do lots of damage with their bombs. "But that's like going into Dodge against the bad guys with one hand tied behind your back," one said. Said another, "I could see the reason behind it—I'd have probably done the same thing if I had been a colonel. But that didn't make me feel any better about it."

And it did not stop the losses, either. Three days after they took away their gun and started sending them into kill boxes in southern Kuwait, another Hog driver took the big hit.

Lieutenant Colonel Jeff Fox, the OA-10 squadron's operations officer, took off from King Fahd at 0730 and went to kill box Alpha Echo Five, which was west of the tri-border intersection and just a few miles into Iraq. He arrived there for his TOT of 0830 and was given a five-minute tour by the FAC he was relieving, 1st Lt. Patrick Olson. Said Fox, "He told me there were vehicles in the southern part of the kill box and some artillery and what looked like vehicles in bunkers in the north. Out of my twenty-six missions I had been in that kill box at least a half a dozen times and I was convinced there weren't people down there.

"Our fragged targets were, first priority, artillery, then tanks, and then thin-skinned vehicles [trucks, etc.]. I had a list of the targets ready and a list of the fighters that were supposed to come in the target area—a list of their different TOTs. But no one showed up. Not a soul.

"I entered the kill box at 17,000 feet. I took the briefing at 17,000 feet and in the course of forty minutes of flying around I was down to 8,000 to 9,000 feet. As I went lower my SA [situational awareness] should have had a corresponding increase, but it didn't. At 0900, at the end of my TOT, I was getting ready to climb back up to exit altitude and head for KKMC for gas. I had just checked the last target that had been passed on to me and had placed my binoculars on the right glare shield when I felt a very solid thump under the airplane. It must have been a SAM of some kind—probably an SA-13—and I would bet a month's pay that it had hit just aft of the cockpit.

"The airplane didn't move or budge. It just kept going straight ahead—I was exiting to the south. For a tenth of a second, I said to myself, What the hell was that? There was no clanging or grinding, but the lights on the panel began to illuminate. Then the airplane was pitching up ever so slightly and I padlocked exclusively to the hydraulic gauges because the stick was losing control. Both hydraulic gauges were going to zero and I reached and placed the airplane in manual reversion. The stick was dead now and it pitched up to where it finally rolled off to the right. I am now making radio calls, 'Mayday, Mayday, I'm hit, Alpha Echo Five, I'm heading south.'

"The airplane is spiraling around now, I have no control, and the nose is just seeking the ground. I'm desperate now, trying to get a hold of this thing. All I can see is sand. There is no more sky. Then, with the airspeed increasing you get into sensory overload. If somebody had said, 'Jeff, move that switch and the airplane will right itself,' you would go, 'Forget it.' I knew it was time to eject. I pulled the handles—40 pounds of pull—and I remember the canopy leaving the airplane. Whooosh.

"The next thing I knew I was awake in the parachute and simultaneously with coming awake, I heard the airplane hit the ground. Baboom. And I was coming down into the wreck. Also, at this time I was in a little state of shock. During the ejection my right elbow had struck the canopy rail and my hand was hanging. My right heel had struck either the airplane or the ejection seat during seat separation, and my knee hurt very much—later they found a torn ligament that required major surgery. My knee hurts, I'm holding my right arm with my left hand, I'm coming down into the wreck and I can hear the 30mm popping. It is only the casings exploding but in my mind I was going, 'Oh, Christ, I'm going to be killed by these bullets.'

"I was attempting to steer the chute but I physically didn't have the strength nor the inclination to do it. I lucked out; I drifted ever so slightly to the right and missed landing in the crater. But I landed in the blast frag area because the ground where I landed was all black from the blast. You could see maps and papers and other paraphernalia that had floated down. I was out of that parachute harness in about a nanosecond and as I looked around, there wasn't a soul in sight. Off to the south—I could tell by the sun—there was an old vehicle of some kind and I began to move in that direction as fast as I could go—which was not very fast.

"In the meantime, I whipped up the antenna of my radio and did the 'Mayday, Mayday, Mayday' number. And the rest is on tape that guys recorded so I've had the chance to hear it again. I'm saying, 'I'm on the ground, Nail five-three, AWACS come up, where are you? I'm in Alpha Echo Five, come up on this frequency, I don't have the frequency card. Come up on Guard: I'm on Guard; I'm heading south,' and then, God bless them—this is the thing that is a kick in the butt for me—every airplane that was in the air was coming to Alpha Echo Five. You could hear them calling, 'We're inbound, we're coming, we're across the hardball road, call us if you see us overhead, I'm inbound.' 'Yeah, Roger,' Then I looked around and here he comes, a single Iraqi soldier. Distance is hard to judge. He's not very large but he's far enough away where I cannot hear him. But I see him coming. I tell the guys, 'They are coming for me, dudes. Here they come.' They say, 'Okay, fine, we are across the hardball,'—this kind of thing.

"One of the FACs, [1st Lt.] Mike Boyle, said, 'I have a tally ho on your smoke. I am inbound; where are you from there?' I said, 'I'm a hundred meters south.' He said, 'We are inbound.' I say, 'Fine.' But I'm not holding out any hope because this guy is closing. I can begin to hear him in Arabic, screaming, and he's motioning. He has a weapon and I started running. He kept getting closer and he fired his AK-47 in the air in my direction. I stopped, and that's when they said, 'We're inbound; tell me if you hear me overhead.' I said, 'Okay, it's too late guys, he's here.' I have since talked to many guys and they said they listened to that tape a hundred times at home. They didn't know whether I had been shot, beaten or what had happened. They kept listening to the tape and it is to their credit. They were all coming to get me; they just didn't have enough time."

One more Hog driver was now on his way to meet the goons and be beaten and to get an eardrum punctured. He would be the last to suffer that ordeal, but not the last to take the big hit.

# 17

# THE GROUND WAR

*"When the ground war starts, we'll strafe up a storm and get in as close as we need to get the job done. No A-10 pilot should ever have to buy a drink at any Army bar in the future."*
    —Col. Dave Sawyer to General Horner

The ground war was about to start. Like the civilians at home who were glued to their televisions, the Hog drivers, too, were speculating among themselves as to how long it would last.

The pilots, of course, knew something that the civilians at home did not. They knew the extent of the massive Coalition buildup because they were flying over it everyday. They knew that signals had been called for an end-around maneuver, in which armored forces would move swiftly to encircle Kuwait from the west— Schwarzkopf's "Hail Mary" plan, while the Seventh Corps would hold the pivot position and drive up the center.

Also, they knew of the tremendous amount of work done by the planners to anticipate every eventuality. Said Colonel Sawyer, "One day our GLO [Army Ground Liaison Officer] gave Sandy [Sharpe] and me a copy of an Army paper on a breaching strategy—how they would breach the minefields, and so forth. It was incredibly detailed—excruciating detail, really. Those Army guys were precluding everything."

Even with all that knowledge, the majority of the commanders and their pilots thought the ground war would last two weeks or more. "I confess that I was one of the most conservative ones," said Colonel Sawyer. I estimated a month because I expected some fanatic resistance on the ground. I believed that Saddam's plan was to drag the war on, inflict heavy casualties, and when the body bags started coming back home to America, protestors would cause America to pull out like they did in Vietnam. Consequently, I expected something like the Okinawa campaign where we would find pockets of resisters, like those who believed in the emperor—fanatics who would fight to the death rather than surrender. And as far as casualties go, I was afraid we'd get at least a thousand of our guys killed on the ground."

Sawyer's perception may have been pessimistic, but it helps us appreciate the attitude of the pilots who were getting ready to fly during the ground war. They didn't know it was going to be a four-day rout. They didn't know that huge numbers of Iraqi soldiers were just waiting for an excuse to surrender. The pilots had heard that every white article the Iraqi soldiers owned had been taken away from them so that they could not surrender. What they did not know was that these same troops were waiting with white nylon from the LUU-2 flare parachutes that had been dropped over the battlefield—parachutes they had picked up and hidden.

The pilots were most aware of what they had to do during the ground war. General Glosson told them before the air campaign started that they would have to fly low and protect the friendlies. They heard it again from their commanders, after another call from Glosson.

"I just happened to be in the WOC when the call came," said Colonel Sawyer, "and I vividly remember some of his words. He said, 'I'm calling all the wing commanders just to let you know that the ground war starts tomorrow and there will soon be something up there worth dying for—that when our ground troops cross that border our job is get down and do whatever we have to to keep them from dying.' He said, 'That's the time to hang it out if you have to, but just don't do anything foolish.' He also pointed out that he really didn't need to say that to the A-10 community. He said, 'You've been down in the mud all along and I'm in awe of what your guys have done with that airplane. So I know you'll do the job that has to be done when the friendlies need you.'

"Of course, we hadn't known exactly when the ground war was going to start—we were speculating like everybody else, but when that call came down, we went into action. We called the squadron commanders together and gave them the word. 'Guys, we're finally going to do the job we were trained for and were sent over here to do.'"

The same day they began preparing the battlefield for the ground attack, the Hogs received still another assignment they weren't expecting. Lieutenant Colonel Tom Essig explains.

"Saddam had all those fire trenches up there that were a potential threat to the Army. They were full of oil, and when we attacked, he was going to light them and keep them burning with plumbing connected to oil wells. Supposedly, they would serve a dual purpose. The continuous fire would act as a barrier, and the smoke produced would screen them from attacks.

"Our tasking involved two approaches. First of all, we were going to try and interdict the plumbing—cut off the feeder lines that supplied oil to the trenches. We were going to do that with Mark-84s—2,000-pound bombs. Second, with the supply to the trenches cut off, we were going to ignite the oil that was there and let it burn out before the attack. Of course, we hadn't done anything like that before, so we didn't quite know how to go about it. I know I was scheduled for a mission where I was going to shoot the trenches with Willy Pete [white phosphorous] rockets. I didn't get to try that; the mission got weathered out. But I think some other guys did it."

The Hogs did try to drop the big bombs on the oil feeder lines and in some cases were successful. Eventually, however, the Stealths—F-117s—were brought in with smart bombs to do that job.

However, the Hogs tried as best they could to ignite the oil that was already in the trenches. They tried dropping Mark-82s, but from high altitude. "It was like trying to drop bombs on a hairline," said one pilot. "We tried many times, and maybe some of the guys had some luck but we didn't."

In addition, they tried shooting the trenches with the gun. Captain Cliff Grafton, who had been down in Riyadh and had done the RFOA-10G signs, was now back flying and he describes one of those missions.

"I had heard that somebody had strafed the trenches and caught them on fire so that's what I did. My lead stayed east while I lined up and shot some bullets into a trench. It flared up but then went out. I realized then that I was going to have to get a hundred-round burst in the trench to light it.

"The next time I went down pretty low and this time I got maybe 150 bullets in it and it lighted up with a huge fireball—a real explosion. I was at 2,500 feet and my slant range was probably a mile, so I pulled real hard to get out of this big fireball—it came up real high, but it dissipated a lot as I rolled upside down and looked at it. I then went to the next trench and shot it while I was upside down. I rolled and then pulled up and shot a little farther down the next trench—again 150 rounds. Each time I got big, huge explosions. It was like *Apocalypse Now;* it was exciting. Then the artillery people told us we had to vacate the area right then. But I ended up getting three or four of the trenches to totally light before we went north. And the nice thing was that the smoke was going north; it was blowing into the enemy's face."

But the enemy got even, at least with one of the pilots. Captain Rich Biley, with wingman 1st Lt. Mike Greco, was sent up to the oil trenches armed with four pods of Willy Pete rockets hanging from their planes. "We had never fired them, except when we were training in the A-10 in Tucson," said Biley. "We didn't know the mil settings or anything else. But we called the OA-10 squadron and got some of that information, then motored up. There was a Nail-FAC ahead of us and it was reported that he got one burning [with Willie Pete] but we couldn't contact him. We went on into the kill box, found some trenches, dropped our Mark-82s and missed, then each of us rolled in and fired the rockets. I got two of them in the trench but they just plopped into the oil and disappeared. We learned later that they have to have oxygen in order to ignite and burn. But we kept at it. Two went in, shot and missed, and I rolled in again for my second pass with rockets—the third pass all together—which was a mistake.

"On that pass I pushed the pickle button and nothing happened. I thought I had hit the switches wrong, so I did it again. Nothing. So I pulled off, rolled from inverted to right side up, and turned south. Then, all of a sudden the airplane shook like we were going through severe turbulence. I didn't hear a noise but it shook like the devil and I immediately lost control.

"The stick was completely inop. The plane started to pitch up and when I pushed forward there was nothing. Then Mike called saying, 'Lead you're on fire.' I didn't have any fire lights and the master caution panel only had a couple of lights lit. I was thinking that maybe some Willie Pete rockets blew up. But I looked back and they were fine. Then I looked and saw my hydraulics [gauges] were zero.

"I went up and over the top in a big wingover and was doing a split-**S** out when I hit the manual reversion switch and gained aileron control. It was a lot sloppier and I still had no pitch control. Somehow I recovered but I felt like a leaf in the wind. I headed south to KKMC, but all I could do was a series of lazy eights, using bank angle to control my altitude. In level flight I was pitched 10 to 15 degrees nose high, so all I could do to keep from climbing was put the plane in a steep bank and bleed off some altitude. For every mile of forward progress, I had to go about a mile left and a mile right. And I couldn't get a good damage assessment because I had to keep Two at a safe distance.

"I got south of the border and now I could eject in good-guy territory. I didn't think there was any way I could get the plane on the ground. Already I had worked up to 23,000 from 9,000—it would have taken 90-degree banks to peel off altitude and I wasn't comfortable with more than 60-degree banks in manual reversion—aileron control was too heavy and too sloppy. Then, I thought of trying a 60-degree banked turn for three-sixty degrees. I did that and Two finally came in close enough to see my damage. He said it looked like Colonel Sawyer's plane, which had gotten its tail feathers blown off with an SA-13. I thought, 'Great, at least he had his hydraulics.' I rolled level again and continued toward KKMC, thinking that I would do a controlled ejection near the base.

"Then I remembered that we had emergency pitch trim for when our regular pitch trim was inop. That was on the left console and I tried it. The nose came down and I discovered that I had some pitch control. It wasn't much—it took two or three seconds for it to respond, but at least I could get the nose up or down. I eased off power, got down to 10,000, and contacted Alamo Ops at KKMC. They had the Dash-1 [operating manual] and they began helping me through the checklist. I continued the descent to 5,000, flying in a landing configuration. I did the emergency gear extension, got three greens, checked the controls and decided I was on the razor's edge, with just enough control at each phase to go on to the next. About 15 to 20 miles out, Mike, who was low on fuel, went on in to land and [Capt.] John Scott came in to fly chase.

"I started on the approach but began to get a bit of PIO [pilot induced oscillation]—the nose would get low and I would do a couple of clicks of up trim, then the nose would overrespond, going from being too low to too high—and it was getting worse. At about 1,000 feet I went about 3 [degrees] high—I really wanted to get that thing on the ground. Then I went 5 [degrees] low at about 500 feet and saw a windscreen full of desert. I hit the pitch trim back as far as it would go and shot up, then went around."

Captain Scott, who was flying chase, said, "When I came up on him, I was amazed that he was still flying. The tail stinger was totally gone and there were cables hanging out in the wind behind it. The whole back end was just full of holes. He had no linkage at all to the elevator; all the cables were blown away. He just had electrical control to the trim tabs which gave him some delayed pitch authority.

"After the go-around, he came in again and did a spectacular job of flying. It was a stable, smooth approach and he set it down hard, just like you are supposed to do when in manual reversion. Both wheels hit, then the nose came down hard like the book says it will. I was maybe 200 feet above him when, in the calmest voice he says, 'Well, gentlemen, I have no brakes.' Theoretically he should have had emergency accumulator braking but for whatever reason it didn't work. So he goes rocketing down the runway, drifts off the right side, directly toward a C-130 that was warming up."

"I was going about 165 knots on the hard-packed caliche [a rock-like layer of material] right toward this C-130," said Biley. "I learned later that he ran up to full power but didn't know which way to go. I was freaking, along just for the ride, and the cockpit was shaking like crazy. I stood on the rudder even though I knew I had no control, and somehow it started bouncing back to the left. I came back across the runway at a 30-degree angle, still going, maybe 155 knots—it would not slow up. As I crossed the runway my nosewheel hit a runway light and blew. I was on the rim but even that didn't seem to slow it. I was back in the caliche and the dust again, and then I started heading toward some soft desert—sand and bushes—and when I hit that, the nose gear sheared, the nose went down into the dirt and I went IFR, with dirt and rocks going over the canopy. Then the tail started to come right and the main gear sheared because of the side loading and the right wingtip with the ECM pod dug into the dirt. Without that pod, I might have started cartwheeling, but digging into the dirt, it acted as a stabilizer. Then it spun out. It did a 180 [turn to the opposite direction] and stopped in a cloud of dust and nobody could see me. The canopy seals were broken and tons of dust came in the cockpit. I shut off the engines, unstrapped, jumped over the side, and was 200 feet away from the plane before a fireman arrived. Looking back, I would never do that again if I knew I wouldn't have brakes. But the problem is, how are you going to know that?"

Everybody breathed a sigh of relief when Biley walked away from that airplane. And not just for Biley's sake. The KKMC ramps were loaded with huge fuel bladders, stockpiles of bombs and ammunition, and numerous planes in various stages of rearming and refueling. Biley's out-of-control landing could have created a disaster, and it was a cause of many nightmares for those who were potentially threatened by it. However, they had not seen the worst. In just a few days they would see a tragedy that would remain etched in their minds forever.

The ground war kicked off on February 24, Saudi time, and nothing happened the way the Hog drivers expected. First, the weather was, in their phrase, Delta Sierra. Low clouds, rain, thunderstorms, lightning, wind shears, severe turbulence, icing conditions—all of these meteorological conditions occurred at one time or another during the four-day ground war.

Also, they had the black filth and muck left by Saddam's criminals to depress and hinder them.

One of the world's most massive oil spills blackened the beautiful blue waters and white beaches that had provided optical relief from the depressing moonscape over which they flew most of the time. The dense, black clouds of smoke from the oil well fires the Iraqis had set, colluded with the ragged, low, nimbus clouds to create a true "darkness at noon," eerie, sinister, low-visibility environment where the threat of a midair collision, with so many planes down in that muck trying to do CAS, was as hazardous as the Iraqi AAA and missiles.

And besides all that, the Army was moving too damned fast.

In the traditional CAS scenario, the Army moves a distance, stops and consolidates, then moves again—always with reasonably well-defined positions and doctrine-dictated lines where CAS aircraft work and are subject to control.

However, in this war, the doctrine rarely got past the textbooks where it was printed. This war was almost a stampede, with troops and machines racing to see who could create the most mayhem upon the enemy. Captain Rob Givens probably best described what the Iraqis were up against when he said, "Most people see the American soldiers when they are eating ice cream and pizzas and having fun. And they think, 'Oh, those are good-natured, fun-loving, friendly young people,' and they're right. But what they don't realize is that when you tear those same Americans away from their homes and families and put them in a war, they become the most violent, bloodthirsty fighters on the earth."

For four days the Hogs flew around the clock. They killed hundreds of tanks, many of which were out of their revetments and running. Now they were showing up white-hot on their TVMs and easy targets for their IR Mavericks. At the low altitudes they were flying, they were also killing lots of armor with their guns, and were getting confirmation of these kills from the ground FACs who were coordinating the attacks.

They were also earning the free drinks they expected to get at the Army bars when they returned home. Time after time they answered desperate calls from ground FACs who were taking fire from Iraqi artillery. Flying through the muck, sometimes as low as 50 feet and with as little as 1 mile visibility, they went in and either killed the artillery or marked its position so the friendlies could kill it.

Captains Paul Johnson and John Whitney flew a mission that was typical of some of the wild flying that was done during the ground war. Said Whitney, "We were working with the Brits—they were pushing northeast and the wind had shifted bringing all that oil smoke over their area. It created a cloud bank from about 50 feet to

300 feet and we had to get under that. I felt very uneasy about going in there, not having flown below 5,000 feet since September, and having never seen life below 100 feet in my entire career. But I followed PJ in and somehow he located the Brit's position in all the haze, smoke, and disorienting desert geography. When we got there, they were taking fire from some Iraqi tanks and they called us on them. As we came in, they attacked them with multiple rocket launchers and TOW missiles, then we hit them with Mavericks. It was tough, because my mil settings were for a down angle, and in order to fire my Mavericks I had to raise the nose, but that would put me in the oil. But we got three of them. PJ shot the first, I shot the second, and he shot the third. The Brit FAC confirmed all three and PJ flew right over one of his and confirmed that they were T-64s.

"After taking out one more tank, the FAC wanted us to overfly the target area to survey the situation, and PJ unhesitatingly agreed. Fortunately for us, the Iraqi's had already given up, waving white cloth as we overflew them at 50 feet. They scattered as PJ dropped a flare marking their position for the FAC and, of course, the flare was still burning as it hit the ground, bouncing between the soldiers, making them even more anxious. The Brits rolled in and we were called to assist in another area. However, I made it absolutely clear that I'd had enough of that kind of fun for the day—besides we were low on fuel."

The pilots who were probably the most courageous and who had the most demanding flying of them all were the FACs who had to fly by themselves, without the security of a wingman to cover them, and who had to hang out over the battlefield, in low visibility, within the envelope of all the Iraqi AAA, and direct all the other fighters in to their targets. "It was almost an out-of-body experience," said Lt. Col. Bob George, the commander of the Nail-FACs. "I guess you're just a coward and don't show up, or you go out and do what you have to and ignore the danger.

"I know one day I was out there—I think this was typical—and I was working with a ground ALO [Air Force Liaison Officer who is a ground FAC] low over this area where I called in guys that killed twelve tanks. Then the Army guys said, 'There's some artillery down there shooting at us and we need coordinates on them.' I rogered and at 1,500 feet, which is pattern altitude [the altitude one flies in the traffic pattern over an airport], and at 250 knots I went boring through a rain storm, popped out the other side, rolled over to take a look, and I was right over an active Iraqi artillery battery. They were shooting the gun and I was close enough to see their faces looking up at me. It was sort of like the hunter and the bear seeing each other at the same time. I rolled off, marked the coordinates and gave them to the Army. That was the end of that battery."

Some of the pilots were working so low and so close to the Army that they could not use their bombs or their Mavericks, but had to work strictly with their guns. Two Vultures, Lt. Col. Jack Shafer and Capt. Tom Atkins, found themselves in that position north of Kuwait near the Ar Rumaylah Air Base. Said Atkins, "The friendlies were going against a long line of dug-in T-72s and the battle was going good when we got there. We could see our tanks firing, then our Apaches popping up and firing. Our guys were holding their own but they wanted us to go against a second echelon of tanks.

"We made one pass, came back around, took both 23mm and 37mm fire and one IR missile that we outmaneuvered, then went in on a different heading. This time we were so low we couldn't use the bombs or the Mavericks; our only option was the gun. But we just rolled around and took turns driving bullets through tanks—it was almost like shooting at the rag [range target] except people were shooting back at us. On two passes I actually got to see the tanks erupt into flames and the turret pop off. Apparently the turrets aren't bolted on; they must just sit on there with their weight holding them on because when the tanks blew, you could see the turrets sail through the air and tumble on the ground. Also, to keep the bullets away from friendlies, we would pull the plane around, using a little rudder and aileron, and pull the bullet stream to the target. Just on that one attack we got six T-72s that were confirmed by the HeliFAC [helicopter FAC] who watched our attacks."

That same day two Vanguards, Capt. Eric Salomonson and 1st Lt. John Marks set the all-time one-day record for A-10 tank kills by a two-ship flight. Salomonson describes that action:

"We had flown three missions the day before so they put us on CAS alert and, quite truthfully, I wanted to cock the plane [preflight it and have it ready to go instantly], then go take a nap. We were doing the preflighting just before 0500 when we went Alarm Red and had a Scud attack. But we had gotten complacent by then and said the heck with it and finished the preflight. Then they launched us and we flew off in the dark with no idea where we were going.

"We contacted all the agencies, got some coordinates, then met some guys from the 74th [Flying Tigers Capts. Mike Mangus and Ralph Hansen] who had been up there on a night mission and found a column of tanks. They passed a fighter-to-fighter handoff [they passed target information directly rather than through ABCCC] which was nice. They said they had popped the first and the last tank in the column to bottle them up and that there should be plenty of targets left.

"We got up there and contacted Nail 66 [Capt. Ted Bale]. He was coordinating with the Army units to make sure where the friendlies were. Then we started hitting them. We had four Mavericks and full gun, but no bombs, which made it nice because we didn't have that extra weight to carry around. I immediately rolled in and the tanks were beautiful hot targets against a cool background—it had just quit raining and the ground was muddy. They were very easy to lock up and we just kept rolling in in a shooter-cover attack. It was an A-10 pilots dream—an air-to-mud pilot's dream to have twenty-five or thirty operational Soviet tanks that had just been running. The secondaries were fabulous. Sometimes star-cluster shells would pop out or real bright magnesiumlike stuff would come spewing out on the ground and burn white hot for fifteen or twenty minutes. Turrets were blowing off like tops blowing off pop bottles. When we left the area we had eight burning, blowing up and spewing stuff, and we had put bullets down on four others that we called damaged—they were probably killed but we were always conservative.

"We went to KKMC, shut down, went into Ops and were immediately sent back out. The Marines in the MarCent area [southern Kuwait along the coast] needed help.

"This second mission was hair-raising. The weather was worse; it was raining with a low overcast and there was AAA everywhere. A Marine FastFAC [F/A-18] was working the area and he starts telling us about a row of tanks, which were right in the heart of the AAA."*

"There were bullets all over the place but we shot our Mavericks and emptied our guns and just kept the jet moving all the time. As long as we could see the stuff [AAA] moving on our canopy, we knew it wasn't going to hit us, so we just kept after them and got eight more tanks.

"Then we did a third mission, worked with another FastFAC and we came out that day with a confirmed twenty-three tanks destroyed and ten others damaged. Getting that many was partly luck but we had also gotten very good with the gun by then. We had figured out how to hammer them on a 45-degree or steeper wire [dive angle] where we could put bullets through the top. It was a record, of course, and there was a lot of hoopla about it, but we didn't do any-

---

* Wingman Lieutenant Marks said, in a separate interview, "It was very dark and eerie because of the oil smoke, low clouds, and rain, and while we were circling around looking at all the AAA and Fish [Salomonson] was asking about threats, the Marine FAC just says, 'Look, are you coming in or not?' Of course, when you say something like that to two Hog drivers, it's like a slap in the face, so we went in.

thing that any other A-10 pilots couldn't have done in the same situation. We just lucked out and had three target-rich environments on all three missions."

Some of the pilots' most memorable missions were flown during the ground war, and their memories had nothing to do with the tanks they killed or the ordnance they expended. Captain Paul Rastas, a Vulture, describes one such experience.

"We were tasked to support the Seventh Corps as they moved north and hit the Republican Guard. [1st Lt.] Brad Whitmire was on my wing and we had let down through a solid overcast to designated coordinates, and the FAC who was down there brought us in over the battle. It was really unfortunate that we had cloud cover because a satellite photo of that scene would have been awesome. It was just like a map with General Schwarzkopf's plan in the sand. You could see the tank tracks going north, then hooking right into the Republican Guard. It was laid out perfectly. We saw a unit break off to the right and hit revetments, then we saw the burning stuff. We were right over these M-1s charging the revetments in a line. I'm going, 'Wow!' It was amazing! I'm seeing behind me about thirty armored vehicles, tanks, APCs in perfect formation just charging for the front line. The Army really impressed me that day. It was absolute discipline."

Captain Greg Benjamin had another memorable experience. "I was flying with [Capt.] Mark Hedman and we were working with a FAC who was marking targets for us. But every time he would mark the target, thirty guys would come out with their hands up waving white flags. That happened three or four times. Finally, a ground FAC called us in on a target and the air FAC came to confirm it. Again, as he shot a rocket in, the ground FAC goes, 'Wait, wait, wait, I think they are surrendering.' Sure enough, they came out waving white flags. Then the ground FAC calls us in again on a target a little farther away but we can't drop because our bombs would be too close to the prisoners. And that's the way it went. We never did get any of our ordnance off. They were just waiting for us to get there so they could surrender."

One group of Iraqis who surrendered made world headlines and, afterwards, contributed to Warthog lore. Captain Don Fann, who was at TACC in Riyadh tells the story. "One day during the ground war this Army Blackhawk helicopter was out scouting an area when these Iraqi soldiers see it and they started waving white flags. The crew didn't know what to do but they ended up accepting the surrender and used the helicopter to herd the prisoners away. That evening the Army guy who was giving the brief to General Horner had made a special slide for the briefing. It was a drawing of an

A-10 towing a banner over the battlefield at low level, the banner reading, 'The Blackhawk departs at 1300.' When he presented the slide, he said, 'Sir, we are respectfully suggesting another job for the A-10 since it has been doing everything else in this war.' It was a great joke, but it made us feel good because other people recognized all the things we had done."

The war was within one day of being over but there was still time for another pair of Hog drivers to make a spectacular contribution to the victory.

Out west, Lt. Col. Greg Wilson, the former Raven FAC and, according to one of his many admirers, "the compleat warrior," was up near the Syrian border, looking for Scuds, with Lt. Stephan Otto of the Panther Squadron. "We were right up where the Euphrates River comes in from Syria," said Wilson. "We had dropped our CBUs on Hicksville on the way up, and I really didn't have much hope of finding Scuds at the coordinates we were given. I was actually hoping to get another locomotive or two [he had already killed several]. Near the town of Al Kiem we found what I thought was a FROG missile site and while I was firing a Maverick on one of those, Steve Otto says, 'Hey look over here; here is some other stuff.'

"I climbed back up and went over there and put the glasses down on what looked like SAM sites. Then, in between these two complexes, the first time I dragged the binoculars across I got the image of four Scuds sitting out in the open. I couldn't believe it. I rubbed my eyes and kind of cleaned off the lenses, looked again and there they were—only there were about twenty of them.

"I fired a Maverick at one of them and it went off with a huge secondary. It was red smoke which we hadn't seen before. Obviously they were fueled and ready to fire. Otto had two Mavericks and he fired and got two more. Then something flew by my airplane, kind of fishtailing. About that time on Guard I got a warning that there was a Hawk launch south of the target. It must have been one of our Hawk missiles they had stolen out of Kuwait, and it must have been an optical launch by a guy who didn't know how to control it. By that time we were out of gas and had to head south.

"We went back, refueled and rearmed, hit a tanker on the way up and went back in. This time we had an SA-3 launched at us but we defeated it. By the time we got up there the third time, seven Navy F/A 18s were coming into the target. Altogether we busted them up pretty good. It was a long day, with twelve hours in the airplane, but I think it might have been a very important mission. I think there was a good chance Saddam was going to launch one last, massive attack on Israel as sort of a last-ditch effort to bring them into the war. But that's just a guess."

As the war was nearing its end, the Hog drivers were having more and more difficulty employing their ordnance. They flew as cover, but the tanks and Apache helicopters with Hellfire missiles were "just awesome," to use an almost universal description by the Hog drivers who flew over the advancing armor units.

Captain Greg Durio, the Cajun who discovered Home Depot, describes one scene. "With my wingman, 2d Lt. Mark Mikelonis, we were covering the ground attack of the Jalibah airfield near the Euphrates River north of Kuwait. It was truly a John Wayne episode if I ever saw one. Tanks were rolling at almost full speed, firing to the side, to the front, back to the side, and the chatter on the radio was wild, with the ground FACs telling how they were overrunning the MiGs that were still on the airport. We had a God's eye view of the whole scene. We saw some enemy tanks waiting for them and wanted to go in—we knew the friendly markings and felt secure doing this, but we were told to hold fire. They wanted to take them out themselves, and they did. There were guns blazing and fires everywhere, and at any given time there were twenty or more tanks in our field of view. Soon it grew dark from the black smoke, and the muzzle flashes of the tanks, which are very, very bright, were tremendously impressive. As we were preparing to leave, one of the ALOs down there was telling us about one of the MiGs. He was saying, 'It's in almost flying condition. Oops, no, it's not any more.' It was quite a sight. It was pure Hollywood, but even Steve Spielberg couldn't recreate that scene."

First Lieutenant Scott Fitzsimmons, Nail 80, was flying in that same area when he heard a Mayday call on Guard frequency. It was an F-16 pilot [Capt. Bill Andrews] and he had been shot down near the Ar Rumaylah airfield west of Basrah. "I knew where he was," said Fitzsimmons, "so I started heading up there. The visibility was low but he picked me up when I was about 3 miles away. They had fired at him while he was in his chute coming down, and when he hit the ground he broke his leg. So here he was, with a broken leg, with the Gomers still shooting at him on the ground, and he answers my call with something like, 'I gotcha, break, missiles, Zeus!'

"Zeus is what we call the ZSU 23-4, the radar-guided, four-barrel AAA gun that sends out a red stream of bullets. Actually, all I really heard was, 'Break, missile, Zeus,' and I broke as hard as I could and started puking out flares. As soon as I broke, this wall of fire went over the top of the canopy from the ZSU. I haven't talked to him but when he gave me that warning, the missiles and bullets must have been in the air. At the low altitude I was flying, if he had even waited a breath for the warning I would have been dead. He saved my life, and he won an Air Force Cross, the highest Air Force award given during the war and one of only two that were awarded. I never had the chance to thank him personally but I made sure he got a fine bottle of single-malt after the war when he returned to Germany."

It was a melee on the ground for the entire four days and all the A-10 pilots who were interviewed expressed relief that there weren't some midair collisions because of the large number of aircraft providing CAS during the fray. In regard to their other worry—the inadvertent killing of friendlies—they were not so lucky. One of the A-10s was called in on what he believed was an enemy APC by a ground FAC. Since the pilot did not see an orange panel or any other marking device that was supposed to be displayed on the top of all friendly vehicles, he fired on it with a Maverick. The result was tragic. It was a British "Warrior" APC and some of its occupants were killed. Further details on this incident have been withheld until completion of a British coroner's inquest, which was under way as this book went to press.

Another major tragedy hit the A-10 community. Tragically, it happened in the last hours of the war. First Lieutenant Patrick Olson, Nail 69, was flying his OA-10 in the same general area where the F-16 was shot down. AAA and shoulder-fired missiles from the cornered Republican Guard divisions were murderous, but he remained low over the battlefield and coolly sorted out the mix of fighters threading through the smoke and haze and, according to his colleagues, bravely ignored the threats that were being fired at him. Then he got hit, and Capt. Dave Hanaway who, with his wingman Capt. Jim McCauley, was in the air with him, describes the scene.

"Olson joined us and the three of us flew in low over a battle. MRLs [multiple rocket launchers] were going off and one 55mm artillery was firing—there were M1A1s charging and firing, with lots of smoke and muzzle flashes everywhere. It was an awesome sight and after Olson, working with a ground FAC, talked us in, we made two or three passes, then he said, not in code, 'I'm hit.' I said, 'Roger, turn to heading two-seven-zero and where are you?' He had been out in front of us trying to find more targets. We finally got visual on him and started escorting him back.

"He was in manual reversion and was telling us he had no hydraulics and that oil pressure on his right engine was dropping. I'm in fingertip with him now, 3 feet away—we're over friendlies— and looked him over. He had a bunch of holes in the bottom of the fuselage, his rudders were gouged from fragments, and there was frag damage on the engines—it was pretty much like Sawyer's plane—it was probably an IR missile that exploded just before contact. Olson was calm. We talked about punching and I told him to relax, that he was over friendlies now. If anything went wrong [with the plane] no big deal. I wasn't really worried about him. We were about thirty minutes out of KKMC. However, he wasn't getting full power. We had power way back and we were doing about 200 [knots] indicated.

"Coming into KKMC I cleared my wingman to land. I was low on gas but flew chase about 200 feet above him as he approached. He had talked with the SOF [supervisor of flying—in the tower] all along, had done the controllability checks and his approach looked good."

As Olson talked to the SOF it was also established that he had no upward elevator authority, nor did he have the emergency elevator trim that Rich Biley had used to raise the nose during his manual reversion landing. The only upward pitch authority he had was engine power; when he increased power, that increased lift which brought his nose up. According to Lt. Col. Lee Brundage, who subsequently investigated the incident, "They [the SOF and Olson] began discussing the option of him making a controlled ejection in an area near the field. He [Olson] didn't come right out and say it, but in my opinion, from listening to the tape, he really didn't want to do that. He wanted to land the airplane. After all, Jim Rose had done it in manual reversion, and so had Rich Biley. The difference was that they had some up elevator authority—they could flare during the touchdown phase. He could not, at least with the elevator. All he had was power to increase lift [and that would have dramatically increased his landing speed]."

Major Greg Durio, who had been up north watching American forces overrunning the Jalibah airfield, heard Olson talking on the radio as he was limping home. Durio and his wingman, after determining that they were not needed as an escort, hurried to KKMC so that they could turn for another mission, and would already be on the ground in the event that Olson had trouble landing and ended up closing the only runway.

"I had just begun my refueling," said Durio, "and I was sitting on the parallel taxiway when he came in sight about 4 or 5 miles away on a left downwind. Then he turned on final and I was the closest one to the runway where he would touch down. There were two planes behind me, and there were fuel bladders, ammo, and bombs stacked everywhere—we had no other paved places to put them.

"I watched his whole approach and it seemed to be a fine approach. I didn't know his limitations in the plane but obviously he felt that he could make the landing.

"He almost did. He was coming in and it looked like a stable approach; it looked like he was going to make it to the runway. But he hit short—I don't think it stalled; I think it just dropped short, but it didn't hit nose wheel first and it didn't appear to me that he hit abnormally hard. He hit in the overrun, which was soft, and it looked to me like his right gear sunk into the ground, and then sheared off. The plane started sliding and turning a little sideways, then the left wing started getting lift and the plane got airborne again—almost 50 feet by my estimate. However, the left wing just kept getting lift and the plane rolled inverted and was coming right toward me. I could see the canopy and, now that he was inverted, it was too late for him to eject.*

"I could see him in the cockpit and I literally watched the canopy impact the ground. Then the plane kept coming straight for me with a massive fireball erupting from it. Actually, it was headed more for my wingman and it stopped maybe 150 feet away from him—close enough for him to feel the heat of the fire before we pulled away. It's horrible to say this after his tragic death, but there were a lot of us who were very, very fortunate. With the fuel bladders and Mavericks stacked all over, it would have been almost impossible to plan a crash that would have done less damage."

First Lieutenant Olson was killed instantly in the crash, and it was a bitter loss to those who knew him. Six months after the war they were still talking about the loss. Said his squadron commander, Lt. Col. Bob George, after a flagpole was dedicated to Lieutenant Olson at the main entrance of Davis-Monthan Air Force Base, "He had a great natural talent for leadership, he was intelligent, and he was intensely patriotic—I mean he flew every mission with a folded American flag under his seat. There is absolutely no question in my mind that he had the quality of leadership that could have taken him to the top job in the Air Force. We lost a potential chief of staff."

---

* Hanaway, who was watching from above, called for him to eject at this time.

# 18

## The Bitter End

*"The single most recognizable, and feared aircraft was the A-10. This black-colored jet was deadly accurate, rarely missing its target. Seen conducting bombing raids 3 to 4 times a day, the A-10 was a seemingly ubiquitous threat. Although the actual bomb run was terrifying, the aircraft's loitering around the target area prior to target acquisition caused as much, if not more anxiety since the Iraqi soldiers were unsure of the chosen target."*

*—Seventh Corps debrief of a high-ranking Iraqi prisoner of war.*

By the evening of the 27th of February it was almost over. Coalition ground forces had blitzed through Kuwait and were now in Iraq, blazing away, trying to annihilate the surviving armor of the Republican Guard divisions that were engaged in a fighting retreat. When darkness arrived the president's goal of liberating Kuwait had probably been accomplished. But the Republican Guard's armored forces were like a gut-shot lion; they were mortally wounded but still extremely dangerous. So the battle raged on into the night, and the destruction or capture of that armor was on the mind of every Coalition warrior.

And that included the Night Hogs.

Said Lt. Col. Jim Green, "For me, this was the scariest night of the war. [First Lieutenant] Eric Paul and I took off at about 1900 and there was a line of huge thunderstorms along our whole route to the northwest. They were vicious, with lots of lightning and we had to pick our way through those. Finally, we got up near Kuwait, tankered, then headed north of Basrah, to the highway along the Euphrates River where a convoy of about two hundred vehicles— mostly tanks—were trying to escape. When we got there it was like a feeding frenzy with A-10s, F-16s and F/A-18s all trying to get in to destroy that convoy. I ended up orchestrating the affair since we were beyond the army and the ground FACs. The Iraqi guys jumped out of their vehicles and ran while the mix of planes in the area just systematically decimated that column.

"Then I went bingo and we headed to KKMC to refuel. Only we were not tracking the course I had planned. The winds that night were 100 knots out of the west and, without us realizing it, we were blown over the Iranian border. Then, as we were coming back across the border and over Basrah International Airport, I got SA-6 launch indications on my RWR."

First Lieutenant Eric Paul, his wingman, continues the story. "Colonel Green was yelling that there was an SA-6 launch and I didn't have any indications. But I started looking and saw an orange plume at my three o'clock and I called that out. I didn't know where he was exactly, but he calls back that he sees it and tells me to chaff. I start firing chaff and later he said I looked like Halley's Comet with that chaff coming out behind me, illuminated both by the firing mechanism and the bright moon that was out that night."

"I don't mind saying that I was scared when I saw that orange plume," said [Col.] Jim Green. "It was guiding on me because it wasn't moving in my canopy, so I chaffed, put it in on my beam, waited until it flamed out, then put on some heavy G's and pulled for the ground. Then, at night, all you can do is wait and hope that it misses because you can't see it. Luckily, it did miss us, as did a second missile they fired at us.

"The rest of the night was anticlimactic. We went back and refueled, then headed north again. But by that time the Army was in control and they would not let us employ our ordnance. They pretty much had the Iraqi forces corralled and just didn't need us. From my perspective the A-10 shooting war ended about midnight on the twenty-seventh.

That night Capts. Mark Koechle and Don Henry were among those who were attacking the Iraqi armor column. Said Koechle, "The first time up there we just followed the INS, not really knowing where we were going. We found the armor, bombed it with Rockeye [cluster bombs with armor-piercing bomblets], fired our Mavericks, then came back to KKMC. That is when we plotted our course on the map and found out that we had been north of Basrah on the Baghdad highway. We went back and there was a lot of confusion. But we kept hunting for movers and about 2 miles north of the column we had hit, I saw this mover [on the TVM] heading north. It was a multiple rocket launcher and it burned for an hour after I hit it with my Maverick. Just north of there was a bridge over the Euphrates that F-16s were trying to take out. As they were attacking there was lots of AAA and several SAM launches. Things quieted down about midnight but before that, there was a real war going on."

Early the next morning some of the Hog drivers got airborne and were heading for the battlefield when, at 0500 Saudi time, they heard a codeword broadcast from ABCCC. The codeword was "Wolf Pack," and according to the information they had received in their pre-mission briefing, it meant that a cease-fire had been declared and that they were to return to base.

They had flown over 8,100 missions, an average of 193 missions a day for 42 days. So the phasing down of operations came as an immense relief to their tired bodies and stressworn nerves. However, their commanders were already shifting gears and looking at new challenges. And they were most concerned that their "kids," now older by years after 42 days of combat, would soon become restless and perhaps too nonchalant about the "plain vanilla" peace-time flying that was in store for them. So the commanders preached a slogan, "Not one more life," and they assumed the unpleasant, but necessary task of taming some who had gotten into the aggressive mode during the ground war, who were, by nature, feisty, balls-to-the-wall, freelancing warriors, back into peacekeepers, where restricted flying hours coupled with budget constraints were the new imperatives.

Of course, they still had some work left to do. Several of the A-10s were tasked to fly low CAP over the area where the cease-fire talks were to be conducted. And numerous pilots flew missions deep into Iraq in support of secret operations by the Special Forces and other intelligence-gathering teams.

They also had some fun, albeit without their commanders' knowledge. For example, one pilot, who must of necessity remain nameless, said, "I was flying over this airfield near where the brass was going to meet and this Army colonel came on the radio and told me to make a low pass in front of his troops, which were in a big crowd near the runway. I replied that I couldn't do that—it was an unauthorized flight. He came back, we established that he was a colonel and that I was a captain and he said, 'I believe you understand an order from a superior officer. So I am ordering you to make a low pass in front of my guys because I want them to take a close look at a damned good airplane. Do you understand, Captain?' Of course, I said, 'Yes, sir!' and I put that airplane in a screaming dive and I flew low, right in front of those troops, moving as fast as the jet would go.

Then this colonel comes on and keys his mike and you can hear the cheering in the background. Those guys were just going crazy down there. They appreciated what we had done."

And, officially, just what had they done? That question was asked numerous times at several levels of command, and the author is convinced that we will never get an accurate answer. After the war, teams of investigators combed through the ruins left on the battlefield and tried to make assessments of damage. In many cases, as when a tank was destroyed by a Maverick missile, it was generally credited to the A-10s. But what about artillery sites that were bombed or strafed? Numerous attack planes went after the artillery sites and it was often impossible to tell what kind of ordnance had done the job. And even the gun kills could not always be credited to the A-10s because the Bradley fighting vehicle has a powerful 25mm gun that also makes little round holes in armored vehicles. And, of course, there was the conservative attitude of the A-10 pilots themselves. During the war they were adamant; they were not going to claim anything killed that might still have some life.

But there is always a demand for statistical analysis so estimates are made whether the data are nebulous or not. The estimate with which A-10 commanders feel the most comfortable is one that credits the A-10 for at least half of the artillery and armor that was destroyed during the war. And that is more of a consensus statement than somebody's official tabulation.

The Pentagon is slightly less conservative. In a "White Paper" published in April, 1991, their analysts said, "Although flying only 30 percent of the sorties, A-10s achieved over half the confirmed bomb damage assessment (BDA). . . ."

In this war, with the exception of air-to-air kills, pilot kills were not recorded. All kills were credited to individual airplanes, which, despite whatever pilot's name happened to be stenciled on it, were flown by a variety of pilots. During the war, symbols for kills of tanks, APCs, Scuds, artillery sites, radar sites and trucks were painted on the sides of the planes. These were removed (along with all the nose art) after the war, but the record remains if anyone cares to dig through the wing records filed under the serial number of the airplane.

And the price for all this glory?

First, the price in machinery. Four airplanes were seriously damaged—those flown by Maj. Jim Rose, Col. Dave Sawyer, Capt. Paul Johnson and Col. Bob Efferson. All four of those airplanes were repaired and flown home, although two of them—Rose's and Efferson's—were more closely inspected and the decision was to take them out of service and make static displays out of them. (Look for them in New Orleans and Sacramento.)

Two airplanes were completely destroyed during manual reversion landings. They were flown by Capt. Rich Biley, who survived,
and 1st Lt. Patrick Olson, who was killed.

In addition, four aircraft were shot down in enemy territory. They
were flown by Capt. Dale Storr, Capt. Steve Phillis, First Lt. Rob
Sweet, and Lt. Col. Jeff Fox. Storr, Sweet, and Fox ejected and were
captured and released. Phillis went down with his plane.

So, altogether, two airplanes were lost from irreparable damage
and four were shot down—for a total loss of six aircraft.

What is both remarkable and of military significance is the fact
that none of the Night Hogs suffered as much as a single bullet
hole.* This, of course, was primarily because of their "relative"
stealth—a factor that might cause a major reevaluation of the A-10's
combat role—more later.

The human price, while tragic, was minimal considering the num-
ber of hazardous missions they flew and all the threats they faced.
Just two pilots were killed in the war: Capt. Steve Phillis and 1st Lt.
Patrick Olson.

The three POWs paid a high price physically and mentally during
their imprisonment in Baghdad. They were all beaten and tortured,
and forced to live in inhumane squalor. Of the three, Lt. Col. Jeff
Fox suffered the most debilitating damage. Upon arrival back in the
States, he had to undergo major knee surgery, and eventually he had
to have a skin graft operation to heal his ruptured eardrum. (The
Iraqis had tried to rupture his other eardrum but failed.) Six months
after the war all three were declared fully recovered and were flying
again. Fox is now working on a book about his experiences and, having heard him describe several of them, the author highly recom-
mends its reading, especially for the episode on the airplane when
the prisoners were flown out of Baghdad.

There was another price paid during the war, and the currency
was the sweat, fatigue and dehydration sickness experienced by the
ground crews who maintained, armed, and fueled the airplanes.
Working around the clock, often in brutal heat, and often with their
faces masked by goggles and scarves to protect them from the hella-
cious sandstorms that frequented the area, they did a magnificent

---

* In the early days of the war, Lieutenant Colonel McDow, on an initial
  flightline inspection, declared that one of the Falcon's airplanes had a
  hole caused by shrapnel. However, he changed his mind later when
  further evidence showed that the damage had been caused by a fragment
  thrown out during a Maverick launch.

job. Despite their many hardships and the extraordinary amount of flying and rough treatment of the airplanes, they maintained a mission capable rate of 95.7 percent, which was 5 percent greater than their peacetime effort. Said Col. Hank Haden, one of the DOs, as he pointed to his flightline at Myrtle Beach, "Percentagewise I had more Code-One jets [planes essentially in perfect condition] during the war than I have out there right now. And the reason is because those folks were as dedicated and as hard-working as any troops I've ever seen."

There had been some skeptics before the deployment. The ground-force ranks included many women, and despite the official propaganda touting the lack of sex bias in the Air Force, many of the veterans felt that the women would be a liability when the going really got tough. The author spent three long days on the flight line with the crews who kept the planes flyable during the war, and repeatedly, in confidential, confessionary statements, the macho males in that fraternity went out of their way to compliment the women. They wanted the author who was going to write a book about their airplane to know that the women really did a job, just like the guys. Said Vietnam veteran C.M. Sgt. Wilson Ewing, Jr., who was the enlisted person in charge of half the airplanes and who himself ended up in the hospital with severe dehydration sickness, "Those women proved a lot to all of us. They worked right along with the men, didn't complain, and handled themselves like real professionals." And said Sr.M Sgt. Luis Salinas, another Vietnam veteran, "You have to remember that in my culture [Hispanic] we have strong traditional views on the role of women. For example, my personal feelings were that I didn't think they should be there, not that they couldn't do the job—I'll tell you, they did fantastic. They never were behind; nobody had to help them out. They pulled their weight and they did it themselves. I was brought up to think different about them. But I'm proud of them now. They proved themselves."

Everybody proved themselves: the air campaign architects, the commanders, the pilots, and the magnificent support crews who kept the campaign running. Technology was also a winner in the war, particularly in the Hog community where the Maverick missile performed superbly as a reliable, stand-off, fire-and-forget weapon. Except for the Maverick that "went stupid" during the Battle of Khafji and killed some of our Marines, the missile performed exactly as it was designed.

So after the war, there were a lot of happy Hog drivers, proud of their achievements with the airplane, and relieved that so many of the Iraqi troops, who for the most part were innocent conscripts, escaped death by remaining out of their vehicles and away from the artillery batteries that they pounded day after day. Nobody knows, of course, how many Iraqis were killed in the war, but the Hog drivers believe that the deaths they themselves caused were mostly the Iraqis who were manning actively firing AAA weapons and artillery, and those who were unlucky enough to be in "movers" that the pilots destroyed at every opportunity. Strictly from the A-10 pilot's perspective, the casualties they inflicted, at least after the first day of the war when the Iraqis were surprised, were light.

After the war, the Hog drivers soon grew restless with their once-or-twice-a-week, short, boring flights to maintain currency, while loved ones at home, impatient and lonely, were plying them with the question they could not answer: Why do they need you now?

Finally, about a month after the war was over, they began to be relieved. It was a "first in, first out" policy, so the first squadrons to deploy—the Panthers and Falcons from Myrtle Beach—were the first to go home. Shortly afterward they were followed by the Vanguards and Flying Tigers from Alexandria, Louisiana. Then the agony set in, especially for the Cajuns, who were reservists with full-time jobs at home and with bosses who had been understanding and patient during the war but who were now questioning, sometimes unkindly, why the reservists were not coming home. Their reasoning, which to some extent coincided with the thoughts of the Cajuns themselves, was that service during peacetime was the job for regulars—that reservists should serve during an emergency, but return to their civilian status when the emergency was over.

Finally, in May, the Cajuns flew home, followed by the Vultures who winged their way back to RAF Alconbury. And what a homecoming it was, for all of the squadrons. Bands played and crowds of flag-wavers greeted them enthusiastically. The pilots spoke at schools, commanders spoke at service clubs, and, in general, the tone was euphoric and the goodwill they encountered was unlike anything they had ever seen or expected as servicemen and women. They were all too young to have seen the same kind of euphoria after World War II.

And they were excited. Their beloved Hog had gained new respect in the eyes of Air Force leadership. In the reduced Air Force that was projected, there were plans to keep 390 A-10s out of the 650 that remained in the inventory. (Before the war, all were scheduled to go to the boneyard.) And all of those were to be upgraded with the new Low Altitude Safety and Target Enhancement (LASTE) mod, which included a radar altimeter, a simple, three axis autopilot, and a computer that greatly enhances shooting and bombing accuracy. Said Col. Dave Sawyer, regarding the LASTE mod, "We were a pretty good gorilla in the Persian Gulf War but we would have been King Kong had we had the LASTE mod over there."

Air Force strategists were also intrigued with the effective ways the A-10 was used as a night fighter. A special developmental unit at Nellis Air Force Base began to experiment with different kinds of forward-looking, infrared devices (FLIRs)—night vision devices that would be much more effective than the "soda straws" used in the war when pilots had only their IR Maverick missiles for night vision. Also, they began to test a variety of night vision goggles that would allow them to increase their night capability. With all of this research underway, many of the pilots, especially the Night Hogs, believe it highly probable that the A-10 will have a significant role in the future as a night fighter.

The summer months began to pass. There were several marriages, including that of Capt. Matt Cavanaugh who, as he was flying through thunderstorms on the way to the war (see Chapter One), was thinking that his girlfriend, Melanie, was the one with whom he wanted to start a family. (The first new member of that family, Luke, arrived September 5, 1992.) And, unfortunately, there were some tragic deaths. Major Jeff Watterberg and Lt. Eric Miller were killed in a midair collision. One of the senior commanders lost his teenage daughter in a head-on collision with a cement truck. But the happiness and sorrow tightened the already strong bonds in the community, even while forces of great magnitude were beginning to tear it apart.

First there was the death sentence that had been imposed by Congress on their air bases. Myrtle Beach Air Force Base in South Carolina was closing. England Air Force Base in Alexandria, Louisiana was closing. RAF Alconbury in England was closing. In addition, the A-10s were being taken away from the Cajuns in New Orleans and replaced with F-16s—not a popular move.

But what really hurt were the squadron inactivations that were ordered. The Panthers, Falcons, Vanguards, Flying Tigers, and Vultures—five of the seven squadrons that fought in the war—were ordered to shut down. In the months ahead they would auction off much of the memorabilia covering the walls of their squadron buildings (each auction winner agreeing to keep the item and return it should the squadron be reactivated). And on the day of the inactivation there would be a ramp ceremony, with a band playing, with Air Force and local dignitaries at the head of a crowd of hundreds of prior squadron members in dutiful attendance, and with a low-level fly-by (a formation with senior veterans and the squadron's youngest pilot). Later, would come a gaggle of parties where young lieutenants and captains, subdued now, would share memories with old-timers who had also worn the coveted squadron patch.

While all of this was pending, anxiety was running painfully deep in the souls of most of the pilots. Almost all of them were worrying about their new assignments after their squadrons went inactivated. Would they be able to stay in the A-10 at some other base even though the numbers of planes were being cut back?

Then, as their concerns grew, the new assignments began to trickle in. And there was some good news. Some of the pilots were, indeed, going to remain in the A-10 at other bases. *Sierra Hotel!* And a few went on to the glamour planes—the F-117 Stealth and the F-15E Strike Eagle. *We'll drink to that!* But many of the new assignments were to the Air Training Command as instructor pilots. This was not good news, and the typical comment heard around the squadrons at that time was, "Oh, no, not back to a Tweet!"—this lamentation referring to the T-37 primary trainer, derisively called the "Tweety Bird" because of its small size and lack of pizazz.

As the months passed and new assignments still trickled in, the pilots began to get worried. At the same time, the word was out that Delta and American Airlines were both hiring and, reluctantly, and for the most part because the future of flying for the Air Force looked like a chancy occupation, several of the pilots elected the security of an airline career. So when the reader flies Delta and American, listen for familiar names coming from the flight deck—names like Cavanaugh, Weidekamp, Sobol, Whitney, Wilson, and Swift.

Later, as the squadrons began to count down their days of existence and pilots had not yet received assignments, the lowly little Tweety Bird began to look more and more inviting. And the comments heard around the squadrons now had a different tone from those heard just six months earlier. The sentiment had shifted and the typical unassigned pilots were often heard to say, "I'd be tickled to death to get a Tweet; at least it's a cockpit."

As this book went to press, all of the unassigned pilots were deeply afraid that the system was going to chain them to a desk somewhere. They had heard horror stories from their commanders of what it was like immediately after the Southeast Asia war was over—how a pilot was lucky to get a job as a commissary officer.

Amid the gloom, there was some good news. At the Gunsmoke competition the A-10s, now with the new LASTE mod, creamed all of the pointy-nosed fighters and brought home the top prizes. Also, wing commanders Sharpe and Sawyer, both popular and respected by their pilots, were recognized for their leadership during the war and were promoted to the rank of Brigadier General. And, down the line, several others in the community received significant promotions in recognition of jobs well done.

But the bitter end was in sight and the pain was mounting, exacerbated when some of the pilots had to fly the most depressing mission of their careers. Let us close this story of the A-10 with an account of one of those missions, which, technically, is fictional, but which is based closely on accounts given by pilots who preferred not to advertise their indiscretions or their pathos.

Low, dark clouds were rolling over the green plains of East Anglia and light rain was falling as the six A-10s departed the runway at RAF Alconbury. They were southwest bound, and behind them followed two spares, ready to replace any of the six should they encounter trouble at the first tanker. They were on their way to the States, heading home over the Atlantic, but the finality of their flight was not on their minds. They were not going to war this time; they were determined that they were going to enjoy this flight, and as they bumped up through the wet, gray clouds and burst out into the dazzling cotton tops of the stratocumulus deck, three of them thumbed the knobs of their Fox Mike radios to the secret frequency that they would use to communicate privately on the trip.

They climbed on up toward the feathery mare's tails that were arrayed in east-west patterns across the sky—cirrus clouds of floating ice crystals, forerunners of a massive low pressure area sitting in the north Atlantic, creating misery for ships plowing through waves created by 70-knot winds. They had been briefed about this system but it did not worry them. Their route of flight to Lajes in the Portuguese Azores, where they would stop for the night, would keep the bad weather on their starboard beam for the entire trip.

They air-refueled once, sent the spares back to England then continued to Lajes without incident. After landing they enjoyed a few beers, a pleasant meal, but a night of intermittent sleep because of howling winds. The Azores were on the edge of the weather system, and the next morning, 95-knot winds were whistling over the mountain peaks, grounding all flights. But the three friends were restless; they wanted to get on with the flight; they wanted to get on with their lives. Bored sitting in their quarters, they braved the wind and set out to climb the highest volcanic peak on the island. And when they reached the top, panting and out of breath, they nestled behind a windbreak, sacrificed two beers to the weather gods, and prayed to them for a break in the weather. And then, as if on cue, the isobars on the next meteorological prognosis charts were farther apart, showing that the pressure gradient was diminishing. The winds were dying and they were going to get to launch at daybreak.

The flight to Myrtle Beach was long, but the war had conditioned them to long confinements in the cockpit. Therefore, they were in a rousing party mood when they were met on the flightline by old comrades offering Budweiser "tall boys"—unavailable in the UK—and treating them like visiting royalty. With a car generously loaned by one of the local pilots, they enjoyed their first night home in the locals' favorite restaurant, and the next day they whacked away in friendly, but bloodthirsty competition on the beautiful Whispering Pines Golf Course. Then they watched the Super Bowl and drank a few more tall boys.

Then it was on to Richards-Gebaur Air Force Base south of Kansas City in separate flights of three. There they were met by more A-10 comrades and were treated to a luncheon where their UK-atrophied palates were reeducated to the tang of Texas-style bar-becued ribs.

After lunch, they took off for Tucson, Arizona—to Davis-Monthan Air Force Base—the last leg of the flight. It was a quiet flight, with little chit-chat, each pilot deep into his own thoughts as the geomet-rically ordered fields of the midwest disappeared behind the wings, and the raw, aimless terrain of the New Mexico and Arizona deserts appeared in the distance.

An hour later the controller monitoring their flight at Albuquerque Center gave his last instructions. "Air Force three-one, contact Tucson Approach three-one-eight point one. So long."

"Three-eighteen-one," the flight lead replied. Then he called Tucson. "Tucson approach, Air Force three-one, flight of three at one-eight-zero checking in."

"Air Force three-one, roger. Radar contact three-four miles north-east. Descend and maintain one-four thousand, fly heading one-nine-zero, vectors for a visual, runway three-zero. Do you have informa-tion Kilo?"

Lead had been monitoring ATIS, the recorded airport informa-tion. "A-firm," he replied.

They backed off power, descended to fourteen thousand, then on Fox Mike, Lead said, "What say guys, shall we arrive like fighter pilots?" He was referring to an overhead approach, which was for-bidden for pilots coming in from a cross-country flight—the theory being that their senses might be dulled by the long flight and that they might not physically be able to cope with the Gs pulled in the approach. But he wanted to bust the reg. He wanted to look sharp on this, his last approach; he wanted to feel the Gs after the boring flight.

The other two did not reply for a moment. Both of them wanted to fly the overhead. Then Three spoke, "Lead you're getting out and Two, you're thinking about it. But what about me? They've got my nuts for four more years."

Lead didn't hesitate. "You're right. Okay, we'll drag it in like good little boys. But ain't it the shits for it to have to end this way?"

*Two:* "Yep."

*Three:* "The runnin' shits, man."

"Air Force three-one," said the approach controller, "descend and maintain eight thousand."

"Leaving fourteen for eight, Air Force three-one," Lead replied. Then on Fox Mike, he said, "Okay, guys take a look at two o'clock. There's a sight that'll make you cry." They were descending between the Rincon and Santa Rita mountains and the 3,000-acre aircraft boneyard loomed ahead and to the right.

*Two:* "Ain't it a shame?"

*Three:* "Yeah. God look at the planes down there."

*Lead:* "See those ugly green ones? That's us guys."

*Three:* "Yeah, I'm counting . . . nine, ten, eleven, twelve. I get twelve.

*Approach control:* "Air Force three-one, you're eight miles east and cleared for the visual, runway three-zero. Contact the tower now on two-five-three point five."

*Lead:* "Two fifty-three-five and cleared for the visual, Air Force three-one." Then to the tower, "Air Force three-one, five miles, gear down, full stop."

*Tower:* "Roger, three-one, cleared to land."

*Three:* "Look at all those F-4s down there guys. There must be two hundred of them."

*Two:* "Yeah, there's enough to start a war."

*Lead:* "Okay, guys forget that shit down there; it's time to get low and slow."

*Two:* "Always slow, boss."

*Three:* "Do you mind if I bounce it one more time?"

*Lead:* "Okay, that's enough; let's make it look good."

They rolled out on the runway, exited on taxiway one-six and Lead waited on the other two. Then, when they had pulled up where they could see him, he tapped his canopy, waited, then nodded, and each flipped their canopy motor toggle switch after pulling it from its detent and all three canopies went up at the same time. Then Lead contacted Ground Control. "Three-one clear the active. How about vectors to the cemetery?"

*Ground Control:* "Roger, taxi straight ahead, follow me will assist."

They taxied south until they saw the "follow me" truck, then trailed behind it down a long taxiway to a ramp in front of some buildings. "That must be the mortuary," said Lead, looking at the largest building.

*Two:* "The place gives me the creeps already."

*Lead:* "Okay, let's shut 'em down."

Lead pulled the left throttle up and over the hump. Then he cycled the flight controls, checking to see that there was no binding of the hydraulics with only the right hydraulics powered. The controls were free and clear. Then he pulled the right throttle up and over the hump and the muted whine of the right engine was replaced by the harsher whine of the inverter as it kicked in. As he sat waiting for the residual fuel to drain from the engines, he looked over to the right where two Navy S-3s were parked, their white and black-striped tail hooks looking stark against the mottled gray planes to which they were attached. He thought they had the same GE engines and he wondered, since they looked heavier, if the S-3's performance was even more doggy than his own bird.

"Lead, are you still up?" It was Two on Uniform radio.

*Lead:* "Yeah, what?"

Two, in a musical voice: "Looook who's catching us."

A blue "six-pack" pickup truck pulled up in front of them and four alert airmen and a staff sergeant piled out.

*Lead:* "Is Plan Alpha still operational?"

*Two:* "I think we've got enough."

*Three:* "I've got some extra Vultures. We're okay."

*Lead:* "Okay, let's do it."

He flipped the toggle switches for the inverter and battery. Then he began unstrapping; first the parachute, then the lap belt, then the right and left survival kit straps, and finally, the G-suit, emergency oxygen, regular oxygen and com cord. After removing his helmet and while he was performing his ritual head-scratching routine, a voice reached him from below. It was the sergeant. "Where did you all come in from, sir?"

Lead turned on his most charming manner. "We started out across the pond and we brought you guys a couple of things."

The sergeant had been bribed before and he responded enthusiastically. "You got some patches, sir?"

Lead didn't reply immediately. He was listening to the musical, soft clink of the fan blades as they spun down, a sound that he would remember the rest of his life. Then, back to reality, he stood up in the seat, turned, reached for the ladder, his booted foot guided by the sergeant, and he remembered the sergeant's question. "Got a couple of patches that you might not have," he said as he stepped down from the ladder. Actually, he had a dozen or so patches in his bag, which was in the travel pod slung under the wing. All pilots carried them on cross-country flights; they were universal trading merchandise and eager collectors seemed to be everywhere.

"I'll get your bags out, sir," said the sergeant as Lead stood, looking wistfully at the row of sleek F-106s on the distant ramp. He had always wished that he could have flown a 106 sometime during his short career.

"Shall we do it now?" asked Two as he approached. One of the alert airmen was also getting his bag out of his travel pod.

"Yeah. Did you see any SPs as you were coming in?"

"No, but they're around. You think these guys will talk them away?"

The sergeant started for the six-pack with Lead's bag when Two yelled at him. "We're going to need those bags, sergeant."

"You want them in at reception?" the sergeant yelled back.

"No, leave them on the ramp," yelled Lead. Then, to Two and Three who had just sauntered up, "Come on, let's get in those bags and start feeding them some patches."

They gave them Vulture and Desert Storm patches and several zaps—paper stick-on squadron insignias—from their base. "Okay, guys, now we have to work on our airplanes a little bit," said Lead to the alert crew. "Are we okay for an hour or so out here on the ramp?"

"No sweat, sir," said the sergeant. Go inside and log in, and when you're ready to go I'll run you to the airport—I guess you'll be flying out tonight."

They logged in with wisecrack remarks then went out on the ramp and took the spray paint and stencils out of their bags. Before leaving the UK the black Vulture stripe under the canopy and the pilots' names had been removed from the airplanes. Now they were going to put them back.

They masked the area with their enroute charts and sprayed the black stripes first. Then, laboriously, using their survival knives, they cut letters for their names out of the stencils they had purchased at the art store in Myrtle Beach. And while they were affixing them over the black stripe, getting them ready to spray with white paint, a truck with two SPs cruised down the ramp. Lead waved and the two SPs smiled and returned the wave as they went by.

"Do you think they shared?" asked Three.

"They probably gave them a zap or two," said Three as they went back to work.

The sun was low when they finished, and they hurried to catch the remaining soft rays of light on the Kodacolor that was in Two's camera. First, Lead posed, sitting in the cockpit behind his name while photos were snapped. Next, Two and Three took their turns while their hero-images were frozen on film for their children and grandchildren to someday admire. Then they took their bags and turned their backs on the green machines that had carried them so many miles through fire and storm. The machines would go to the pickle factory to be embalmed, and, theoretically, they could be brought back to life should they be needed in an emergency. But none of the pilots expected that to happen. With their consciences weighed by guilt, they were leaving their perfectly healthy and faithful bird dogs at the pound and they knew their real fate.

"Lead, we screwed up," Two said as they stood by their bags waiting for the six-pack to pick them up.

Lead frowned. "How?"

"We should have brought some champagne for the occasion."

"You're crazy; you don't drink champagne to a Hog."

Two looked over at the three beautiful, ugly machines sitting silently on the ramp. "They earned it," he said.

# Glossary

AAA—pronounced triple-A; any form of anti-aircraft fire

ABCCC—pronounced A-B-triple-C; a C-130 airborne command post for coordinating air strikes

ADF—automatic direction finding instrument; its needle responds to low-frequency radio transmissions

Aileron—movable control surface on trailing edge of wing; controls roll response; activated by right-left movement of stick

AIM-9—air-to-air, heat-seeking missile; carried by A-10 for defense against fighter attack

Al Jouf—a Saudi airfield about 545 miles northwest of King Fahd and 300 miles northwest of KKMC; served as a base for A-10s hunting Scuds in western Iraq

APC—armored personnel carrier; used to move infantry personnel on battlefield

ATO—air tasking order; the order that specifies the different missions that are to be flown

AWACS—provides airborne radar coverage of strike area; provides vectors for friendly aircraft; detects enemy aircraft and missiles

BAI—battlefield air interdiction; missions are flown behind enemy lines against enemy armor, artillery, and support systems

BDA—bomb damage assessment

Cajuns—the 504th Tactical Fighter Squadron; a reserve squadron permanently based at New Orleans Naval Air Station, Louisiana

CAP—combat air patrol; mostly F-15 fighters patrolling at high altitude, ready to attack enemy aircraft

CBU—cluster bomb unit; canister that opens at a preset altitude and releases bomblets

coordinates—latitude and longitude designations for a specific geographic point on the earth

DF—direction finding; when a low-frequency radio transmits, the needle of the ADF instrument points in that direction; used for navigation and for locating downed airmen

DO—deputy for operations; the officer in an Air Force wing who is responsible for all flying activities

ECM—electronic countermeasures; electronic equipment that jams and confuses enemy radars and communications

elevator—the hinged, movable part of the horizontal tail that controls the up and down (pitch) movement of the aircraft; controlled by back and forth movement of the stick

FAC—forward air controller; ground or airborne person who identifies and marks targets, and coordinates air strikes with ground commanders

Falcons—the 355th Tactical Fighter Squadron from Myrtle Beach AFB, South Carolina; they were the first to be trained for night combat

FIDO—fighter duty officer; a rotating assignment; represented A-10 fighter community in Riyadh

FLIR—forward-looking infrared device; a pod carried by some aircraft that allows them to have limited night vision

FOL—forward operating location; a base closer to the combat area with the essentials for combat—mainly ordnance, fuel, and essential supplies; for the A-10s in the war: KKMC and Al Jouf

FROG—free rocket over ground; a missile fired from ground to ground like artillery

Flying Tigers—the 74th Tactical Fighter Squadron from England AFB, Louisiana; direct descendants of Chennault's original Flying Tigers; second squadron to be trained for night combat

FRAG—the part of the ATO that pertains to one specific unit, e.g., the missions for the A-10

GCI—ground control intercept; radar warning sites used to detect incoming aircraft and missiles

Guard—name for emergency frequency monitored by all aircraft

HARM—anti-radiation missile; used by Weasels against enemy radar; when fired it homes in on waves emitted by the radar

horizontal stabilizer—the horizontal part of the tail that does not move

HUD—heads up display; projects vital flight information and targeting data on pilots' windscreen; allows pilot to keep eyes forward and out of cockpit

IFR—instrument flight rules; acronym used by pilots to describe flying under instrument conditions in clouds or when visibility is poor; technically, pilot should be flying under international rules for instrument flight when IFR

IMC—instrument meteorological conditions; more appropriate term for flying in clouds or with poor visibility; often used interchangeably with IFR

IP—initial point; designated geographic coordinates that pilots use as a reference when they reach target area; also instructor pilot

IR—infrared radiation; heat

INS—inertial navigation system; system that allows pilots to fly to or from geographic coordinates; fairly accurate but tends to drift with time

KKMC—King Khalid Military City; one of two FOLs used by A-10s; located about 245 miles northwest of King Fahd airport where the A-10s were based

KTO—Kuwaiti theater of operations; Kuwait and surrounding area where Iraqi forces were concentrated

log—flare released for marking purposes; burns on ground for about thirty minutes

LUU-2—parachute flare; heat from flare slows descent of parachute; burns for about five minutes

MarCent—Marine Central Command; used by pilots to describe the area along the coast of Kuwait south of Kuwait City

manual reversion—emergency control system used after all hydraulic-boosted controls are inoperable; allows operation of trim tabs—small, hinged control surfaces—on ailerons, elevator and rudders, which, in turn, cause these larger control surfaces to respond

Mark-82—500-pound iron bomb; most common iron bomb employed by A-10; typical load: six

MRE—meal ready to eat; packaged rations; modern version of C-rations

Ops—abbreviation for operations

ORI—operational readiness inspection; major, high-level inspection to determine readiness of Air Force units padlock—term used by pilots who must keep their eyes fixed on an object outside the cockpit so they will not lose sight of it

Panthers—the 353d Tactical Fighter Squadron from Myrtle Beach AFB, South Carolina

rudder—the hinged, movable part of the vertical tail; controls right-left movement (yaw) of nose; there are two of them on the A-10

RWR—radar warning receiver; pronounced "raw" by pilots because of acronym used for original receiver; gives pilot azimuth (direction) and information about the type of radar missile being aimed or fired; of no value for detecting heatseeking missiles

SA—situational awareness; pilots use term to describe their degree of awareness of where they are in space and time

SAM—surface-to air-missile

SAR—search and rescue; certain pilots in every squadron are specially trained to find and support the rescue of downed pilots

SAS—stability augmentation system, a system that helps keep the A-10 stable while the gun is firing and producing recoil

SOF—supervisor of flying; subordinate of DO who is posted in the tower whenever flight operations are being conducted; person responsible for assisting pilots with airborne emergencies

STU—secure telephone unit; used for secure telephone communications

TACAN—distance measuring instrument; measures time of microwave transmissions between the ground and aircraft or between aircraft and produces distance readout for pilots

TACC—tactical air control center; nerve center in Riyadh where all flight operations were controlled

TOT—time over target;  in the A-10s case, usually thirty minutes

TVM—television monitor; small TV screen on right, front panel of A-10; used for viewing what television camera in Maverick missile is seeing

Vanguards—76th Tactical Fighter Squadron from England AFB, Louisiana

vertical stabilizer—vertical, nonmovable part of tail; also called fin; the A-10 has two of them

Vultures—the 511th Tactical Fighter Squadron from RAF
  Alconbury, Great Britain

Willy Pete—term used for white phosphorous marking rockets; used
  by FACs for marking targets

WOC—wing operations center; A-10 command center at King Fahd

# APPENDIX

# THE A-10 PILOTS WHO FOUGHT IN DESERT STORM

*Each squadron was augmented with pilots from other squadrons and from the wing staffs*

**353d Tactical Fighter Squadron (Panthers)**
Lt. Col. Tom Essig
Lt. Col. Ron Kurtz
Lt. Col. John Mokri
Lt. Col. Mike Parsons
Lt. Col. Rick Shatzel, Squadron Commander
Maj. Scott Hill
Maj. Dave Mitchell
Maj. Doug Owens
Maj. Dan Swift
Capt. James Baldwin
Capt. Fred Biddix
Capt. Larry Butler
Capt. Jim Cavoto
Capt. Tom Dean
Capt. Mike Dunn
Capt. Harry Earle
Capt. Don Fann
Capt. Kim Gilbert
Capt. Randy Goff
Capt. Dave Hanaway
Capt. Greg Henderson
Capt. Carl Hickey
Capt. Paul Johnson
Capt. Jim McCauley
Capt. Dan Mulherin
Capt. John Nachtman
Capt. Ken O'Neill
Capt. Trent Palmer
Capt. Bill Pfau

Capt. Steve Phyllis
Capt. Gary Powell
Capt. Glenn Roberts
Capt. Ken Scarborough
Capt. Eric Sobol
Capt. Joe Walsh
Capt. Greg Weidekamp
Capt. John Whitney
Capt. Tom Wilson
Lt. Jim Chambers
Lt. Dan Kolota
Lt. Stephan Otto
Lt. Jeff Scott
Lt. Rob Sweet

**355th Tactical Fighter Squadron (Falcons)**
Col. Hank Haden, DO
Col. Sandy Sharpe, Wing Commander
Lt. Col. Joe Barton
Lt. Col. Danny Clifton
Lt. Col. Chuck Fox
Lt. Col. John Lauten
Lt. Col. Rick McDow, Squadron Commander
Lt. Col. Con Rodi
Maj. John Bingaman
Maj. A.J. Jackson
Capt. Gary Akins
Capt. Dave Bachman
Capt. Bob Buchanan

Capt. Jeff Bucher
Capt. Jim Cobb
Capt. Landis Cook
Capt. John Dobbins
Capt. Gene Dougherty
Capt. Mike Edwards
Capt. Angelo Eiland
Capt. Leon Elsarelli
Capt. Terry Featherston
Capt. Ron Gaulton
Capt. Jeff Gingras
Capt. Rob Givens
Capt. Steve Gray
Capt. Hugh Hanlon
Capt. Carlos Honesty
Capt. Allen Ingle
Capt. Jeff Kanarish
Capt. Ken Lacy
Capt. Mike Lankford
Capt. Kevin Leek
Capt. Tim Lloyd
Capt. John Marselus
Capt. Mike McGee
Capt. Stuart Moore
Capt. Ken Murchison
Capt. Pat Peters
Capt. Leslie Rohlf
Capt. Mark Roling
Capt. Joel Rush
Capt. Jack Thomas
Capt. Jim Thomas
Capt. Dave Vonbrock
Capt. Dave Wappner
Capt. Jeff Wesley
Lt. Scott Hall
Lt. Jim Hurley

**74th Tactical Fighter Squadron
(Flying Tigers)**
Col. Tom Lyon, DO
Lt. Col. Jim Green, Squadron
  Commander
Lt. Col. Mike Wilken

Maj. Jeff Watterberg
Capt. Steve Barbour
Capt. Pat Bertlshofer
Capt. Matt Cavanaugh
Capt. Dave Cundiff
Capt. Arden Dahl
Capt. Pete Edgar
Capt. Dave Feehs
Capt. Phil Fichthorn
Capt. Jim Glasgow
Capt. Ralph Hansen
Capt. Mike Isherwood
Capt. Kevin Jens
Capt. Scott Kelly
Capt. Mark Koechle
Capt. Tony Mattox
Capt. Mike Mangus
Capt. Walton Miller
Capt. Mike Nutterfield
Capt. Ron Patrick
Capt. Eric Paul
Capt. John Russell
Capt. Jo Slupski
Capt. Jeff Snell
Capt. Mike Spencer
Capt. Eric Stoll
Capt. Jim Tillie
Capt. Lee Wyatt
Capt. Kent Yohe
Lt. Bryan Currier
Lt. Cliff Grafton
Lt. Rich Ferguson
Lt. Don Henry
Lt. J. J. Krimmell
Lt. Dave Lucke
Lt. Pat McAlister
Lt. Keith McBride
Lt. Mike Murphy
Lt. Tom Norris
Lt. Steve Olmos
Lt. Dan Osborne
Lt. Dave Ure

**76th Tactical Fighter Squadron (Vanguards)**

Col. Dave Sawyer, Wing
  Commander
Lt. Col. Phil Brown
Lt. Col. Bob Lane
Lt. Col. Gene Renuart,
  Squadron Commander
Lt. Col. Lynn Vanderveen
Maj. Scott Chaisson
Maj. Steve Moffet
Maj. Glen Weaver
Capt. Rich Biley
Capt. Marty Brogli
Capt. Ernie Brown
Capt. Karl Buchberger
Capt. Roger Clark
Capt. Gary Ducote
Capt. Wyatt Fleming
Capt. Dave Foelker
Capt. Byron Greer
Capt. Rick Griffin
Capt. Al Hicks
Capt. Ward Larson
Capt. Blas Miyares
Capt. Keith Moring
Capt. Gary Mullett
Capt. Mike O'Dowd
Capt. Rick Robinson
Capt. Joe Rutkowski
Capt. Tim Saffold
Capt. Eric Salomonson
Capt. John Scott
Capt. John Slaton
Capt. Dale Storr
Capt. Bob Sullivan
Capt. Curtis Viall
Lt. Neal Culiner
Lt. Dan Dennis
Lt. Dave Ferguson
Lt. Mike Greco
Lt. Darren Hansen
Lt. Rick Johnson

Lt. Roy Keller
Lt. John Marks
Lt. Dan Martin
Lt. Craig McCurdy
Lt. Eric Miller
Lt. Greg Mooneyham
Lt. Matt Murray
Lt. Jim Schmick
Lt. Randy Staudenraus

**511th Tactical Fighter Squadron (Vultures)**

Lt. Col. Keith Bennett
Lt. Col. Mike O'Connor,
  Squadron Commander
Lt. Col. Jack Shafer
Maj. John Condon
Maj. Wayne Pepin
Maj. Doug Richter
Capt. Tommy Abbott
Capt. Scott Alexander
Capt. Tommy Atkins
Capt. Greg Benjamin
Capt. George Bennefield
Capt. J. C. Carter
Capt. Rod Glass
Capt. Mark Hedman
Capt. Scott Johnston
Capt. Dar Kemp
Capt. Kevin Kriner
Capt. Sam Martin
Capt. Mike Meier
Capt. Colin Moffat
Capt. Joe Nuti
Capt. Eric Offill
Capt. Jeff Quinn
Capt. Paul Rastas
Capt. Todd Sheehy
Capt. Steve Sikes
Capt. Dave Tan
Capt. Rick Turner
Capt. Brian Welch
Lt. Jeff Clifton

Lt. Todd Decker
Lt. Greg Engle
Lt. Dan Greenwood
Lt. Richard McKinley
Lt. Brad Whitmire
Lt. Charles Wyndham

## 23d Tactical Air Support Squadron (Nail FACs)

Lt. Col. Jeff Fox  Nail 02
Lt. Col. Bob George, Squadron
  Commander  Nail 01
Maj. Gary Buis  Nail 03
Capt. Ted Bale  Nail 66
Capt. Mike Baltzer  Nail 25
Capt. Hoss Barker  Nail 62
Capt. Mike Bartley  Nail 44
Capt. Mike Beard  Nail 55
Capt. Mike Chandler  Nail 60
Capt. Jerry Deemer  Nail 68
Capt. Tony DiPietro Nail 21
Capt. Jon Engle  Nail 33
Capt. Bob Ginnetti  Nail 11
Capt. Jerry Stophel  Nail 13
Capt. Greg Wilhite  Nail 96
Lt. Mike Boyle  Nail 40
Lt. Tom Deale  Nail 90
Lt. Scott Fitzsimmons  Nail 80
Lt. Sean Kavanaugh  Nail 36
Lt. Ed Norwesh  Nail 91
Lt. Pat Olson  Nail 69 (retired)
Lt. Quentin Rideout  Nail 50

### 23d TASS pilots who served as ground FACs during Desert Storm

## lst Cavalry Division

Maj. Jim Wilson Nail 07
Lt. Jeff Cowan  Nail 49
Lt. John Fitzgerrell  Nail 32
Lt. Dean Lee  Nail 26
Lt. Bob Morse  Nail 87

## 3d Armored Cavalry Regiment

Capt. Steve Connolly  Nail 06
Lt. Vince Godfrey  Nail 95
Lt. Mark Register  Nail 47

## 2d Armored Cavalry Regiment

Capt. Greg Andreachi  Nail 28
Capt. Steve Buchanan  Nail 45
Capt. John Rogler  Nail 41
Lt. Scott Stark  Nail 16

## 706th Tactical Fighter Squadron (Cajuns)

Col. Bob Efferson, Group
  Commander
Lt. Col. Johnny Alexander
Lt. Col. Lee Brundage
Lt. Col. Tom Coleman,
  Squadron Commander
Lt. Col. Earl Deroche
Lt. Col. Doug Findley
Lt. Col. Jack Ihle
Lt. Col. Craig Mays
Lt. Col. Greg Wilson
Maj. Greg Durio
Maj. Randy Falcon
Maj. Larry McCaskill
Maj. Rich Pauley
Maj. Sonny Rasar
Maj. Jim Rose
Maj. Richard Sachitano
Maj. Mike Shaw
Maj. Jim Venturella
Maj. Johnny Weaver
Maj. Ron White
Maj. Tim Wroten
Capt. Jim Callaway
Capt. Dave Duncan
Capt. Phil Farrell
Capt. Mark Habetz
Capt. Ed Kinney
Capt. Larry Merington
Capt. Todd Nilsen

Capt. Bob Swain
Lt. Bill Demaso
Lt. Charles Guarino
Lt. Mark Mikelonis
Lt. Will Shepard
Lt. Mark White

# INDEX

# About the Author

WILLIAM SMALLWOOD served in the Air Force in the Korean War and is an experienced instrument- and multiengine-rated pilot with thousands of hours of flying time. An award-winning high school teacher, he is the author of numerous science textbooks as well as *The Air Force Academy Candidate Book*, *The Naval Academy Candidate Book*, and *The West Point Candidate Book*. While researching *Warthog*, he flew his airplane from his home in Sun Valley, Idaho, around the country to interview scores of A-10 pilots, unit commanders, and support personnel.